# Philosophical and Sociological Perspectives on Education

# Philosophical and Sociological Perspectives on Education

J.C. Aggarwal

SHIPRA

(12th Reprint, 2014 Rev. Ed., First Published 2003)

Rs. 1295, US$ 52

ISBN: 978-81-7541-736-6

*2023 Impression*

*Philosophical and Sociological Perspectives on Education*



Published by:
**SHIPRA PUBLICATIONS**
LG 18-19, Pankaj Central Market
I.P. Ext., Patparganj, Delhi 110092, Ind
Tel.: +91 11 2223 5152; 96500 28065
E-mail: info@shiprapublication.com
www.shiprapublication.com

# Preface

This book provides a detailed discussion on the philosophical and sociological perspectives of education in the context of Indian Society. It suggests practical measures for fulfilling the objectives of secularism, socialism and democracy as envisaged in the Constitution. The role of different types of formal, informal and formal agencies of education in this regard is highlighted. 'What', 'Why', of issues like education of the girls and disadvantaged sections of the society will provide proper insight.

Suitable quotes of great thinkers on education enrich the subject matter. Diagrams, tables and illustrations are used to explain issues in a simple and vivid manner. Material in this volume has been drawn from the reports of Committees and Commissions, Resolutions and National Policies on Education. All possible efforts are made to provide authentic and latest data based on national and international publications on education and allied subjects.

Planned as a textbook for students, this can also serve as a handy reference manual for practising teachers and other interested in philosophical and sociological issues of a democratic society. The author extends his thanks to all the authors and publishers whose works he has made use of in preparing this book.

**J.C. Aggarwal**

*Editor's Note*: In this 2014 edition, tables have been revised/updated.

# Contents

## Part I
## Philosophical Perspectives on Education


1. **Meaning, Nature and Scope of Education** 3–12
Significance of Education / 3; Meaning of Education / 4; Wider and Narrow Meaning of Education / 6; What Education is Not / 6; Nature of Education / 7; Scope of Education / 7; Functions of Education / 7; Main Dimensions/Elements of the Process of Education / 8; Meaning of Formal, Non-formal and Informal Education / 9; Important Definitions of Education / 10; Best Definition of Education / 11; Four Pillars of Education: Education for the Twenty-first Century / 12

2. **Aims of Education** 13–20
Why Aims of Education? or Significance of Aims of Education / 13; Factors Affecting Aims of Education / 13; General Aims of Education / 14; Individual Aim and Social Aim of Education / 15; Character Development Aim of Education and Vocational Aim of Education / 17; Aim of Education in India through the Ages / 19; Immediate and Ultimate Aims of Education / 19

3. **Meaning, Nature and Scope of Philosophy: Philosophy and Education** 21–26
Significance of philosophy / 21; Meaning and Nature of Philosophy / 21; Why do we need philosophy / 22; Scope of Philosophy / 22; Relationship between Philosophy and Education / 24; Contribution of philosophy to Education / 25

4. **Concept and Development of National System of Education** 27–42
Concept of the National System of Education / 27; Need for a National System of Education / 28; Development of National System of Education in Ancient Period / 29; National System of Education During the Medieval Period / 31; National System of Education During the British Rule in India / 32; National System of Education during Post-Independence Period / 33; Constitutional Provisions and the Development of National System of Education / 34; National System of Education at the Elementary Stage / 34; Development of the National System of Education at Stages other than Elementary Stage of Education / 37; National

System of Education as provided for in the National Policy on Education—NPE, 1986 / 38; Present Position of National System of Education / 42

**5. Sri Aurobindo Ghose (1872-1950)** **43–47**

Brief Life Sketch of Sri Aurobindo / 43; Main Ideas of Aurobindo's Philosophy / 44; Sri Aurobindo's Main Ideas on Education / 44; National System of Education / 46; Contribution of Sri Aurobindo to Education / 46; Select Quotes of Sri Aurobindo on Education / 47

**6. Swami Vivekananda (1863-1902)** **48–52**

Brief Life Sketch and Work of Swami Vivekananda / 48; Principal Features of Swami Vivekananda's Philosophy / 49; Swami Vivekananda's Philosophy of Education / 49; Swami Vivekanand on Various Aspects of Education / 49; Contribution of Swami Vivekananda to Education: Relevance of his views today / 51

**7. Rabindranath Tagore (1861-1941)** **53–58**

Brief Life Sketch / 53; Tagore's Philosophy of Life / 54; Educational Philosophy of Tagore / 54; Tagore's Views on Different Aspects of Education / 55; An Ideal School / 56; Educational Institutes started by Tagore / 57; Visvabharati (World University) / 57; Contribution of Tagore to Education / 57

**8. M.K. Gandhi (1869-1948)** **59–63**

Brief Life Sketch / 59; Gandhiji's Educational Experiments / 59; Gandhiji's Publications on Education / 60; Principal Features of Gandhiji's Philosophy of life / 60; Factors that Influenced Gandhiji's Philosophy of Life and Philosophy of Education / 61; Gandhiji's Views on Different Aspects of Education / 61; Gandhiji as an Idealist, Naturalist and Pragmatic Educationist / 62; Criticism of Gandhian Approach to Education / 62; Contribution and Relevance of Gandhiji's Views on Education in Modern Times / 63

**9. Zakir Hussain (1897-1969)** **64–67**

Brief Life Sketch / 64; Dr. Zakir Hussain's Views on Various Aspects of Education / 65; Characteristics of a Good School / 66; Contribution of Dr. Zakir Hussain to Education / 67; Main outline of the Seven Years Course of Basic Education as Suggested by the Committee / 67

**10. Idealism** **68–72**

Meaning of Idealism / 68; Chief Exponents of Idealism / 68; Main Principles of Idealism / 68; Idealism and Various Aspects of Education / 69; Limitations and Weaknesses of Idealism in Education / 71; Contribution of Idealism to Educational Theory and Practice / 72; Summing up / 72

**11. Naturalism** **73–78**

Meaning of Naturalism / 73; Chief Characteristics of Naturalism / 73; Prominent Naturalist Philosophers / 74; Naturalism and Its Various Dimensions in Education / 74; Negative Education according to Rousseau / 77; Limitations of Naturalism in Education / 77; Contribution of Naturalism to Education / 78

12. **Pragmatism** **79–83**
Meaning of Pragmatism / 79; Fundamental Principles of Pragmatism / 79; Broad Features of Pragmatism in Education / 80; Limitations of Pragmatism / 82; Contribution of Pragmatism to Education / 82

13. **Humanism: Comparative Study of Idealism, Naturalism and Pragmatism** **84–87**
Meaning of Humanism / 84; Principles of Humanism / 84; Humanism and Modification of Human Nature / 84; Humanism and Democracy / 85; Educational Implications of Humanism / 85; Humanism and Curriculum / 85; Comparative Impact of Idealism, Naturalism and Pragmatism on Educational Theory and Practice / 86

14. **Practical Work: Diverse Issues** **88–109**
Life Sketch and Contribution of Mahatma Gandhi / 88; Critical Analysis of Primary System of Education in India / 93; Child-Centered Education / 103; Moral Education / 109

**Part II**
**Sociological Perspectives on Education**

15. **Meaning, Concept and Importance of Educational Sociology** **119–123**
Meaning and Concept of Educational Sociology / 119; Scope of Educational Sociology and Its Development / 119; Sociological Perspective of Education / 121; Importance of Educational Sociology / 121; Concept of Educational Sociology and Its Relations with Other Disciplines / 123

16. **Sociological Bases of Education** **124–126**
Meaning of Sociology / 124; Society and Education / 125; Sociological Bases of Education / 125

17. **Social Aims of Education** **127–131**
Concepts and Terms Associated with Social Aims of Education / 127; Need for Social Aims of Education / 127; Different Interpretations of Social Aims of Education / 127; Important Social Aims of Education Accepted by Democratic States / 128; Chief Supporters of the Social Aims of Education / 129; Why claims for Social Aims of Education / 130; Critics of Social Aims of Education / 130; Synthesis Between Social Aims of Education and Individual Aims of Education / 130

18. **Contemporary Social System in India: Its Structure (Caste and Class)** **132–137**
Dimensions of Indian Society / 132; Indian Social Structure and Its Meaning / 132; Caste System in India / 133; Caste and Education in

India / 134; Class Structure / 135; Social Classes in India / 135; Class Structure or social classes in India According to General Acceptability / 136; Social Structure and Education / 136

**19. Guiding Principles of Indian Policy** **138–142**

Constitution as the Guiding and Inspirational Source of Indian Policy / 138; Salient Ideals and Values Contained in the Constitution / 138; Major Policy Provisions / 139; Specific Articles in the Constitution Relating to Education Policy / 140; Summary of Policy Directions / 141

**20. Secularism** **143–146**

Introduction / 143; Origin of the Word Secularism / 143; Indian Concept of Secularism and a Secular State / 144; Secular Outlook or Characteristics of a Secular-minded Individual / 144; Constitutional Provisions and Secularism / 145; Constitutional Provisions Regarding Imparting of Religious and Secular Education / 146; Constitutional Provisions Regarding Admission and Establishment of Educational Institutions by Religious Minorities / 146; Reasons for Imparting Secular Education / 146;

**21. Socialism** **147–150**

Meaning and Origin of Socialism / 147; Main Features of Socialism / 147; Methods of Achieving Socialist Goals / 148; Demerits of Socialism / 148; Indian Concept of Socialism / 148; Educational Implications of Socialism / 149; Socialism and Equalisation of Educational Opportunities / 150

**22. Democracy** **151–156**

Meaning of Democracy / 151; Significance of Each Letter of the Word Democracy / 151; Dimensions of Democracy / 152; Democracy and Education / 152; Importance of Education in Democracy / 153; Significant Implications of Democracy in Education / 153; Various Dimensions of Education and Democracy / 154; Measures for Educating and Training the Students for Democracy / 156

**23. National Integration and the Role of the Teacher** **157–161**

Meaning of National Integration / 157; Why National Integration / 157; Hindrances and Obstacles in National Integration / 158; Role of Education in National Integration / 158; Ways and Means of Promoting National Integration through Educational Programmes / 159; Role of the Teachers in Promoting National Integration / 160; Pledge for National Integration / 160

**24. Socialisation and Education** **162-165**

Meaning of Socialisation / 162; Importance and Objective of Socialisation / 163; Main Characteristics of the Process of Socialisation / 163; Education and Socialisation / 163; Difficult Task of Socialisation of the Child / 164; Role of the School in the Socialisation of the Child: Important Programmes of

Socialisation / 164; Role of the Teacher in the Socialisation of the Child / 165

**25. Social Change, Nature, Process, Causes and Effects** **166–170**
Meaning of Social Change / 166; Nature and Characteristics of Social Change / 166; Process of Social Change / 167; Causes/Factors of Social Change / 169; Effects of Social Changes / 170

**26. Education as a Means and Product of Social Change** **171–175**
Education as a Means of Social Change / 171; Broad Areas of Social Change and transformation through Education / 172; Functions of Education in Social Change / 172; Equality of Opportunity in Education and Social Change / 173; Agencies of Education and Social Change / 173; Limitations of Education in Bringing About Changes / 173; Teacher as an Agent of Social Change / 174; Education as a Product of Social Change / 174; Interdependent Role of Education and Social Change / 175

**27. Role of Education in the Preservation of Cultural Heritage of India** **176–179**
Rich Cultural Heritage of India / 176; Meaning of Cultural Heritage / 176; Chief Characteristics of Indian Cultural Heritage / 177; Composite Cultural Heritage of India / 178; Cultural Heritage and Education / 179

**28. Informal, Formal and Non-Formal Agencies** **180–189**
Need for Different Types of Agencies of Education / 180; Broad Classifications of Agencies of Education / 181; No Watertight Division of Agencies of Education / 182; Broad Comparison Between Formal and Non-Formal Agencies of Education / 183; Mass Media as Agencies of Education / 184; Radio as Agency of Education / 184; Television as an Educational Medium / 186; Peer Group and Education / 188

**29. Role of the Family, School, Community (NGOs) and State in Education** **190–200**
Role of the Family in Education / 190; School As an Agency of Education / 191; Functions of the School in Behavioural Terms / 193; Community as an Agency of Education / 194; Interaction Between the Community and the School / 195; Non-Governmental Organisations (NGOs) and Education / 196; Policy Statements on the Role of NGOs / 198; Role of the State in Education / 198

**30. Constitutional Provisions Regarding Elementary Education** **201–206**
Concept of Elementary Education / 201; Importance of Elementary Education / 203; Comparative data on Elementary Education / 204; Implications of Constitutional Provisions on Elementary Education / 205; Problems, Issues, Remedies and Constitutional Provisions / 206

**31. Girl's Education** **207–213**
Importance of Girl's and Women's Education / 207; Constitutional Provisions Regarding Girls Education / 208; Gender Disparity / 209; Variations in Girls Enrolment Rate in States / 209; Causes of Slow Progress of Girls' Education / 210; Measures for the Promotion of Girls' and Women's Education / 210

**32. Problems, Issues and Remedies Regarding Child Labour** **214–218**
Constitutional Provisions Regarding Child Labour / 214; Who is A Child / 214; Poverty and Child Labour / 215; The Preferred Picture of Child Labour and Welfare / 215; What is Child Labour / 216; Child Labour in India / 216; Types of Child Labour / 216; Measures Taken in India for Eliminating and Checking Exploitation of Child Labour / 217; Suggestive Measures for Improving the Condition of Child Labour and Eliminating Child Labour in India / 218

**33. Problems, Issues and Remedies Regarding Children with Special Needs** **219–223**
Meaning of Children with Special Needs / 219; Main Characteristics of Children with Special Needs / 219; Why Education and Training of Children with Special Needs / 221; Constitutional Provisions Regarding Education and Training of Children with Special Needs / 221; Patterns/Systems of Education for Children with Special Needs / 221; Integrated Education for the Disabled Children (IEDC) / 222

**34. Problems, Issues and Remedies Regarding Disadvantaged Sections** **224–228**
Meaning of Disadvantaged Sections / 224; Constitutional Provisions Regarding Deprived Sections / 225; Expansion of Educational Facilities to the SCs and STs / 225; Importance of Promotion of Education among the Deprived Sections / 225; Measures for the Promotion of Education of the Deprived Sections / 226

**35. Practical Work: Diverse Issues** **229–243**
Policy Recommendations on Girls' Education Since Independence: Committees, Commissions and National Policies on Education / 229; Policy Recommendations on Special Education since Independence / 235; Policy Recommendations on Education of the Disadvantaged Sections / 239; Preparation of Profile for School: Guidelines/Hints / 241; Preparation of Reports for Field Trips / 243

# PART I

# PHILOSOPHICAL PERSPECTIVES ON EDUCATION

# 1

# Meaning, Nature and Scope of Education

## 1.1 SIGNIFICANCE OF EDUCATION

According to thinkers of ancient India, education is the 'third eye' of a person. It gives him insight into all affairs. It teaches him how to act justly and rightly. It leads him to realise the true significance of life. It removes darkness and shatters illusion.

A person without education is really blind.

In the words of Rousseau, "Plants are developed by cultivation and men by education."

Education increases our fame. It makes us cultured and pure.

Education nourishes us like a mother. It directs us to the proper path like the father. It guides us to reach our destination like a teacher.

The 'Upanishadas' consider education as a means of Salvation.

सविधा या विमुक्तये

or

सविधा या विमोक्षधति प्रदा

The following is a traditional common saying in India:

*Swadesh pujyate raja,*
*Vidvan sarvatra pujyata*

A king is respected in his own kingdom while a learned man is worshipped every where.

The Hindu law-givers even go further and lay down that the very sight of a learned man is sacred.

Joseph Addison (1672-1719), has very rightly stated, "What sculpture is to a block of marble, education is to a human soul."

The Education Commission (1964-66), the first Commission in India which examined all aspects of education, very aptly began its report with these words, "The destiny of India is new being shaped in the classroom." It further observed, "In a world based on science and technology, it is education that determines the level of prosperity, welfare and security of the people." The National Policy on Education (1992) has emphasised, "Education is fundamental to our all-round development, material and spiritual."

## 1.2 MEANING OF EDUCATION

The meaning of education may be explained by stating its origin. The term education is derived from the following three Latin words:

1. *Educare*: This means : to bring up, to nourish, to rear and to train.
2. *Educere*: This implies : to draw out; to lead out.
3. *Educo*: The letter 'E' means out of and 'duco' to lead. This denotes: to extract out, to lead forth.

Thus education implies:

(i) Act of bringing up
(ii) Act of drawing out
(iii) Act of extracting out
(iv) Act of leading forth
(v) Act of leading out
(vi) Act of nourishing
(vii) Act of rearing
(viii) Act of training

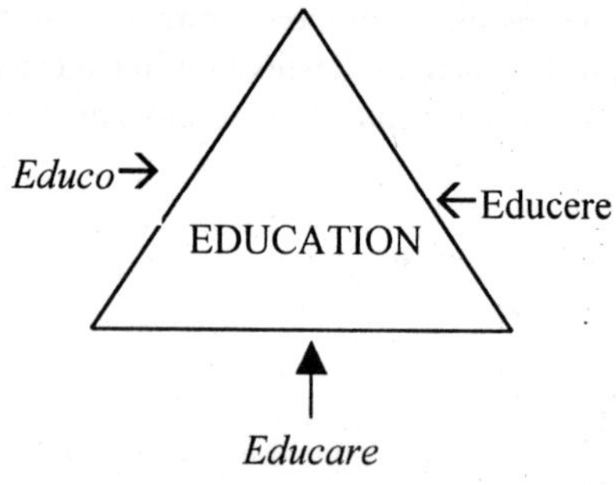


*Fig. 1.1: Showing Origin of the Term Education (Derivation or Etymology of Education)*

A synthesis of the above words relating to the origin (derivation) of education provides us a comprehensive view of the meanings of the term education. Several great educators and thinkers have followed this approach of synthesis. Plato (427-347 B.C.) stated, "Education develops in the body and in the soul of the pupil all the perfection he is, capable of." A great Swiss educator, namely Pestalozzi (1746-1827) has expressed the meaning of education in these words, "Education is the natural, harmonious and progressive development of man's innote powers." According to Froebel (1782-1852), a German educator, "Education is unfoldment of what is already enfolded. It is the process through which the child makers' internal external." Tagore (1861-1941) has observed, "Education gives us the wealth of inner light." Aurobindo (1872-1950) states, "Education means helping the growing soul to draw out that is in itself." Swami Vivekananda (1863-1902) has said, "Education is the manifestation of divine perfection already existing in man."

Gandhiji (1869-1948) gives the meaning of education as, "By education I mean an all-round drawing out the cost in child and man—body, mind and spirit."

*Meaning of the term 'Drawing Out'*: It is accepted by all educators that the nature has given (endowed) children a tremendous energy. They have within them the springs of action, joy and vigour. They have the God-given curiosity to know and explore things for themselves. It will be wrong to suppress these powers. They must be 'drawn out'.

*Meaning of the term 'Best in the Child'* : This implies that maximum use should be made of the innate powers of the child—body, mind and soul.

*How to draw out the best?* Now the key question arises as to how the innate powers are to be brought out, developed, nourished and trained. Here comes the environmental factor which includes the family, the neighbourhood, the school, the community and the society. Thus, education is a means to provide the proper environment for the all round development of the individual. The development of the individual has to be a balanced one and not lop-sided. An individual is one whole.

The following figures illustrates the over all meaning of education.

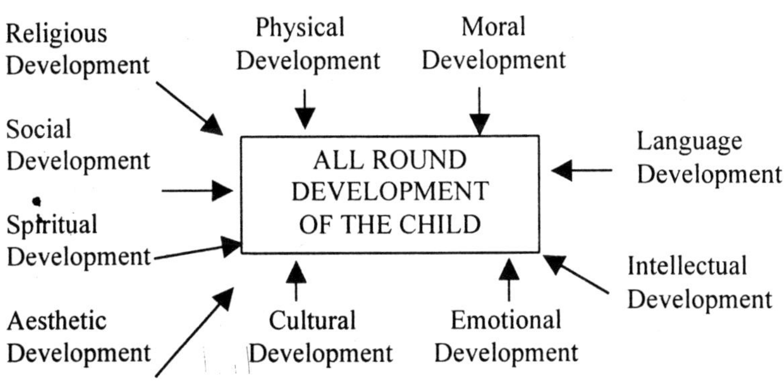


*Fig. 1.2: Meaning of Education as the All-Round Development of the Child*

The all-round concept of education has been explained by Gandhiji in his book *'Basic Education'* as "I hold that true education of the intellectual can only come through a proper exercise and training of the bodily organs, e.g., hands, feet, eyes, ears, nose etc. In other words an intelligent use of the organs in a child provides the best and quickest way of developing his intellect. But unless the development of the mind goes hand in hand with a corresponding awakening of the soul, the former alone would prove to be a poor lop-sided affair. By spiritual training I mean education of the heart. A proper and an all round development of the mind, therefore, can take place only when it proceeds 'pari passu' with education of the physical and spiritual faculties of the child. They constitute an indivisible whole."

*Summing up:* Education implies drawing out the best in the child with the aim of producing individuals who are aesthetically refined culturally well behaved, emotionally stable, ethically sound, mentally alert, morally upright, physically strong, religiously pious, socially efficient, spiritually enlightened and vocationally self-sufficient.

## 1.3 WIDER AND NARROW MEANING OF EDUCATION

*Wider Meaning of Education*: In the wider sense all experience is educative. R.C. Lodge in his book *Philosophy of education* even includes the experience of bite of a mosquito, the taste of watermelon, falling in love, flying in the aeroplane etc. in the educative process. Everything we say, think or do educates us. Likewise what others say to us or do to us should be treated as educational experiences. Consciously or unconsciously we always learn and receive education.

John Stuart Mill states that every environment, every surrounding and every activity is educative to some extent. Every interaction results in education.

It is said that a child gets one-fourth of his education from his teachers, one-fourth from his own intellectual efforts, one fourth from his fellow students and the rest through his life experiences in the environment.

*Narrow Meaning of Education*: Education means only specific influences and experiences which are deliberately planned to modify the behaviour of the child. Following are the characteristics of the narrow meaning of education.

1. Schooling is education.
2. Education is confined to the experiences proved in the classroom.
3. It is limited to the teaching of ready-made instructional material.
4. It is imparted in organised institutions like school.

## 1.4 WHAT EDUCATION IS NOT

1. *Education is not mere Schooling*: Education takes place within the four walls of the school and outside also. Education is not mere spending a few hours in the school and learning some subjects.
2. *Education is not Information*: Information must lead to constructive thinking and wisdom.
3. *Education is not Instruction*: Instruction is confined to classroom. Education is life-long and ends with death.
4. *Education is not Indoctrination*: Indoctrination is confined to a particular belief but education is very broad and leads to broad mindedness.

5. *Education is not merely Training of mind*: Education is concerned with the development of body, mind and soul.

## 1.5 NATURE OF EDUCATION

Following are the chief characteristics of the nature of education:

1. *Education is Purposive* i.e. there is a definite purpose underlying all educational activities.
2. *Education is Deliberate* i.e. education involves care and guidance.
3. *Education is Planned* i.e. education is not haphazard. It is systematic.
4. *Education is Life-long* i.e. education starts from the time of conception and goes on till death—education from cradle to grave as is sometimes said.
5. *Education is Influence Exerted* i.e. the mature person (parents, elders and teachers) influence the learners.
6. *Education is Balanced Development* i.e. education is concerned with the development of all faculties of the child.
7. *Education is Bi-polar* i.e. both the teacher and the pupil influence each other. Of course, the influence of the teacher is very prominent.
8. *Education is Tri-polar* i.e. education involves the teacher, the taught and the environment or the subject-matter.
9. *Education is Psychological as well as Social* i.e. the endowments or the capacities of the child—his needs, interests etc. must be interpreted in a social setting.
10. *Education is Growth* i.e. education modifies the behaviour of the child.

## 1.6 SCOPE OF EDUCATION

Scope of education is as vast as life itself. There is no aspect or dimension of life which is not covered under education. In fact all education is life and all life is education. Education is a life-long process. Education is formal, non-formal and informal. Likewise agencies of education are formal, non-formal and informal.

Every year, every month, every day, every moment, step by step we learn from every source.

Education is concerned with the aesthetic, cultural, ethical, intellectual, physical, religious, social, spiritual and vocational development of the individual.

Education has moved away from preparing pupils to fit into a particular society but it seeks to make then feel they belong to the larger world family.

## 1.7 FUNCTIONS OF EDUCATION

Education is expected to perform the following functions:

1. Individual development functions.

2. Social development functions.

*Individual Development Functions of Education* : These functions of education are:

(i) Maximum development of the innate or natural abilities and powers of individuals.
(ii) Development of character and personality of the individuals.
(iii) Preparing individuals for living present life amicably and happily.
(iv) Preparing individuals for taking up gainful employment/self-employment.
(v) Development of suitable leisure time activities.
(vi) Development of qualities of followership and leadership.
(vii) Development of emotions of individuals of individuals so that they are emotionally stable.

*Social Development Functions of Education* : These may be stated as:

(i) Development of skills of the individuals that help them to harass the natural resources of the country.
(ii) Development of community sense among the students.
(iii) Conservation of social heritage by providing suitable curriculum to the students.
(iv) Promotion of cultural heritage by broadening the outlook of students.
(v) Involvement of students in community service and welfare activities.
(vi) Development of ideals and values of emotional integration and national unity.
(vii) Development of social awareness.
(viii) Development of values of secularism, socialism and democracy.

## 1.8 MAIN DIMENSIONS/ELEMENTS OF THE PROCESS OF EDUCATION

1. *Why to Educate*: This includes aims of education. The educator and the educand must be clear about the aims of education so that efforts are made in the right direction. Aims of education depend upon a host of factors: political, economic, social, geographical, religious etc. In a nutshell, education must produce socially efficient individuals.

2. *Whom to Educate*: The educator must understand the educand child thoroughly—his aptitudes, interest, temperaments etc., so that the 'best of him' is 'drawn out'.

3. *Who is to Educate*: The teacher is to educate and he must thoroughly understand himself also. He must get rid himself of all the blemishes and remember 'Woe to the teacher who teaches one thing with the lips and carries another in the heart.'

4. *Where to Educate*: The child is to be educated in a school which must 'simply', 'purify' and 'idealise' the environment. Likewise there are several other agencies that supplement school's work.

5. *What to Educate*: This leads to the contents of the curriculum which has been described as 'the environment in motion'. In a broader sense it includes all the courses, readings, associations and activities that go in the school—in the classroom, library, laboratory, workshop, playgrounds and in the numerous informal contacts between teachers and pupils.

6. *How to Educate*: This involves the knowledge and technique of various methods of teaching for making the teaching-learning process dynamic, effective and inspirational.

7. *When to Educate*: This is concerned with the different stages of the child so that 'motivational' aspects may be handled and attended to psychologically.

## 1.9 MEANING OF FORMAL, NON-FORMAL AND INFORMAL EDUCATION (FORMS OR TYPES OF EDUCATION)

Education

(1) Formal Education (2) Non-formal Education (3) Informal Education

*Fig. 1.3: Forms or types of education*

**Comparative Study of Formal and Non-formal Education**

| *Aspect* | *Formal Education* | *Non-formal Education* |
|---|---|---|
| *Aim* | Aim is generally clear and specific. It is examination oriented. | No specific aim. Not examination-oriented. Enrichment of knowledge and skills. |
| *Contents* | Fixed curriculum | Flexible curriculum |
| *Period* | There are several stages of schooling like elementary, secondary etc. | There is no fixed stage. |
| *Agencies* | Educational institutions like schools and colleges | `Clubs, radio and T.V., social education centres. |
| *Admission Requirements* | Points of entry and exist age and entry qualifications | Flexible points of entry and exist. No special qualifications |
| *Employment* | Usually employment-oriented | Usually growth aspect. |
| *Role of the Teacher* | Very predominent | Process of sharing |
| *Lessons* | Fixed according to syllabus | Very flexible |
| *Mental strain* | Heavy mental strain on the teacher and pupil | Little mental strain |
| *Formalities* | Several | Very few |
| *Time Table* | Specific and fixed | Flexible |
| *Time* | Usually full time | Usually part-time |

*A Balanced View*: The use of new information technology in education has narrowed down the difference between formal and non-formal education. T.V., once a medium of non-formal education is gradually used in the normal classroom teaching. Distance education, correspondence education and open education employ formal approach to teaching. Homes are becoming educational institutions with the use of computers and internet modes of learning.

**Meaning of Informal Education**

The following characteristics of informal education bring out its meaning:

1. Informal education is 'not planned' education.
2. Informal education is 'not deliberate' education.
3. Informal education is 'incidental'.
4. Informal education has 'no boundaries'.
5. Informal education is 'spontaneous'.
6. Informal education is not imparted in specialised institutions.
7. Informal education does not involve any conscious effort.
8. Informal education does not follow 'any prescribed time-table.'
9. Informal education has 'no set syllabus'.

Informal education is that education which an individual acquires without attending any educational organisation, system or institution.

*Examples*: Courteous manners, gentleness etc. learnt even in a market place or in a hotel or in one's sitting room talking with others constitute informal education. We get lot of informal education through films, radio and television. It consists of experiences and actual living in the community.

## 1.10 IMPORTANT DEFINITIONS OF EDUCATION

**Definitions and Meanings of Education Given by Indian Thinkers**

(i) *Yajnavalkya* (6th Century B.C.). Education is that which makes a man of good character and useful to the world.

(ii) *Kautilya* (4th Century B.C.). Education means training for the country and developing love for it.

(iii) *Sankraacharya* (788-820). Education means the realization of the self.

(iv) *Swami Dayanand* (1824-1883). Education is a means for character formation and righteous living.

(v) *Swami Vivekananda* (1863-1902). Education is the manifestation of divine perfection already existing in man.

(vi) *Gandhiji* (1869-1948). By education I mean an all-round drawing out the best in child and man—body, mind and spirit.

(vii) *Tagore* (1861-1941). Education is that which makes one's life in harmony with all existence.

(viii) *Aurobindo* (1872-1950). Education means helping the growing soul to draw out that is in itself.

**Definitions and Meanings of Education as Given by Western Thinkers**

(ix) *Plato* (427-347 B.C.). Education develops in the body and in the soul of the pupil all the perfection he is capable of.

(x) *Aristotle* (384-322 B.C.). Education is the creation of a sound mind in a sound body.

(xi) *Pestalozzi* (1746-1827). Education is the natural, harmonious and progressive development of man's innate powers.

(xii) *Froebel* (1782-1852). Education is the process through which the child makes internal, external.

(xiii) *Nunn* (1870-1944). Education is the complete development of the individuality of the child so that he can make an original contribution to human life according to the best of his capacity.

(xiv) *Dewey* (1859-1952). Education is the development of all those capacities in the individual which will enable him to control his environment and fulfil his possibilities.

(xv) *Montessori* (1870-1952). Education means helping in the complete unfolding of the child's personality.

## 1.11 BEST DEFINITION OF EDUCATION

Going through the various definitions of education, one finds that there is a wide difference among the scholars and thinkers. This difference has arisen as education has been defined in the light of the needs of times in different countries. Keeping into account all the definitions, an attempt is made here to give a comprehensive definition of education. Education is a conscious as well as unconscious, deliberate or non-deliberate process of balanced harmonious and maximum development of the innate powers of the individual—aesthetic, cultural, emotional, intellectual, physical, religious, social, spiritual and vocational, according to individual and social needs.

Chief merits of the above mentioned definition are:

1. It takes note of the innate powers of the individual i.e. heredity.
2. It accepts that education may be formal, informal and non-formal i.e. an individual receives education in educational institutions and even without them.
3. It attaches due importance to the environment—environment may be specially designed as is provided in educational institutions or may be natural and unplanned.
4. It includes all aspects of the individual i.e. it treats an individual as a whole.
5. It is based on the needs of the individual as well of the society.
6. It stresses the words 'balanced and harmonious'.
7. This definition is based on the fact that 'drawing out' of the innate

powers i.e. hereditary and 'pouring in' i.e. environmental influences are complementary and supplementary.

## 1.12 FOUR PILLARS OF EDUCATION: EDUCATION FOR THE TWENTYFIRST CENTURY

*Present Tensions*: The International Commission on Education (IEC) for the twenty-first century (1993-96) appointed by UNESCO that considered various aspects of education needed for the 21st century, listed the following tensions that should be taken note of.

1. Global *vs.* Local tension.
2. Universal *vs.* Individual
3. Tradition *vs.* Modernity
4. Long-term consideration *vs.* Short-term consideration
5. Need for competition *vs.* The concern for equality
6. Spiritual *vs.* Material

*Four Pillars of Education*: The Commission proposed the following four pillars of education to meet the changes.

*Learning to Know*: This means 'learning to learn' so as to benefit from the opportunities education provides throughout life. It also implies to acquire education by combining a sufficiently broad general knowledge with the opportunity to work in depth on a small number of subjects.

*Learning to Do*. This means to acquire not only an occupational skill but also competence to deal with many situations and work in teams. It also implies learning to do in the context of young people's various social and work experiences. These social and work experiences may be formal or informal.

*Learning to Live Together*: This means (i) Developing an understanding of other people, (ii) Carrying on joint projects, (iii) Managing conflicts, (iv) Developing a spirit of respect for the values of others' culture.

*Learning to be*: This means developing one's personality and to be able to act with full sense of responsibility. In the connection education to pay due regard to all aspects of individual's potential: aesthetic sense, communication skills, memory, reasoning and physical capacities.

# 2

# Aims of Education

## 2.1 WHY AIMS OF EDUCATION? OR SIGNIFICANCE OF AIMS OF EDUCATION

It is accepted by all that without the knowledge of aims, the educator is like a sailor who does not know his destination and the child is like a rudderless vessel which will be drifted along somewhere ashore.

Educational aims are important for the following reasons:

1. Educational aims given direction to educational activity.
2. Educational aims provide meaning to the educational programme.
3. Educational aims help in acting intelligently.
4. Educational aims provide motivation to take up educational programmes.
5. Educational aims are necessary for efficient school organization, administration and supervision.
6. Educational aims are necessary to assess the outcomes or results of the process of education.
7. Educational aims are useful for parents, students and teachers to contribute their best to achieve these aims.
8. Educational aims give continuity and significance to education.

## 2.2 FACTORS AFFECTING AIMS OF EDUCATION

Aims are related to the needs of the individual and the society. Education to be effective must meet the many-sided needs of the individual and the society. Since change is the law of nature, needs also undergo changes. A child is educated in a society. So to become a useful member, he must be educated according to the changed needs. Educational aims change with the cultural, economic, geographical, political, philosophical, religious and sociological changes in the society. Thus educational aims may differ from time to time and country to country.

The moral and religious aims dominated education in ancient India.

There were two diametrically opposed aims of education in ancient greek states. On account of internal as well external in security, Sparta, aimed at developing courage, endurance, obedience and above all physical strength of its pupils under the supreme control of the State. The immediate aim of education was to train Spartan youth as good soldiers. On the other hand, Athenian education was finer and richer. It laid more stress on inculcating in pupils such qualities as obedience to elders, ability to discern the beautiful and to enjoy life, fortitude and truthfulness. The sophists overstressed system aimed at acquainting the pupils with several subjects. Ability to argue and debate was strengthened.

The educational system of the Romans was more utilitarian in nature. Moral aim was also given due attention. It was more state welfare oriented than individual development oriented.

Education in middle age was on the whole religion-dominated.

During the 18th, 19th and first half of the 20th century, the imperialists powers of Europe had established their rule in several parts of the world. Accordingly their interest was to establish that system which catered to their needs and those of the conquered nations. It was natural that after gaining independence, the independent countries established third educational system which suited their aspirations and needs.

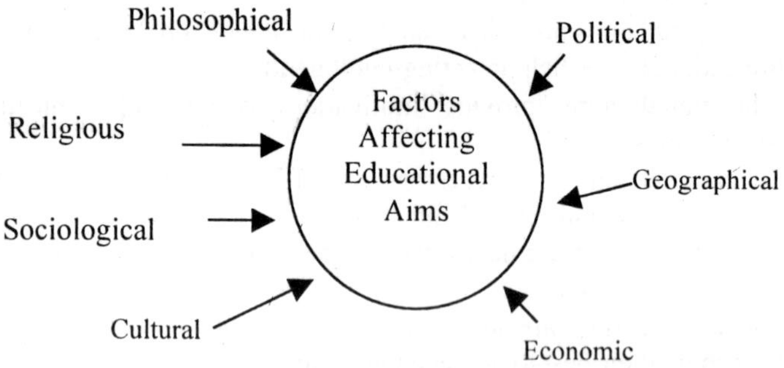


*Fig. 2.1: Factors affecting educational aims*

## 2.3 GENERAL AIMS OF EDUCATION

1. Aesthetic aim.
2. Complete living aim.
3. Cultural aim.
4. Harmonious and all-round development aim.
5. Happiness aim.
6. Individual aim.
7. International understanding aim.
8. Knowledge aim.
9. Leisure aim or recreational aim.
10. Moral aim.
11. Physical health and well being aim.

12. Political aim.
13. Religious aim.
14. Self-realization aim.
15. Social aim.
16. Spiritual aim.
17. Vocational aim.

*Summing up*: Education to be effective cannot have a single aim. An ideal balance among various aims has to be struck.

*Aesthetic Aim of Education*: It consists of developing the aesthetic senses of the child for instance appreciation of the beauty of the sun-set or song or an object of art etc.

*Cultural Aim of Education*: Although culture has different meanings, here it is taken as a way of communicating with others i.e. use of refined etiquettes and manners.

*Knowledge Aim of Education*: Some sort of knowledge is necessary for a well-adjusted life.

*Moral Aim of Education*: It is related to the development of values like honesty etc.

*Vocational Aim of Education*: According to this aim, education must enable an individual to earn his livelihood.

*Physical Strength Aim of Education*: Sparta, a Greek State followed the physical strength as the chief of education in ancient times. This was account of the reason that it faced external as well internal dangers to its freedom. So the state prepared its citizen to become efficient soldiers and fighters.

## 2.4 INDIVIDUAL AIM AND SOCIAL AIM OF EDUCATION

### Individual Aim of Education

*Meaning of Individual Aim*: Individual aim of education implies that education should train the individual first. The primary task of education is to provide such an environment in which the individuality of the pupil is most completely developed.

### Supporters of Individual Aim of Education

1. *Biologists' Support to Individual Aim*: Prof. G. Thompson is the ardent supporter of this aim. According to him education must enable the individual to survive.

2. *Naturalists' Support to Individual Aim*: Rousseau's is the champion of this view. According to him, "Everything is good as it comes from the hands of nature but everything degenerates in the hands of man." Likewise Percy Nunn states, "Nothing good enters into the human work except in and through the free activities of the individual."

3. *Psychologists' Support to Individual Aim*: According to psychologists,

each individual is a separate and unique identity. Accordingly education should be in accordance with individual needs.

4. *Spiritualists' Support to Education*: The spiritualists, in general stress that the aim of life is self-realisation. Education, therefore, must provide opportunities for self development and self-realisation.

**Criticism of the Individual Aim of Education**

1. According to Raymont, an individual is only a figment of imagination. An individual cannot be conceived in isolation from society.

2. Absolute freedom to the individual should not be given. The individual may begin to assert that 'I must have what I want.'

3. The critics of individual aim believe that the individual left to himself is an animal, selfish and indisciplined. The animal instinct of man, if given, a loose rein is sure to lead him to the state of primitive barbarism where the law of jungle prevailed.

4. The exaggerated claim of the individual may have an adverse effect in the politics and economy of a country. The policy of *'Laissez faire'* i.e. 'let things go alone' is not conducive to national interests in the modern times.

**Social Aim of Education**

*Meaning of Social Aim of Education*: Social aim has several dimensions. (1) Society is supreme and an individual exists in the society and for the society, (2) State should provide for citizenship training, (3) Social efficiency should be the main aim of all training.

Social aim of education finds expressions in such terms 'education for citizenship' and 'education for social service'.

**Supporters of the Social Aim of Education**

1. According to Prof. Dewey, a socially efficient individual is an asset to himself as well as to society. He is able to earn his livelihood. He conforms to moval and social standards of conduct.

2. Raymont says that a individual is a social being. An isolated individual is 'a figment of imagination'. An individual lives in the society. So he should be trained through social contacts.

3. The Education Commission 1984-66 emphasized that education cannot be considered in isolation. It is to be planned in social settings. It must contribute to national development.

**Criticism of the Social Aims of Education**

1. Social aim of education ignores the fact that every individual has his unique individuality.

2. Undue stress on social aim of education is against the concept of universal brotherhood.

3. Extreme form of social aim has led to the concept. "My country!

Wrong or right" This emphasis became responsible for the rise of Nazism in Germany and Fascism in Italy. As a result of this, Second World War took place. Rise of communism led to lot of bloodshed.

4. Social aim of education envisages the individual as a non-entity and leaves little scope for his personality development.

**Synthesis Between Individual and Social Aim of Education**

The individual and the society, both be regarded as realities. Neither of the two is absolutely independent of the other. Instead of being regarded as isolated entities, the individual and the society should be considered as related to each other. The individual acts on the society, and the society reacts on the individual. The individual is the product of society. The society in the own turn finds its advancement in the development of its individual members. In the words of John Adam, 'Individuality requires a social medium to grow. Without social contact we are not human."

According to Ross, "Individuality is of no value and personality is a meaningless term apart from the social environment in which they are developed." Self-realization can be achieved only through social service. Social ideas of real value can come into being only through free individuals who have developed valuable individuality. The circle cannot be broken.

Following points should be noted in this regard:

1. Individuality and society are interdependent.
2. Equal importance should be given to the individual and the society.
3. Synthesis is always an ideal condition.
4. The good of all is the good of each and the good of each is the good of all.

## 2.5 CHARACTER DEVELOPMENT AIM OF EDUCATION AND VOCATIONAL AIM OF EDUCATION

**Character Development as an Aim in Education**

*Meaning of Character*: Broadly speaking, each letter of the word as given below signifies some characteristics of a man of character:

C denotes—Cooperativeness, Constructiveness. Creativity. Clarity.
H denotes—Hard work, Humility. Honesty.
A denotes—Affectionate
R denotes—Rational.
A denotes—Adaptability
C denotes—Cleanliness (Ethical)
T denotes—Truthfulness. Tolerance
E denotes—Ethics
R denotes—Reasonable

Character has two aspects: personal and relationship with society

**Importance of Character as an Aim of Education**

Gandhiji has observed, "All our learning or recitation of the Vedas, correct knowledge of Sanskrit, Latin, Greek and what not will avail us nothing if they do not enable us to cultivate absolute purity of heart. The end of all knowledge must be building up of character."

According to Swami Vivekananda, "We want that education by which character is formed".

Dewey has stated, "The formation of character is a comprehensive aim of education."

The Secondary Education Commission has observed, "Education is the training of character to fit the students to participate creatively as citizens."

*Building of Character*: It is very difficult to build character.

Character is the product of daily, hourly actions and words and thoughts; daily forgiveness, unselfishness, kindness, sympathies, clarities, sacrifices for the good of others, struggles against temptations. What is character without elementary personal purity?

In India today we find a lack of character at various levels so much so that the actions of the V.I.P.'s also create doubts in the mind of the common man. State of affairs is very shocking. The present saying is 'As the ruler, so that people'. Perhaps after independence, morality or character has been the greatest causality. Education, therefore, must be devoted to character building activities.

*Criticism of Character Development Aim*: The aim is one-sided. A man of character but empty stomach will face frustration.

**Vocational Aim of Education**

*Meaning of Vocational Aim:* It implies preparing students for livelihood. It is also called 'bread and butter aim'.

*Importance of Vocational Aim in Education*

(i) An individual must be prepared to earn his livelihood, otherwise he will not be a happy man.

(ii) Vocational education contributes to increase production and national wealth.

(iii) As Gandhiji observed, "True education ought to be for them (boys and girls) a kind of insurance against unemployment.

(iv) Vocational education develops values of dignity of labour.

(v) Vocational education reduces verbalism and memorisation.

(vi) Vocational training is also suitable for persons with low intelligence.

*Criticism of Vocational Aim of Education*: Man does not live by bread alone. This aim is very narrow.

*Synthesis of Character Formation and Vocational Aim of Education:* Vocational aim in education has its own importance but man does not live by bread alone. Education must take into consideration the entire personality of the pupil and not one segment of it. Man has to develop himself aesthetically, intellectually, morality, physically, socially and vocationally. The University Education Commission 1948-1949 has very rightly observed, that vocational aim alone would starve the spirit and lead to '*Rakshas Raj*'.

Pt. Nehru has stated, "Education has mainly two aspects, the cultural aspect which makes a person grow, and the productive aspect which makes a person do things. Both are essential. Everybody should be a producer as well as good citizen." Gandhiji, it is true, stressed the vocational aspect but at the same time he was very emphatic, "By education I mean an all-round drawing out of the best in child and man—body, mind and spirit". He was convinced that without character, vocational efficiency had no meaning.

## 2.6 AIM OF EDUCATION IN INDIA THROUGH THE AGES

*Aim of Education in Ancient India*: Aim of life in the Vedic period and the Buddhist period was *'mukti'* or *'nirvana'* i.e. salvation. Accordingly education was imparted for the realization of this aim. Development of personal purity was the common feature. Of course, contents and methods of education differed in both the periods.

*Aim of Education during the Medieval Period*: Religious aim was the supreme aim.

*Aim of education during the British period*: Aim of education was to prepare individuals who would serve the British rulers faithfully.

*Aims of Education in Democratic Free India*: The ideals and values embodied in the Preamble to the Constitution of India are the guiding sources of educational aims in India. These may be expressed as under:

1. Development of democratic values.
2. Development of egalitarian values (values of equality).
3. Development of secular values.
4. Development of values related to dignity of individual.
5. Development of values conducive to the unity of the country.
6. Development of skills and values related to vocations/professions.
7. Development of values related to universal brotherhood and understanding.

(*Details are discussed in the subsequent chapters*).

## 2.7 IMMEDIATE AND ULTIMATE AIMS OF EDUCATION

*Immediate or Functional Aims of Education*: The specific aims or immediate or functional aims which need immediate attention are:

1. Development of language abilities of listening, reading, writing and thinking and communication skills needed for social living.
2. Development of mathematical abilities to develop a logical mind that would help learn perform mathematical operations and apply them in daily life.

3. Development of scientific temper.
4. Development of environmental understanding
5. Development of qualities necessary for self-learning.
6. Development of appreciation of small families.
7. Development of healthy sex related attitudes.
8. Development of the capacity to process, understand, reflect and develop insight.
9. Development of qualities needed for living a harmonious social life.
10. Development of attitudes and skills necessary for keeping physically and mentally fit.
11. Development of understanding and appreciation of composite culture of India and diversity in language etc. of the people of India.
12. Development of respectful attitude for freedom fighters.
13. Development of appreciation for the need of a balanced synthesis between technological advancements and humanistic values.
14. Development of appreciation for the need of a balanced synthesis between globalisation and localisation.
15. Development of respect for the national symbols.
16. Development of patriotic ideals to preserve national unity.

*Ultimate or Universal Aim of Education*: The ultimate or universal aim of education is the emotional, ethical, intellectual and physical integration of the individual into a complete individual. In other words 'education is for complete living'.

*Concluding Observations*: The immediate aims of education should become the stepping stones for the ultimate aims of education.

# 3

# Meaning, Nature and Scope of Philosophy: Philosophy and Education

## 3.1 SIGNIFICANCE OF PHILOSOPHY

The subject matter of philosophy is as wide as human experience. It is as old as human life. There is no aspect of life, natural or supernatural, animate or inanimate which falls outside its domain. This wide scope in itself indicates the significance of philosophy. On account of this fact, Francis Bacon (1561-1626), a great English philosopher considered philosophy as the 'great mother of the sciences.' Philosophy is so deeply involved into human life that Aristotle (384-322 B.C.), the great Greek philosopher remarked, "Everyone follows a philosophy, whether he is aware of it or not."

Thousands of years ago, Indian seers and thinkers developed a very comprehensive and well-organised system of philosophy for the guidance of an individual.

## 3.2 MEANING AND NATURE OF PHILOSOPHY

Sanskrit word *'Darshan'* (philosophy) means 'direct perception' of the truth. Seers of ancient India used to see or perceive the truth. The same thing may be said about Socrates (469-399 B.C.), Plato (427-347 B.C.) and Aristotle (384-322 B.C.)—trio of Greek philosophy.

The word 'philosophy' has a Greek origin. *'Philosophia'* a Greek word consists of two words, i.e. *'phileo'* meaning love and *'sophia'* meaning wisdom. Therefore, the literal meaning of philosophy is 'love of wisdom'.

The following definitions of philosophy help us to understand the true meaning of philosophy.

1. In the words of Plato, "Knowledge of the true nature of different things is philosophy."
2. According to Aristotle, "Philosophy is a science which discovers the real nature of supernatural elements."
3. Kant (1724-1804) regards philosophy as "the science and criticism of cognition".
4. Dr. Radhakrishnan (1872-1970) considers philosophy as a "logical inquiry into the nature of reality."

5. Henderson (1947) thinks that philosophy is a search for "a comprehensive view of nature, an attempt at a universal explanation of the nature of things".

From above we conclude that:

1. Philosophy is a search for reality and truth.
2. Philosophy is based on enquiry.
3. Philosophy is local.
4. Philosophy is a dynamic and living force.
5. Philosophy is an art as well as a science.
6. Philosophy is closely related to education.
7. Philosophy is an intellectual attempt to interpret and understand nature.
8. Philosophy is love of knowledge.
9. Philosophy is love of wisdom.
10. Philosophy is a guide to a way of life.

## 3.3 WHY DO WE NEED PHILOSOPHY

Philosophy gives a direction to life. Philosophy in India emerged as a result of reflection over the experiences and problems of life. Dr. Radhakrishnan, the great Indian philosopher has suggested this meaning of philosophy through the titles of two of his books. *"The Indian View of Life"* and *"The Idealist View of Life"*. Human life is always purposeful. The purpose of life is determined by the philosophy of life.

We need philosophy to take decisions wisely and to act consistently. One need wisdom to distinguish between two extremes—falsehood and truth, ugliness and beauty, night and wrong etc. Philosophy enables us to live by values for we do not live only by bread, vitamins and technological discoveries.

## 3.4 SCOPE OF PHILOSOPHY

Scope of philosophy is so vast that Cicero (106-43) B.C., a Roman scholar called it as 'the mother of all arts" and "the true medicine of mind." Francis Bacon, a great English philosopher regarded the philosophy as, "the great mother of the Sciences". Coleridge (1772-1834) a noted poet considered it as the 'Science of Sciences'.

Broadly speaking following types of problems come under the scope of philosophy.

1. Problems of reality
2. Problems of knowledge
3. Problems of value

## Scope of Philosophy (Various Branches)

**Metaphysics**

It deals with questions like

i) What is soul?

ii) What is a living being?

iii) What is the relationship between body and soul?

**Ideology**

It thinks of God and discuss following types of questions:

a) Does God exist?

b) If yes, What are the proofs?

c) What is the nature of God?

**Cosmogony**

It deals with various problems investigated are?

i) What is origin of universe?

ii) Is the universe created?

**Cosmology**

It deals with issues like:

i) Is the universe one?

ii) Is the universe made of spiritual elements?

**Ontology**

It deals with issues like

i) What are the eternal element of universe?

ii) What is the mutual relationship between the elements of universe

**Epistemology**

It deals with questions like

i) What is truth?

ii) What is doubt?

iii) What are the sources of acquiring technolgy

**Ethics**

It deals with questions like

i) What is good?

ii) What is evil?

iii) What is good behaviour?

**Aesthetic**

It deals with questions like

i) What is beauty?

ii) What is ugly?

**Logic**

It deals with questions like

i) What is nature of logical thinking

ii) What is the relationship of inductive and deductive logical methods

## 3.5 RELATIONSHIP BETWEEN PHILOSOPHY AND EDUCATION

Education and philosophy are inseparable. This is explained as:

1. Education and life are interdependent. The aim of education is the all round development or promotion of life. Likewise philosophy and life are inseparable. It is, therefore, natural that education and philosophy are inseperable. It is aptly remarked that without philosophy, education would be a 'blind effort' and without education philosophy would be 'cripple'.

2. Philosophy points out the way, and education follows it. Education thus becomes the best means for the promotion of philosophy. For the good of life, for the good of the individual and for the good of society, we need direction. This direction is provided by philosophy, which is the mother of all sciences including education. This, however, does not mean that education is a slave of philosophy. The field of education provides a testing ground to test the truth of wisdom or direction provided by philosophy. Without the testing ground of education, philosophers would remain arm-chair theorists. A constant mutual interaction goes on between the two.

It is stated that when we define education as the modification of behaviour, the direction in which modification is to be carried out is determined by philosophy. Philosophy deals with the end and education with the means.

3. Education and philosophy are two sides of the same coin—life. Sir John Adams said that education is the dynamic side of philosophy. As Ross put it, "Education is the active aspect of philosophical belief, the practical means of realising ideals of life." T.P. Nunn has also said, "Educational aims are correlative to ideals of life". Henderson has expressed similar views, "Educational aims cannot be determined apart from the ends and aims of life itself for educational aims grow out of life's aims. To determine what constitutes worth living has been one of the chief tasks of philosophy."

Gentile feels that "Education without philosophy would mean a failure to understand the precise nature of education".

4. Fichte right rightly observed, "the art of education will never attain complete clearness without philosophy." Dewey said, "Philosophy is the theory of education is its most general phrases. Education is a laboratory in which philosophical directions become concrete and are tested".

5. If education is a set of techniques for imparting knowledge, skills and attitudes philosophy is the foundation to vitalise these. Philosophy is the foundation and education is the super-structure.

6. Philosophy determines what is worth-living. Education then prepares for that.

**Almost all Great philosophers are Great Educators and Great Educators as Great Philosophers**

A close analysis of the concept of education as given by various philosophers and educators will make clear that their views on education are based on their varying concepts of reality, of knowledge, of wisdom and of values. The great philosophers of all times have also been great educators.

Most of the educational movements were the outcome of their philosophical beliefs. Views of great thinkers like Socrates, Plato, Aristotle, Comenius, John Locke, Rousseau, Froebel, Dewey, H.G. Wells, Bertrand Russell, A.N. Whitehead and Aldous Huxley, offer an interesting example of the intimate connection between philosophy and education. The ancient sages in India were all educational philosophers. In recent times, this is fully illustrated in the case of Swami Dayananda, Swami Vivekananda, Sri Aurobindo, Rabindranath Tagore, Dr. Radhakrishnan, Mahatma Gandhi etc.

## 3.6 CONTRIBUTION OF PHILOSOPHY TO EDUCATION

The contribution of philosophy to education may be taken up under the following heads:

1. Philosophy and Educational Aims
2. Philosophy and Curriculum
3. Philosophy and Textbooks
4. Philosophy and Methods of Teaching
5. Philosophy and the Discipline
6. Philosophy and the Teacher
7. Philosophy and Educational Organisation, Administration and Supervision

1. *Philosophy and Educational Aims*: The aim of education has a reference to the ideals or philosophy of a nation. In independent India, philosophy of life is enshrined in the Preamble of its Constitution. Educational aims according draw their inspiration from it. The aims of education in the U.S.A. are based on its democratic philosophy. The philosophy of fascism determined the aims of education in Germany during Hitler's time. The philosophy of communism influenced the aims of education in Russia and China.

2. *Philosophy and Curriculum*: The philosophical approach to life is the guiding factor in the determination of the curriculum. Gandhi's scheme of basic education was an expression of his philosophy. He was against the lopsidedness of the system of education as propounded by Lord Macaulay and was moved by the illiteracy and poverty of the people. His scheme of studies, therefore, emphasised crafts and the environment. He was very keen to make education self-supporting besides developing moral character. The National Policy on Education 1986 lays stress on a Core Curriculum keeping in view the needs of emotional and national integration.

Introduction of self-government in school programme is the outcome of democratic philosophy.

Various philosophies like humanism, idealism, pragmatism and naturalism have influenced curriculum in varying degrees.

3. *Philosophy and Textbooks*: The contents of the textbooks must mirror the philosophy or way of life of the people. In a socialist society textbooks emphasise socialist philosophy. In a state dominated and ruled by religious

leaders, textbooks reflect tenets of scriptures. In India, since independence, there has been a great stress on emotional integration and national unity. Accordingly textbooks are being screened from time to time to ensure that they include only that matter which promoters emotional integration and national unity.

4. *Philosophy and Methods of Teaching*: Every school of philosophy has its own methods of teaching. Accordingly to the philosophy of idealism, question-answer method, lecture method and discussion method are the most suitable methods of education. Naturalism recommends learning by doing, learning by self-experience and direct experience. Pragmatic philosophy advocates project method, problem solving method and socialist techniques.

5. *Philosophy and Discipline*: Philosophy has a great bearing on discipline in educational institutions. In a democratic set up, discipline is viewed as inner discipline as well as social discipline based on group work. In the totalitarian state, discipline is regimented and assumes the form of a military discipline, and is based on fear of the teacher and the head. There is little concern for the individuality of the child in a totalitarian type of discipline. The idealists emphasise the impact of impression of the teacher on his students. 'Free discipline' is the slogan of the naturalist.

6. *Philosophy and the Teacher*: A teacher is said to play an important role in shaping and moulding the ideals, habits, manners, tastes and ways of life and above all the character and personality of the students. It is, therefore, very essential that he must have a consistent and sound philosophy in accordance with the philosophy of the nation to which he belongs.

A teacher with fatalistic negative philosophy cannot help in the realisation of such an aim as 'complete living' or 'harmonious development'. A teacher without a democratic philosophy would not be able to develop democratic ideals in his students. There is no doubt that the philosophy of a teacher affects everything with which he is connected—the educand, the aims, the curriculum, the textbooks, the methods of teaching, the discipline and the class management.

Philosophy helps the teacher in the following ways:

It provides a way of life to the teacher.

It provides direction to the teacher.

It provides insight to the teacher to comprehend the problems of education in general.

It guides the teacher to undertake experiments.

It enables the teacher to think constructively and rationally.

It serves as a guide to the teacher to solve disciplinary problems.

7. *Philosophy and Educational Organisation, Administration and Supervision*: Democratic philosophy lays emphasis on the participation of the staff and the students in running some programmes of the educational institutions. Philosophy of communism provides little scope for such involvement and the head decides everything.

# 4

# Concept and Development of National System of Education

## 4.1 CONCEPT OF THE NATIONAL SYSTEM OF EDUCATION

National system of education is that system which is in accordance with the national needs and its aspirations. Each nation differs from the other in various respects. Therefore, each nation may have a different national system of education. Education is considered as an important instrument of fulfilling the needs and aspirations of a nation.

National system of education reflects the philosophical and sociological perspectives of a nation.

National system of education is based on the ideals and values of a nation as given in the constitution.

The concept of the national system of education as given in the National Policy on Education, 1986 and as amended in 1992 is explained as under:

1. The concept of national system of education implies that upto a given level all students, irrespective of caste, creed, location or sex, have access to education.
2. The education provided must be of a comparable quality.
3. The national system of education must embody the principles as laid down in the constitution of a nation.
4. The national system of education should have a national curricular framework. This should contains a common core.
5. The contents of education should take into consideration local and regional needs.
6. The contents should reflect unity in diversity.
7. The structure of education should be uniform. Structure implies during of different stages of education, for instance primary stage of five years, upper primary of three years or elementary of eight years, etc.
8. The curriculum should promote common national values.
9. The curriculum should include elements of equality of the sexes.
10. The curriculum should include elements of protection of the environment.
11. The curriculum should include elements which lead to removal of social barriers.

12. The curriculum should include secular values.

13. There should be a common national language or link language to be learnt.

14. All regional languages should be given maximum opportunity to flourish.

15. There should be no domicile restrictions on entry into any educational institution.

16. There should be network of educational institutions of all types in the country.

17. There should be inter-regional mobility of scholars.

18. There should be important educational institutions and organisations at the national level to provide effective direction and guidance.

19. There should be a meaningful partnership in education at the national level, state level and local level.

## 4.2 NEED FOR A NATIONAL SYSTEM OF EDUCATION

Education is considered as the mirror of a nation and an educational institution as a nation in miniature. Education is also considered as one of the most important agents of social change or national progress and prosperity. The Education Commission 1964-66 observed, "The destiny of India is being shaped in her classrooms." The National Policy on Education observed, "Education is fundamental to our all round development, material and spiritual." On account of the important of education, it is essential that there should be a national system of education.

A national system of education is needed on account of the following considerations:

1. Every individual is different from every other. Similarly nations differ. Every nation wants its own identity. This identity must be preserved. Education plays a pre-dominant role in preserving its identity.

2. Nationalism promotes national feelings and education develops values of nationalism among the students.

3. National system of education develops feeling of harmony among people residing in different regions and belonging to different sections.

4. National system of education is needed to develop a feeling of patriotism among students.

5. National system of education is needed to develop a feeling of oneness.

6. National system of education is needed to develop a feeling of solidarity.

7. National system of education is needed to develop a feeling of tolerance of each other's belief.

8. National system of education is needed to provide equality of opportunity irrespective of any consideration.

9. National system of education is needed to acquaint the students with the national heritage.

10. National system of education is needed to establish an egalitarian Nation by developing values of equality and socialism.

11. National system of education is needed to pay equal attention to the development of all regions by establishing all types of educational institutions.

12. National system of education is needed to develop democratic and secular values.

13. National system of education is needed to bring about a synthesis between moral and scientific values.

14. National system of education is needed to facilitate admission of students on transfer or migration of people.

## 4.3 DEVELOPMENT OF NATIONAL SYSTEM OF EDUCATION IN ANCIENT PERIOD

### High Standard of Education in Ancient India

Education in ancient India was wide-spread. From all accounts it was universal. The standard of education was so high that the foreign students and scholars used to come to India for receiving education and enlightenment. On account of its achievements in education and learning, India was called *'Jagat Guru'* (world teacher). To use the modern phraseology, foreigners who got their education in India, took pride in calling themselves 'India Returned' as some of us take period in introducing ourselves as 'U.K. Returned' or 'U.S. Returned'. It is, therefore, no wonder that an English scholar Dr. F.W. Thomas in his book *History and Prospectus of British Education in India*, published in 1891 in England, made the following observations:

1. There is no other country in the world where the love of learning had so early an origin as in India.
2. Learning has exercised a powerful influence in India.
3. Education is not imported in India.

According to the *Encyclopedia Britanica,* Vol. 7, there was note-worthy progress in learning in all fields including science.

*National System of Education.* In spite of all round advancement in learning and education in ancient India, there was no national system of education in the sense as we use this term-nowadays. The rulers in ancient India gave liberal support to scholars and educational institutions, especially of higher learning (Universities). However, they did not interfere in the working of educational institutions.

*Secondly*, there was the religious influence as well as spiritual influence which guided all educational pursuits. This served as a great cementing force—a necessary element in the development of the national system of education. Education was an instrument of *'Mukti'* or *'Nirvana'* (Salvation). This was the common goal.

*Thirdly*, the national system of education had uniform contents in the study of Vedas and other scriptures.

*Fourthly*, the system of education provided lot of flexibility in content and approach.

*Fifthly*, Sanskrit language brought about uniformity during the Vedic period and Prakrit and Pali during the Buddhist period.

**Notable Features of National System of Education in Ancient India**

1. *Education Free and Accessible*: Education was free and accessible to all who sought it.

2. *No State Control on Education*: Rulers of the country subsidised and supported education, if they thought fit to do so, with grants of land or money, but imposed no conditions or control on teachers affecting their freedom of work.

3. *High Status of Teachers*: Teachers were a highly honoured class—honoured even by kings. Kings rose from their thrones to receive great teachers. A well-known Sanskrit verse goes so far as to say:

"The teacher is Brahma. The teacher is Vishnu. The teacher is the Great God Shiva. The teacher is the Great Brahman (Supreme Divine Soul) incarnate. Bow to that teacher!"

4. *Teachers as Parents*: Teachers behaved as parents to their pupils and pupils behaved as members of the teachers' family. The attitude of the pupil was to be one of complete submission.

5. *Residential Schools*: Teachers and pupils lived together and so identified themselves with one another.

6. *Aim of Education—Self-Realisation*: The ultimate aim of education in ancient India was not knowledge preparation for life in this word or for life beyond, but for complete realisation of self—liberation of the soul.

7. *Immediate Aim—Vocational*: The immediate aim of education, however, was to prepare the different sections of people for their actual needs of life.

8. *Education—Moral, Religious and Spiritual*: Education was for education's sake, not for a public examination or for paid public or private service, as it is generally considered to be at present. It was not merely intellectual. It was also moral, religious and spiritual.

9. *Curriculum*: The subjects of instruction varied according to the religious, spiritual and vocational needs of the different classes as far as immediate aim of education was concerned.

10. *Method of Instruction*: The method of instruction generally consisted of recitation by the teacher and repetition by the pupil. This was followed by explanation by the teacher, questioning by the pupil, and discussion between the teacher and the pupil.

11. *Individual Teaching*: Pupils were taught, individually, not *en masse* by the class method.

12. *Method of Study*: The method of study consisted in listening to the teacher, reflection on what had been listened to and its constant revision.

13. *Forests as Centres of Education*: The place of education was generally the forest "far from the madding crowd's ignoble strife".

14. *Role of Travel in Education*: Travel was regarded as necessary to give a finishing touch to education.

15. *Sanskrit as the Medium of Instruction*: The medium of instruction in institutions conducted by Brahmans was Sanskrit.

16. *Self-Control and Self-Discipline*: Self-control or self-discipline was considered to be the best discipline.

17. *Wide-Spread Education of Women*: In the earlier Vedic and Upanishadic times, girls were free to go through the *'Upanayana'* ceremony. They studied Vedas, Vedangas and other subjects along with their brother pupils.

18. *Science Education in Ancient India*: It goes back to the Indus Valley Civilisation, about 5 thousand years ago, when people were familiar with mining and metal-work, simple architecture, manufacturing of gypsum, cement and permanent paints. Vedic science included the element of astronomy, mathematics, chemistry and biology.

19. *Commercial Education in Ancient India*: There were no organised educational institutions, though most of the trades had formed efficient guilds during the first millenium of the Christian era. Training was usually imparted in the family by the elders in real learning situations.

20. *Mathematics Education in Ancient India*: Ancient India quite earlier evolved a system of geometry. Shulvasutras are the oldest mathematical works, probably composed between 400 B.C. and 200 A.D. Aryabhata (476-52) is the first great name in Indian mathematics. To the period immediately proceeding him belongs one of the most significant of human discoveries, the zero, though the name of the discoverer is unknown.

## 4.4 NATIONAL SYSTEM OF EDUCATION DURING THE MEDIEVAL PERIOD

*Religion-dominated Education*: During the medieval period also, there was no such concept of national system of education as we find to-day. Generally, State or the rulers did not interfere in the functioning of educational institutions. Of course, they did give liberal grants to scholars and educational institutions.

### Main Features of Education During the Medieval Period

Following were the distinguishing features of education in India during the Medieval period.

1. *Religion-Centred Education*: In the words of S.N. Mukerji, "The whole educational system was saturated with religious ideals which influenced the aim, the contents of study, and even the daily life of the

pupils." The pupils acquired knowledge as a religious obligation.

2. *Countryside as the Centres of Education*: By and large, educational institutions flourished in the countryside.

3. *Pursuit of Various Disciplines*: Though education was primarily religion-oriented, it included the study of subjects like mathematics, astronomy, grammar, polity and politics. Art and literature were also encouraged.

4. *Norms of Behaviour*: Adequate stress was laid on well-defined norms of behaviour, pattern of thought, building up personality and character of the pupils.

5. *Learned Teachers*: Teachers took to teaching for love of learning. They were held in high esteem. Prof. S.N. Mukerji has observed, "Learning was prized for its own sake and as a mark of the highest human development.

6. *Close Relation between the Teacher and the Pupils*: The relations between the teacher and the pupils were based on affection and respect. The teachers used to pay individual attention to the students.

7. *No Set Machinery for Educational Administration*: The rulers neither claimed any authority over the educational institutions nor interfered and their management.

8. *Patronage of the Rulers*: The rulers helped in the spread of education. they also built educational institutions and universalities. They endowed them with funds. Big landlords also provided financial help for the spread of education. The rulers patronised the men of learning.

9. *Discipline*: Punishments were quite severe. Truants and delinquents were caned on their palms and slapped on their faces. A strange mode of punishment was to make the children hold their ears by taking their hands from under their thighs while sitting on their tiptoes. Whipping was also quite common. Any form of punishment devised and thought of by the ingenuity of the teacher was permissible.

10. *Vocational Education:* The construction of so many magnificent buildings clearly shows that vocational education in different crafts had reached a high water mark.

## 4.5 NATIONAL SYSTEM OF EDUCATION DURING THE BRITISH RULE IN INDIA

Some scholars go to the extent of saying that the system of education was not national but 'anti-national'. It was foreign in aims and contents of education. This is borne out from the observations of Lord Macaulay (1800-1859) who is considered to be the architect of the system of education. Lord Macaulay was the Law Member of the Council of Governor Guard and Chairman of the Committee of Public Instruction appointed by the Lord William Bentinck, the Governor General of India:

1. A single shelf of a good European literature was worth the whole

native literature of India and Asia."

2. About India's literature and religion he said, "A false history, false astronomy, false medicine because we find them in the company of false religion."

3. "We must at present do our best to form a class of persons Indian in blood and colour, but English in Eastes, in opinion, in morals and in intellect."

4. "There is no Hindu who may keep real faith in his religion after studying English."

Some attempts were made by freedom fighters and social and religious reformers in India to evolve the national system of educator.

A National Council of Education was set out in 1905. Hundreds of students studying in Government educational institutions joined national institutions.

Swami Dayanand's followers established a chain of D.A.V. Institutions in different parts of India. In 1905, during the agitation against the Partition of Bengal efforts were made to establish nationalist educational institutions. The Non-Cooperation Movement (1920-22) also created an urge to establish educational institutions free from British Control.

Several national universities like the Bihar Vidyapeeth, Gujarat Vidyapeeth, Jamia Millia Islamia and Kashi Vidyapeeth came into existence during 1920-22. Viswabharti was also established during the period.

## 4.6 NATIONAL SYSTEM OF EDUCATION DURING POST-INDEPENDENCE PERIOD

### National System of Elementary Education

While discussing the National System of Education in the Post-Independence period, following points need attention:

1. Strictly speaking of there was no national system of education or talk of national system of education till the appointment of the Education Commission 1964-66.

2. Basic System of Education became the corner stone as well as the national system of education at the elementary stage immediately after independent. This was declared by the Government of India. During the struggle for freedom several attempts were made to formulate a system of education that would meet the requirements of India. Gandhiji took a keen interest in educational matters. Accordingly, *Nai Talim*, or Basic Education or Wardha Scheme of Education emerged. This scheme was put into operation when Congress Ministries were formed in 9 provinces out of 11 in 1937. However, the Congress Ministries resigned in 1939 when the British rulers involved India in the Second World War without any valid reason to do so.

3. The philosophy as outlined in the Preamble of the Constitution of India adopted in 1950 became the guiding philosophy of education.

4. The University Education Commission (1948-49) dealt with the higher system of education and the Secondary Education Commission (1952-53) dealt with the Secondary Education. Several Committees examined the elementary system of education.

5. No education Commission or Committee at the national level examined the entire structure of education till 1964.

## 4.7 CONSTITUTIONAL PROVISIONS AND THE DEVELOPMENT OF NATIONAL SYSTEM OF EDUCATION

The Constitution of India which came into force on January 26, 1950, is the chief source which provides direction to the development of the national system of education also. In this regard, following points should be specifically noted.

1. Constitution is the mirror of the philosophical and sociological perspective of all areas of life including education. It lays emphasis on (a) Democracy, (b) Socialism, (c) Secularism, (d) Justice, (e) Liberty, (f) Fraternity. The system of education must be in accordance with these objectives and values.

2. Constitution lists the role of the Central Government, State Governments and Union Territories in running the educational system.

3. Upto 1977, education excepting a few areas was the responsibility of the State i.e. it was a 'State' subject. Thereafter it became a 'concurrent subject' i.e. responsibility of the Central Government and the State Government.

4. Article 45 of the Constitution laid down, "The State (here State means the Central Government as well as the State Governments) shall endeavour to provide, within a period of 10 years from the commencement of this constitution, for free and compulsory education for all children until the complete the age of 14 years."

## 4.8 NATIONAL SYSTEM OF EDUCATION AT THE ELEMENTARY STAGE: BASIC EDUCATION

Basic Education became the national system of education at the elementary stage immediate after independence. All elementary schools in the country were converted into basic pattern. Several schemes were launched for its promotion. A number of specialised agencies and institutions were set up to popularise this system. However, there were several doubts about the merits of this system. On account of various reasons, the system failed to become popular. Ultimately after the recommendations of the Education Commission 1964-66, it virtually collapsed.

*Reasons for the Formulation of the Basic System of Education*: Gandhiji was not only an outstanding political leader and statesman, but also an outstanding educator. He found the following defects of the system of education:

1. It is artificial and unreal.
2. It does not meet the requirements of the country.
3. It stuffs the minds of the children with all kinds of useless information.
4. It is dominated by English language.
5. It makes children foreigners in their own land
6. It is not related to production.
7. It does not develop love for manual work.

*Formulation of the Scheme*: Gandhiji views were considered by a Committee headed by Dr. Zakir Husain who later on became the President of India. The Committee prepared the scheme which was accepted by the Congress. The Congress Ministries adopted this scheme in 1937.

**Fundamental Features of Basic Education**

The fundamental features of the scheme that emerged after changes are as follows:

1. A school of say 5½ hours could roughly be divided on the following basis:

| | |
|---|---|
| Physical activities | 20 minutes |
| Mother Tongue | 40 minutes |
| Social Studies and General Science | 60 minutes |
| Art | 40 minutes |
| Arithmetic | 20 minutes |
| Craft work including study of correlated subjects | 2½ hours |

2. Free and compulsory education to be given for 8 years (from 6 to 14 years) in two stages. The junior stage to cover five years and the senior 3 years.
3. The medium of instruction is to be the mother-tongue.
4. Education to centre round some form of productive work. The social and physical environment to be used for correlation in addition to craft.
5. The self-supporting aspect not to be over-emphasized. The sale proceeds of the finished goods to be able to help the school to cover some part of its expenditure.
6. External examinations to be abolished. The day-to-day work of the students to be the determining factor.
7. Textbooks to be avoided as far as possible.
8. Cleanliness and health, citizenship, play and recreation to be given sufficient importance.

**Merits of the Basic Education Scheme**

Following merits may be summed up:

1. Basic system of education is craft and production centred.
2. It is related to community life and needs.
3. It is based on the concept 'learning while earning'.
4. It is work centred.
5. It stresses dignity of labour.
6. It advocates mother-tongue as the medium of instruction.
7. It imparts education through correlation.
8. In it, learning is by doing.
9. It is based on democratic values.
10. It provides greater freedom to the teacher and the taught.
11. It is not a class education. It is for the masses.
12. It attempts to create a social order in which there is no unnatural division between 'havens' and 'have nots'.
13. It is for rural as well as urban areas.

*Significance of the World 'Basic' in Basic Education*: The word 'Basic' is derived from the word 'Base' which means the bottom or the foundation of a thing upon which the whole thing rests or is made.

1. It is basic because it is closely related to the basic needs and interests of the child.
2. It is basic because it comes first in the primary period of our education.
3. It is basic because it makes use of the native potentialities of the child.

**Demerits, Limitations and Causes of the Failure of Basic System of Education**

Inspite of Government support, the scheme failed on account of the following factors.

1. *Economic Aspect Over-emphasised*: Too much emphasis was laid on economic aspect. Teachers remained busy either in the garden or in the workshop and they lost sight of educational objectives of the craft.

2. *Lack of Competent Teachers*: Most of the teachers who taught in basic schools were not trained for this type of education.

3. *Dearth of Textbooks*: Suitable books to teach in accordance with the requirements of Basic Education were not made available.

4. *High Cost of Basic Education*: A good Basic school can only be established with a good deal of initial cost on the purchase of equipment for different crafts. In additional to this cost, there is always a recurring expenditure on the successful running of a good craft.

5. *Lack of Provision for Individual Differences*: It failed to provide for the individual differences of the pupils and, therefore, the drawbacks of traditional system of education continued to harm the individuality of the child.

6. *Artistic and Aesthetic Aspects Neglected*: In some of the Basic schools, these aspects were not attended to. Children did very little art work which was generally confined to the drawing of charts.

7. *Rigidity*: The scheme was rigid in several aspects. Techniques for primary school children must be flexible.

8. *Neglect of the Child*: In a hurry to pay more attention to craft, it has neglected the child. Child was considered as a means—the end being earning capacity. In the training for teachers, child psychology was conspicuous by its absence. It ignored 'effective' aspects of human nature.

9. *Setback to Artisans*: The scheme hit the professional artisans hard by creating competition.

10. *Faulty Correlation*: It is absurd to hang all knowledge from the peg of a single craft.

11. *No Religious Element*: It had no religious element.

12. *Neglect of Knowledge*: Literacy and knowledge of subject matter are considered to be of secondary importance.

13. *Not suitable in Industrial Age*: The emphasis on craft is out of place in a community which has its face turned towards developing its economy to the full.

## 4.9 DEVELOPMENT OF THE NATIONAL SYSTEM OF EDUCATION AT STAGES OTHER THAN ELEMENTARY STAGE OF EDUCATION

After considering reforms in elementary education, the Government of India thought it necessary to bring about reforms at the higher level of education. Accordingly, it appointed the University Education Commission in 1948 to suggest reforms in University Education. The Commission took note of the philosophical as well as sociological perspectives and gave valuable suggestions to strengthen higher education. The report of the Commission remained an importance source of inspiration till the recommendations of the Education Commission 1964-66. It is also true that even now, references are often made to its recommendations. The Commission recommended that first University degree should be obtained after a study of three years. Admission to this degree should be after years of schooling.

The University Education Commission listed the following aims of higher education:

1. To provide an integrated way of life.
2. To impart knowledge and wisdom.
3. To enable the students understand the social values of the society.
4. To train students for self development.
5. To train students for democracy.
6. To enable the students to understand that education is a life-long process.
7. To develop values.

8. To acquaint the students with the cultural heritage.
9. To enable the students to understand the past as well as the future.
10. To provide general professional and vocational education of higher standard.

In 1952, the Government of India appointed the Secondary Education Commission to suggest reforms at the secondary stage of education. The Commission gave its recommendation in 1953. It explained the aim of secondary education, keeping in view the philosophical and sociological perspectives. It suggested the establishment of multipurpose schools on a large scale. It also stressed seven streams out of which students could choose any one stream having several subjects to choose from. A core curriculum at this stage was also recommended.

1. Development of democratic citizenship.
2. Improvement of vocational efficiency.
3. Development of all round personality.
4. Development of qualities for leadership.

Only a few minor recommendations could be fulfilled.

## 4.10 NATIONAL SYSTEM OF EDUCATION AS PROVIDED FOR IN THE NATIONAL POLICY ON EDUCATION—NPE, 1986

### Background

The first major attempt to formulate a national system of education in India was made to appoint the Education Commission in 1964. The Commission examined all aspects of education at all levels and gave its recommendation in 1966.

The Commission listed the four aims of education:

1. To relate education to productivity.
2. To strengthen social and national integration through education programmes.
3. To consolidate democratic values through education.
4. To develop social, moral and spiritual values.
5. To modernise society through awakening of curiosity, developing proper attitudes and skills needed for changing times and increasing the capacity to think and judge for oneself.

The recommendations became the basis of the formulation of the National Policy on Education, 1968. However, much could not be achieved for a number of years. Ultimately in 1986, the Government of India, Department of Education, Ministry of Human Development Resources earlier known as Ministry of Education, declared the National Policy on Education. This was done after a countrywide debate on educational reforms. Slight modifications were made in the NPE in 1992 in the light of its implementation.

## Characteristics of the National System of Education

Following are the important characteristics of the National System of Education as given in the NPE, 1986.

1. *National System on the Principles Embodied in the Constitution*: National System of Education will be based on the philosophy as contained in the Constitution of India.

2. *Common School System*: Up to a given level, all students, irrespective of caste, creed, location or sex, will have access to education of a comparable quality. Effective measures will be taken in the direction of the common system recommended in the 1968 policy.

3. *10+2+3 Structure*: The National System of Education envisages a common educational structure i.e. 10+2+3; elementary system comprising 5 years of primary education and 3 years of upper primary, followed by 2 years of high school.

4. *National Curricular Framework*: There will be a national curricular framework with a common core alongwith other components that are flexible.

5. *Secular Values*: All educational programmes will be carried on in strict conformity with secular values.

6. *Education for Peace and Understanding*: Education will be aimed at strengthening the ideas of peace and understanding.

7. *Equality in Education*: To promote equality it will be necessary to provide for equal opportunity to all not only in access but also in the conditions for success.

8. *Minimum Levels of Learning*: Minimum levels of learning will be laid down for each stage of education.

9. *National Integration*: Steps will be taken to foster among students an understanding of the diverse cultural and social systems of the people living in different parts of the country.

10. *Promotion of Languages*: Besides the promotion of the link language, programmes will also be launched to increase substantially the translation of books from one language to another and to publish multi-lingual dictionaries and glossaries.

11. *Facilitating Inter-regional Mobility*: In higher education in general, and technical education in particular, steps will be taken to facilitate inter-regional mobility by providing equal access to every Indian of requisite merit regardless of his origins.

12. *Network Arrangements in Research Development*: In the area of research and development and education in science and technology, special measures will be taken to establish network arrangements between different institutions in the country to pool their resources and participate in projects of national importance.

13. *Life Long Education*: Life-long education is the cherished goal of the educational process. This pre-supposes universal literacy.

14. *Open and Distance Learning*: The future thrust will be in the direction of open and distance education

15. *Involvement of National Institutions*: Integrated planning will be instituted among all these bodies (University Grants Commission, All India Council of Technical Education, the Indian Council of Agricultural Research, the National Council of Educational Research and Training, the National Institute of Educational Planning and Administration and the International Institute of Science and Technology) so as to establish functional linkages and reinforce programmes of research and post-graduate education.

16. *Involvement of the Nation as a Whole*: Nation as a whole will assume the responsibility of providing resource support for implementing programmes of educational transformation.

17. *Meaningful Partnership between the Centre and the States*: Concurrency signifies a partnership which is at once meaningful and challenging. The National Policy will be oriented towards giving effect to it in letter and spirit.

18. *Education for Equality*: The new policy will lay emphasis on the removal of disparities and to equalise opportunity by attending it to the specific needs of these who have been denied equality so far. This includes education for women's equality, scheduled castes and tribes, backward sections, minorities and the handicapped.

19. *Adult Education*: The nation must pledge itself to the eradication of illiteracy, particularly in the 15-35 age group. A vast programme of adult and continuing education will be implemented through various ways and channels.

20. *Early Childhood Care and Education*: Programmes of ECCE will be child centred. A full integration of child care and pre-primary education will be brought about both as a feeder and a strengthening factor for primary education and for human resource development in general.

21. *A Resolve as Regards Primary Education*: It shall be ensured that all children who attain the age of about 11 years by 1990 will have had five years of schooling, or its equivalent through the non-formal stream. Likewise, by 1995 all children will be provided free and compulsory education upto 14 years of age.

The structure of formal education may be explained as under: (Fig. 4.1)

| *Stage/Level* | | *Duration* |
|---|---|---|
| 1. Anganwadi pre-primary | | Usually between 2 to 5 years of age. |
| 2. Primary | Elementary | 6 to 11 years of age—5 years |
| 3. Upper Primary | | 11 to 14 years of age—3 years |
| 4. Secondary | New pattern of | 15-16 years of age—2 years |
| 5. Higher Secondary | Education 10+2+3 | 17-18 years of age—2 years |
| 6. First Degree | | 19-21 years of age—3 years |
| 7. Post-graduation, M.A., M.Sc. etc. | | 21-23 years of age—3 years |
| 8. B. E/B. Tech | | 19-22 years of age—4 years |
| 9. M. Tech etc. | | 23-24 years of age—2 years |
| 10. B.Ed. | | 22 years—one year |
| 11. M.B.B.S. | | 19-23 years of age—4 years |
| 12. M.D./M.S. | | 24-25 years of age—2 years |

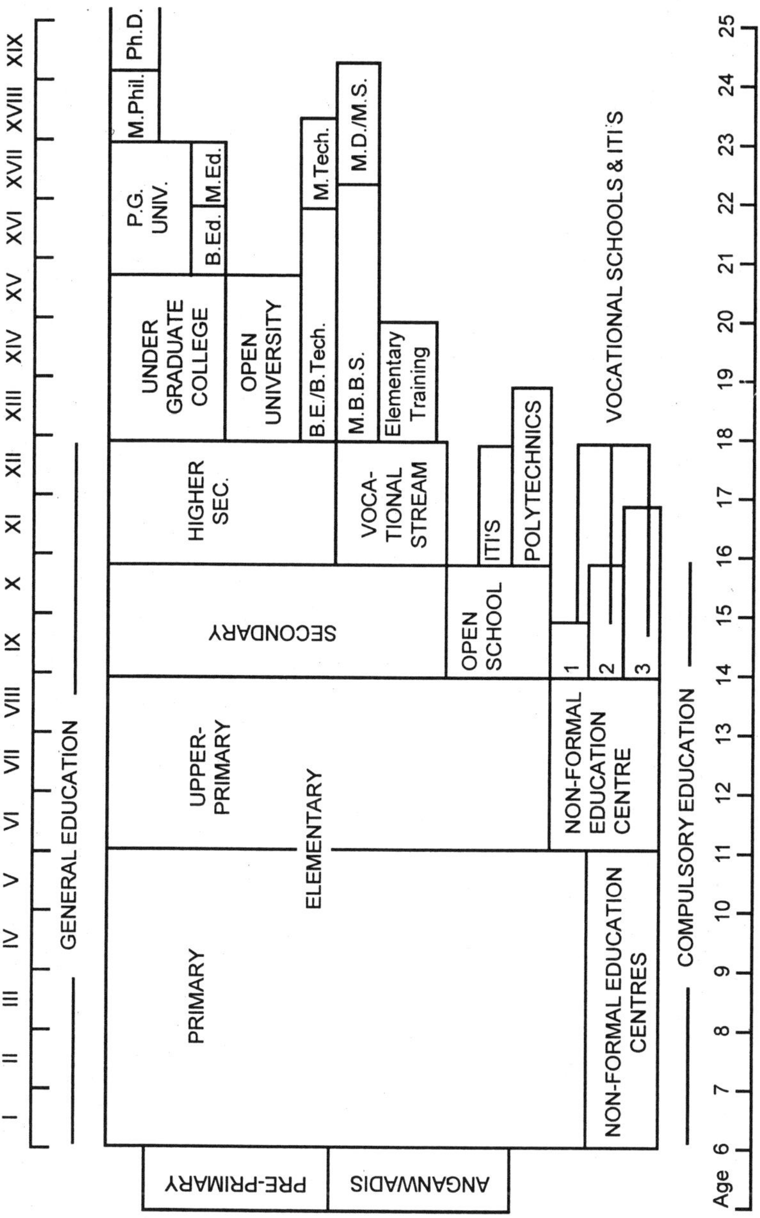


*Fig. 4.1: Diagrammatic representation of educational diagrammatic representation of educational structure at varios levels in india*

Thus it takes four years after Senior Secondary level to become a teacher; likewise four years to become an engineer and 6 years to become a doctor.

## 4.11 PRESENT POSITION OF NATIONAL SYSTEM OF EDUCATION

Strenuous efforts have been made to carry out the directions of NPE. A uniform structure of education has come into being in almost all the States and Union Territories of India. Several new steps have been taken to achieve the goal of universalisation of elementary education and 'education for all'. A number of schemes for the qualitative improvement of education have been introduced. A core curriculum has been prescribed. Special measures for the promotion of education among women and deprived sections of the society have been initiated. Value education and education for emotional and national integration are given due attention. Nevertheless, still a lot of work remains to be done for achieving the objectives as contained in the NPE.

Following core curricular areas find an important part of the national curriculum:

1. History of India's Freedom Movement.
2. Constitutional Obligations.
3. Fundamental Duties.
4. Content Essential to Nurture National Identity.
5. India's Common Cultural Heritage.
6. Egalitarianism, Democracy and Secularism.
7. Equality of the Sexes.
8. Protection of the Environment.
9. Removal of Social Barriers.
10. Observance of Small Family Norm.
11. Inculcation of the Scientific Temper.

# 5

# Sri Aurobindo Ghose (1872-1950)

## 5.1 BRIEF LIFE SKETCH OF SRI AUROBINDO

*Early Life and Education of Sri Aurobindo*: Aurobindo was born in an educated middle class family of Calcutta (Kolkata) in Bengal on August 15, 1872. At the age of 7, he went to England and lived there for 14 years. He received his education at Cambridge. Besides English, he mastered Latin and Greek and learnt French, German, Italian and Spanish.

Aurobindo was a very brilliant student. At the age of 18, he passed the entrance examination of the Indian Civil Service (ICS)—the most coveted service during the British rule. He, however, did not appear in the riding test. This was perhaps on account of his hatred for the foreign rule.

*Literary and Cultural Activities*: On his return to India in 1893, he joined service in the Princely State of Baroda (Vadodara). He became the Professor of English at Baroda College. He devoted himself to cultural and literary activities. He learnt Bengali, Gujarati, Marathi and Sanskrit. He drank deep in the culture and philosophy of India. He began yoga also.

*Political Work—A Revolutionary*: It response to the call of the Indian National Congress, he joined as the principal of Bengal National College at Calcutta (now Jadavpur University). He became an active freedom fighter. He was disappointed with the moderate leaders of the Indian National Congress. He even justified an armed revolt against the British rule. He was considered the most dangerous leader by the British Government.

He started the Bengali daily *'Yugantar'* and an English daily *'Bande Mataram'* to promote revolutionary ideas. He played a notable role against the Partition of Bengal (1905). He was arrested in 1908 in connection with the Alipore Bomb case. He was acquitted after one year.

*Freedom Fighter—Revolutionary Turned Philosopher and Seer*: During one year in jail he spent most of his time in yoga, meditation and study of religious philosophical and spiritual literature. It led to a transformation in his life. In 1910, he left his political activities and went to Pondicherry (a French settlement in India at that time) and spent the remaining forty years (1910-1950) at his Ashram at Pondicherry. He devoted himself to study, and writing. He advocated moral and spiritual regeneration. He propounded theories of education which catered to Indian needs. He set up an

International Ashram and International Centre of Education at Pondicherry and started several educational and social activities. He also started a new experiment known as Aurovill as a city of human unity.

**Aurobindo's Important Publications on Education and Allied Subjects**

1. *'A System of National Education'*
2. *'Sri Aurobindo and the Mother on Education'*
3. *'The Human Cycle'*
4. *'Ideal of Human Unity'*

## 5.2 MAIN IDEAS OF AUROBINDO'S PHILOSOPHY

1. Everyone has in him something Divine.
2. The task is to find it, develop it and use it.
3. This Divine can be obtained by a spiritual discipline, called yoga.
4. Aurobindo's concept of yoga is not that of a *'sanyasi'* who turns away from life in order to turn towards God.
5. Yoga is for the ordinary man, while he carries on his wordly pursuits.
6. If a merchant wishes to follow yoga, he regards his work as Divine and does not use unfair practices to earn money.
7. If a student, looks for higher values, he must observe *'Brahmacharya'* (self-control).

## 5.3 SRI AUROBINDO'S MAIN IDEAS ON EDUCATION

1. *Aim of Education*: According to Sri Aurobindo the aim of education is the spiritual development of the individual, the nation and the universal humanity. Their aim can be achieved by bringing out to full advantage all that is in the individual.

The individual has to enter into night relationships not only within himself but also with the people of his country and with the universal society to which he belongs.

The human race is composed of people or nations and a nation is composed of individuals. The nations make the universal humanity.

The education should enable an individual to realize his inner self which is a part of the universal consciousness.

2. *Functions of Education*: Following are the chief functions of education:

(i) To bring out the real man.
(ii) To build the powers of the human mind and spirit i.e. the evoking of knowledge, character and culture.
(iii) To enable the individual to establish a clear continuity between the past, present and the future.
(iv) To enable the individual to establish right relations with life.

3. *Principles of Teaching*: Sri Aurobindo has stated the following three

principles of teaching:

The first principle of true teaching is that nothing can be taught. The teacher is not an instructor or task master, he is a helper and guide.

The teacher's work is to suggest and not to impose on the mind of the student. He does not actually train the mind of his student but helps him to perfect his mind and encourages him every way in this process. Thus he does not impart knowledge, but shows the way how knowledge can be acquired. Knowledge is within the pupil and the pupil has to help himself to bring it out, but he needs help. Somebody must tell him where it is and how it can be 'habituated to rise to the surface'. Teacher alone can do this work.

The second principle is that the mind has to be consulted in its growth. The idea of hammering the child into the shape desired by the parent or teacher is a barbarous and ignorant superstition. It is wrong and rather immoral to force adult will on the child. The divine in the child should not be ignored and mutilated. To force the nature of the child to abandon its own *'Dharma'* is to do permanent arm.

The third principle of teaching is to work from the near to the far, from the known to the unknown. Man's nature is moulded by his soul's past, his heredity and his environment. The past is the foundation, the present is the material and future is the aim and each must find its due and natural place in any national system of education.

4. *Main Principles of Learning*

(i) Concentration is the first principle of learning.

(ii) *'Abhyasa'* or steady natural practice is the second principle of learning.

5. *Moral Education*: This should be on the following methods:

(i) Personal examples of the teachers and elders.

(ii) Study of books having lofty examples.

(iii) *'Satsanga'* i.e., good company.

(iv) Suggesting and not commanding and imposing.

6. *Discipline*: '*Chitta Shuddhi'* i.e. purification of the mental and moral habits should be the basis of discipline. This means to discriminate between right and wrong impressions and to absorb right ones in the mind.

Sri Aurobindo advises teachers not to be arbitrary, despotic, impatient and ill tempered.

7. *Physical Education*: Perfection is the true aim of education and physical development is an integral part of perfection. Moreover without physical development, *'Dharma'* cannot be performed. Only a healthy body can contain a healthy mind. As the Sanskrit goes, *'Shariram khalu dharmasadhanam'* (the body is the means of fulfilment of dharma).

8. *Curriculum.* It should include the following:

(i) Physical development studies.

(ii) Mental development studies.

(iii) Cultural development studies.

(iv) Vital i.e. sciences relating to preservation of body etc.
(v) Vocational development studies.
(vi) International understanding programmes.

9. *Teacher—A Guide and Helper*: The teacher is not an instructor or task-master; he is a helper and guide. His business is to suggest and not to impose. He does not actually train the pupil's mind, he only shows him how to perfect his instruments of knowledge and helps and encourages him in the process. He does not impart knowledge to him; he shows him how to acquire knowledge for himself. He does not call forth the knowledge for himself. He does not call forth the knowledge that is within. He only shows him where it lies and how it can be habituated to rise to the surface.

## 5.4 NATIONAL SYSTEM OF EDUCATION

*Prevailing Defects in Education*: Shri Aurobindo found the following defects in the prevailing system of education:

1. It was denationalising
2. It was degrading.
3. It was impoverishing the mind; soul and character.
4. It was bad in kind.

*Main Characteristics of the National System of Education*: Aurobindo pointed out the following elements:

(i) Human and spiritual values are complementary and supplementary.
(ii) Education does not become national by tagging the word 'national' to the system.
(iii) Education should pay due attention to modern knowledge and scientific progress.
(iv) Mere knowledge of Science does not make us educated in the true sense. This must be related to powers of the human mind and spirit.
(v) There should be a balanced understanding of the national and international relationships of universal humanity.

## 5.5 CONTRIBUTION OF SRI AUROBINDO TO EDUCATION

*The Ashram School*: The school was originally started in 1943 for the children of Sri Aurobindo's disciples. It expanded gradually from a Primary School to a full-fledged High School. There are resident as well as day-students.

*The International Centre of Education*: The objectives underlying the centre are:

1. To evolve a system of education for making it dynamic, ideal for society.
2. To organise an environment which may provide inspiration and facilities for the exercise and development of the five aspects of personality—the physical, the vital, the mental, the psychic and the spiritual.

3. To emphasise the unity of all knowledge.
4. To develop the sense of oneness of mankind.
5. To discover and prepare for the role India has to play in the formation of the new international harmony.

## 5.6 SELECT QUOTES OF SRI AUROBINDO ON EDUCATION

1. "To bring out the real man is the first business of education".
2. "The chief aim of education should be to help the growing soul to draw out which is best and make it perfect for a noble cause."
3. "The best method of moral education is by personal example, daily converse and the books read from day-to-day."
4. "Perfect liberty would be desirable for the child."
5. "The teacher is not an instructor or task master, he is a helper and guide."
6. "Indeed if the education is to have its maximum result, it must begin even before birth."

# 6

# Swami Vivekananda (1863-1902)

## 6.1 BRIEF LIFE SKETCH AND WORK OF SWAMI VIVEKANANDA

### Early Life

Swami Vivekananda's original name was Narendranath Dutt. He acquired the new name in 1886 when he took *'sanyasa'*. His father was a lawyer who practised at the Calcutta High Court. As a child he developed great taste for music and was adopt in sports. Under the influence of his mother he made a deep study of the Hindu scriptures. He was provided the best of education. He graduated with honours from Calcutta University.

He had an excellent command over Bengali, English and Sanskrit. He was a voracious reader and had a sharp memory. He could often display a verbatim familiarity with the *'Encyclopaedia Britannica'*. His principal Rev. W.W. Hastie once remarked, "Narendranath is really a genius. I have travelled far and wide but I have never yet come across a lad of his talents and possibilities, even in German Universities, among philosophical students."

### Meeting with Shri Ramakrishna—A Turning Point in Life

He was deeply interested in the study of philosophy and religion. He studied eastern and western philosophy and religion. For sometimes he was a classroom teacher also. His search for truth led him to Ramakrishna Paramhansa, at Dakshineswar in 1882. Though not literate, Swami Ramakrishna was an enlightened soul. During the next six years of his association with the master, he had a spiritual transformation and emerged as Swami Vivekananda. He left home and travelled all over India. His wandering left him deeply affected by the despair and poverty of the masses of India.

Swami Vivekanand organised the Ramakrishna Mission in 1886, after the passing away of his master.

*Soul-stirring Address at the World Parliament of Religions at Chicago (USA) in 1893*: On September 11, 1893, on the opening day of the Parliament, he sat rapt in silent meditation. In the afternoon session he rose to speak. He bowed down to Saraswati, the Devi (goddess of learning) and addressed the audience as, "Sisters and brothers of America." Before he could utter another word, people were so much mesmerised that there was applause for full two minutes. When silence was restored, he began his address. His wisdom coupled with universal message of love and tolerance made him a world teacher.

*Message of Spirituality and Social Service*: He addressed several meetings in the U.S.A., U.K., Sri Lanka and spread the spiritual message.

Swami Vivekananda devoted the rest of his strenuous life in communicating his message of unity and tolerance.

In India, he organised social work also in addition to spiritual pursuits.

## 6.2 PRINCIPAL FEATURES OF SWAMI VIVEKANANDA'S PHILOSOPHY

1. God resides in every human heart.
2. The best worship of God is service to mankind.
3. Ethics and morality should be the real basis of life.
4. Love and renunciation should permeate the universe.
5. Religion means self-realisation through self-control.

## 6.3 SWAMI VIVEKANANDA'S PHILOSOPHY OF EDUCATION

Following are the main points of the philosophy of Swami Vivekananda:

1. All knowledge is in the human mind.
2. Education is the manifestation of the perfection already in man.
3. Knowledge is inherent in man. No knowledge comes from outside.
4. Like fire in a piece of flint, knowledge exists in the mind. Man discovers it.
5. The infinite library of the universe is in our mind.

Swami Vivekanand explains this as, "We say Newton discovered gravitation. The falling of an apple gave the suggestion to Newton and then he studied his own mind. He rearranged all the previous links of thought in his mind and discovered a link among them, which we call the law of gravitation."

## 6.4 SWAMI VIVEKANAND ON VARIOUS ASPECTS OF EDUCATION

### I. Aims of Education

1. Development of spirituality in social setting i.e. development of a spirit of fellow-feeling.
2. Development of character which implies doing good to others, courage, fearlessness and strength and above all strong will-power for a noble cause.
3. Development of balanced human relationships.
4. Development of the attitude of considering work as worship.
5. Development of spirit of service to the poor and the neglected.
6. Development of a spirit of renunciation, giving up pride and ego and acquiring spirit of self-sacrifice.

7. Development of vocational proficiency.
8. Development of physical health.

*Character-building as the most Important aim of Education*: "If you really want to judge the character of man, look not at his great performances, watch a man do his most common actions. Those are indeed the things which will tell you the real character of the great man." 'Intellectuality' is not the highest good. 'Morality' and 'spirituality' are the things for which we strive'. "Our women are not so learned, but they are more pure." He does not consider a man as educated if he can only pass some examination and deliver good lectures. The basis of all system, social or political, rests upon the goodness of man. No nation is great or good because its Parliament enacts this or that, but because its men are great and good.

**II. Role of the Teacher**

Vivekananda laid stress on the following qualities that a teacher should have:

1. The first condition is that he should be sinless.
2. The second condition is that he should know the spirit of scriptures.
3. The third condition is the spiritual force of the teacher based on love for the students.
4. The fourth condition is that the teacher should think that he is only helping the child grow. He is the external teacher and he offers the suggestion which arouses the internal teacher i.e. in the mind of the child.

**III. Principles of teaching-learning:**

Swami Vivekananda emphasised the following:

1. *Self-teaching*—"No one was ever taught by another. Each of us has to teach himself. A child educates itself."
2. *Living Examples of Teacher*—"Words even thoughts, contribute only one-third of the influence in making an impression—the man two-thirds."
3. *Teaching through Positive Suggestions*—"We should give positive ideas. Negative ideas only weaken men. If you speak kind words to them and encourage them, they are bound to improve in time."
4. *Concentration as the only method of education*—"The power of concentration is the only key to the treasure-house of knowledge."
5. *Qualities of the Learner*: "The conditions necessary for the taught are purity, a real thirst after knowledge and perseverance."

**IV. Physical and Health Education**

"Be strong, my young friends....you will be nearer to Heaven through football than through the study of Gita."

**V. Education to be based on Western Science coupled with Vedanta**

"Living with the Guru and a similar system of imparting education are needed. What we want is western science coupled with Vedanta—*'Brahmacharya'* as the guiding motto and also *'Shraddha'* (faith) in one's own self."

**VI. Education of the masses**

Vivekananda gave prime importance to the education of the masses. He asserted, "The chief cause of India's ruin has been the monopolising of the whole education of the land, by dint of pride and royal authority, among a handful of men." He further observed, "If we are to rise again, we shall have to do it in the same way, that is, by spreading education among the masses." He considers that "The great national sin is the neglect of the masses, and that is one of the chief causes of our downfall. No amount of politics would be of any avail until the masses in India are once more well-educated, well-fed, and cared for. They pay for our education, they build our temples, but in return they get kicks. They are practically our slaves, if we want to regenerate India, we must work for them."

**VII. Women's education**

Vivekananda was an ardent champion of the education of women. He remarked, "Women have many and grave problems but none that cannot be solved by that magic world: education!"

**VIII. Secular Education**

Vivekanand had great regard for all religions. "Let us take in all that has been in the past, enjoy the light of the present and open every window of the heart for all that will come in the future. Salutation to all the prophets of the past, to all the great ones of the present and to all that are to come in the future."

## 6.5 CONTRIBUTION OF SWAMI VIVEKANANDA TO EDUCATION: RELEVANCE OF HIS VIEWS TODAY

1. He laid stress on the character development education.
2. He advocated the education of the masses which implies adult education and free and compulsory education regardless of caste creed or colour. He said, "I consider that the greatest national sin is the neglect of the masses".
3. He revived the spirit of humanism in education.
4. His clarion call to the educated people was, "So long as the millions live in hunger and ignorance, I hold every man a traitor who, having been educated at their expense, pays not the least head to them."
5. He considered the education of women as the chief instrument of national regeneration.

6. He stressed the teaching of western learning.
7. He emphasised social service, "Service to mankind is the highest goal of religion." 'Assimilation' and 'toleration' were the key points in religion and religious education.
8. Ramakrishna Mission established by Swami Vivekananda is running several educational institutions and spiritual centres, hospitals and dispensaries and doing several types of social work.

*Summing up*: Swami Vivekananda's views on education may be summed up in his own words, "We want that education by which character is formed, strength of mind is increased, the intellect is expanded and by which one stands on one's own feet."

# 7

# Rabindranath Tagore (1861-1941)

## 7.1 BRIEF LIFE SKETCH

### Early Life and Education

Tagore was born on May 6, 1861 at Calcutta. The family of Tagore was known for its enlightened and progressive views. He was the youngest son of (Maharshi) Devendranath and grandson of Dwarkanath Tagore. His father was a prominent leader of the Brahmo Samaj. He studied Sanskrit, astronomy and the Upanishadas from his father. He attended the seminary and the Bengal Academy for his other studies. However, his school days were not happy. About his school he wrote, "All of a sudden I found my world vanishing." Regarding school, he uses the words "cage, dreadful and lifeless." It glorified 'mechanical memorising of facts without original thinking'. Hence in disgust, he left the conventional studies.

After private education, in India, he was sent to England in 1877 to study law for becoming a barrister but he soon returned to India. While still young, he started writing for Bengali magazines. He wrote his first verse in English while he was just eight.

*Educational Experiments*: In 1901, he established his school with 5 students at Bolpur, about 150 km. from Calcutta. This school, later on developed into the famous 'Shantiniketan'—a World University called "Visbabharati".

*Bursting into International Fame*: Tagore become a world figure when his book *'Gitanjali'* won him the Nobel Prize in 1913. Tagore utilized the entire amount of the award of £ 8000 for the upkeep of his school.

*Renouncing Knighthood (Title of Honour)*: The British Government made him 'Knight' in 1915 but he was so pained and stirred by the Jallianwalan Bagh Massacre of Amritsar in 1919, that he returned the Insignia of Knighthood. At that time he wrote to the Viceroy of India. "The time has come when badges of honour make our shame glaring in their incongruous context of humiliation, and I for my part wish to stand, shorn of all special distinctions, by the side of those of my countrymen who, for their so-called insignificance, are liable to suffer a degradation not fit for human beings."

*Founding of Educational Institutions*: On December 22, 1921, Tagore founded the Visvabharati—an international university to being about understanding between eastern and western cultures.

From 1921 to 1941 i.e. till his death, he laboured hard to develop a number of institutions such as Kala Bhawan, Sangit Bhawan and Cheena Bhawan etc.

*Multi-splendoured Personality*: Tagore has left his deep impression on several facets of life i.e. artistic, cultural, educational, intellectual, political and social. There is no field of literature which he has not enriched by his contribution. He was a great artist, educationist, a poet, a patriot, a philosopher and social reformer.

## 7.2 TAGORE'S PHILOSOPHY OF LIFE

1. *Tagore's Humanism*: Tagore observed, "He (God) is there where the tiller is tilling the hard ground and where the pathmaker is breaking stone."
2. *Tagore's Naturalism*: He said, "He lives in a prison house whose walls are alien to him." Tagore loved nature immensely.
3. *Tagore's Spiritualism*: Tagore said, 'I believe in the spiritual unity of man and therefore I ask you to accept this task from me."
4. *Tagore's Individualism*: Tagore believed that every being has the right to shape his life in his own way.
5. *Tagore's Universalism*: He wanted to break down barriers between cultures. He said, "Before we are in a position to stand a comparison with the other cultures of the world, or truly co-operate with them, we must base our own culture on a synthesis of all the different cultures we have."
6. *Tagore's Internationalism*: Tagore advocated synthesis between the East and the West. The Visvabharati at Shantiniketan is an embodiment of his international outlook.

## 7.3 EDUCATIONAL PHILOSOPHY OF TAGORE

*Sources of Information*: Apart from his several publications on different aspects, we get valuable information about Tagore's views on education from the following sources relating to education. Essays were written mostly in Bengali.

1. *'Shiksar Herpher'* (Our Education and Its Incongruities)
2. *'Shiksha Samasya'* (The Problem of Education)
3. *'Abaran'* (Culture or Covering)
4. *'Tapovan'* (Forest Colony)
5. *'Dharmashiksha'* (Religious Education)
6. *'Hindu Visvavidyal y'* (Hindu University)
7. *'Strishiksha'* (Women Education)
8. *'Shiksar Bahan'* (The Vehicle of Education)
9. *'My School'*

10. *'Shiksar Milan'* (The Meeting of Cultures)
11. 'A Poet's School'
12. 'Shiksar Vikiran' (Diffusion of Education)
13. *'Ashramer Shiksha'* (Education in Ashram)
14. *'Bodher Sadhana'* (Education of the Feeling)
15. *'Several Convocation Addresses'*

*Factors Influencing Tagore's Philosophy of Education*: Tagore's philosophy of education was influenced by the following factors:

1. Influence of the Home Environment
2. Influence of the School Environment.
3. Love for Nature.
4. His Extensive Visits.

## 7.4 TAGORE'S VIEWS ON DIFFERENT ASPECTS OF EDUCATION

On account of the above influences, Tagore may be described as an idealist, a naturalist, a modernist, a pragmatic, a traditionalist and above all a humanist and an internationalist.

1. *Aims of Education*: Following were the other aims of education according to Tagore:

(i) Education should develop a creative mind.
(ii) Education should aim at developing aesthetic sense.
(iii) Education should develop values of simple living.
(iv) Education should prepare an individual for a vocation.
(v) Education should develop international understanding.
(vi) Education should develop freedom of mind.

2. *Curriculum*: Tagore recommended a curriculum for the full man satisfying the spiritual, the creative, the aesthetic and the vocational aims of education. Besides providing for the teaching of ordinary schools, Tagore developed many educational ideas, years ahead of others. Now-a-days educationists talk so much about the educational value of crafts, projects, music, dancing, fine arts, etc. But it is indeed very significant to note that the poet provided for the teaching of most of these subjects from the very beginning in his school at Shantiniketan.

3. *Methods of Teaching*: Tagore strongly criticised the bookish and examination oriented teaching. He stressed movement of the whole body in various learning activities. He followed the activity principle, and advocated constructive and creative activities.

4. *Children as Children*: It is a mistake to judge children by the standards of grown-ups. Adults ignore the natural gifts of children and insist that children must learn through the same process as themselves. This is man's most cruel and most wasteful mistake.

Children's have their subconscious mind which is more active than their conscious intelligence.

5. *Discipline and Freedom*: Living ideals cannot be set into clock-work arrangement. Tagore wrote, "I never said to them. Don't do this, or don't do

that... I never punished them".

6. *An Ideal School*: An ideal school is an Ashram where men gather for the highest end of life. Tagore observed. "To give spiritual culture to our boys was my principal object in starting my school at Bolpur."

7. *Role of the Teacher*: In teaching, the guiding spirit should be personal love based on human relations. In education the teacher is more important than the method.

Tagore pointed out, "A teacher can never truly teach unless he is learning himself. A lamp can never light another lamp unless it continues to burn its own flame."

8. *Religious Education*: Tagore stressed religious education through practice. He wrote, "Teaching of religion can never be imparted in the form of lessons, it is where there is religion in living—where life is simple."

According to Tagore, "Real training consists not in foisting moral teachings but in making religion and morality an integral part of life."

## 7.5 AN IDEAL SCHOOL

Tagore attempted to make his school at Bolpur as an ideal institution. According to him an ideal school should have the following characteristics:

1. The school should be situated in natural surroundings. There should prevail the atmosphere of nature's own beauty with her varied gifts of colour and dance, flowers and fruits, with the joy of her mornings and the peace of her starry nights.
2. It should cultivate love of nature among the students.
3. It should provide spiritual training to students.
4. It should educate children by providing an environment of freedom.
5. It should impart education in the mother-tongue of the students.
6. It should provide an environment after the fashion of ancient *'tapovans'*—forest schools about which he had read so much in the Upanishads.
7. It should be a community school where there is no distinction of caste and creed.
8. It should teach crafts like sewing, book-binding, weaving, carpentry etc.
9. It should include drawing, art and music as an integral part of the curriculum.
10. It should provide students adequate opportunities for choosing their hobbies and occupations.
11. It should be a self governing institution—has a dairy farm, post office, hospital and workshop. Students hold their own courts.
12. It should provide for close personal contact with the teacher. The number of students in classes should be very small.
13. It should have a well-equipped library.
14. It should provide for manual labour.

## 7.6 EDUCATIONAL INSTITUTES STARTED BY TAGORE

Following institutions were started by him to carry out his experiments in education:

1. Sisu Bhawan (Nursery School)
2. Path Bhawan (School Section—Matriculation Examination)
3. Siksha Bhawan (Higher Secondary)
4. Vidya Bhawan (College of Undergraduate and Post-Graduate Studies and Research)
5. Vinya Bhawan (Teachers' Training College)
6. Kala Bhawan (College of Fine Arts and Crafts)
7. Sangit Bhawan (College of Dance)
8. Sriniketan (Department of Rural Reconstruction)
9. Siksa Satra (Rural High School)
10. Silpa Sadana (College of Industrial Training)
11. Cheena Bhawan (School of Languages, *e.g.*, Chinese, Tibetan etc.)

By and large, all formed part of Visvabharati University.

## 7.7 VISVABHARATI (WORLD UNIVERSITY)

The word Visvabharati consists of two Sanskrit words. *'Visva'* means world and *'Bharati'* means cultures. Thus Visvabharati would mean world culture. The motto of this university is *'Yatra Visvam bhavati ekamidam'* i.e. where the world meets at one place.

*Main Features of Visvabharati*: Tagore describes these as:

1. It wants to hold before the world the ideal of the universality of man.
2. The greatest distinction is the direct and immediate emotional contact of pupils with their teachers and with external nature.
3. A speciality of our institution is that it wants to bring up our pupils in inseparable association with nature.
4. It is intended not only to be the intellectual centre of the intellectual life of India but also the centre of her economic life.
5. It is envisaged to be the nucleus of an international university and as one of the means of promoting mutual understanding between the East and the West.

*Growth of Visvabharati*: In 1863, Rabindranath's Tagore's father founded the Ashram at Bholpur. It was called Shantiniketan (Abode of Peace). It was meant for the seekers of truth. In 1901, Tagore started the experimental school. In 1921, it became the Visvabharati.

## 7.8 CONTRIBUTION OF TAGORE TO EDUCATION

1. Tagore established a number of educational institutions at Shantiniketan.
2. Tagore founded the Visvabharati.
3. Tagore was a great practitioner. He worked out his ideas and ideals

in a constructive way.

4. He drew attention to the listless environment of the traditional school.
5. He tried to synthesise the ancient Indian ideals of education and the western arts and sciences.
6. Tagore pointed out the significance of providing an environment of freedom in the school.

# 8

# M.K. Gandhi (1869-1948)

## 8.1 BRIEF LIFE SKETCH

Mohandas Karamchand Gandhi (Karam Chand was his father's name) is popularly known as 'Gandhiji' out of reverence, *'Bapu'* out of affection, *'Mahatma'* on account of saintly nature and *'Father of the Nation'*, for his role in the freedom of India from British rule.

*Early Life and Education*: Gandhiji was born on October 2, 1869 at Porbander in Gujarat. His father was a Dewan (Chief Administrator and Chief Revenue Officer) of a small state. At school, he was slow, hesitant and shy. He was married to Kasturba at the age of thirteen. His mother was very pious and he was greatly influenced by her.

*Education in England*: When 18 years old, he was sent to London to study law where he remained for three years. His mother made him promise that in England, he would not take meat and alcohol and indulge in sex. Gandhiji kept his promise.

*Work in South Africa*: After returning from England, he started his law practice at Bombay. However, he was not very successful.

In April, 1893, he went to South Africa in connection with a civil law case of a firm. In 1893 itself, he was thrown out of a first class compartment in Durban (South Africa) for he was a coloured man. He stayed there for about 20 years. This was a turning point in his life. Gandhiji found that the Indians in South Africa were treated very cruelly and in fact like animals. They had no political rights. Gandhiji took up cases which were not entirely political but touched intimately the life of the people. Gandhiji gave up his legal practice. He completely devoted himself to the service of the people. He put into practice 'satyagraha' and 'Ahimsa'.

## 8.2 GANDHIJI'S EDUCATIONAL EXPERIMENTS

1. Gandhiji's philosophy of life including philosophy of education took shape in South Africa. His educational experiences at the Tolstoy Farm at Transwal in South Africa proved very valuable to him in formulating a new system of education suited to the needs of masses. On the Farm, he undertook the responsibility of educating his own sons and other children. The children had to devote 8 hours a day for vocational training and only 2 hours to book learning.

'Learning by doing' and 'learning by cooperation' became the chief methods of education.

2. Gandhiji came to India in 1914. Thereafter though he was deeply involved in the freedom struggle. He continued his educational experiments for a short time at Shantiniketan, then at Sabarmati Ashram and finally at Sewagram Ashram established by him. Sewagram Ashram is located 16 km from Wardha. This place has a great significance as Gandhiji not only formulated his scheme of Basic Education but also fought the battle for freedom from here.

### 8.3 GANDHIJI'S PUBLICATIONS ON EDUCATION

Important publications on education and having hearing on education are:

1. *My Experiments with Truth.*
2. *Basic Education*
3. *Towards Need Education*
4. *True Education*
5. *To the Students*
6. *Task Before Indian Students*
7. *India of My Dreams*
8. *Medium of Instruction*
9. *Tasks fore India*

Gandhiji also wrote extensively on education in *'Harijan'*—a paper founded by him.

### 8.4 PRINCIPAL FEATURES OF GANDHIJI'S PHILOSOPHY OF LIFE

1. *Supreme God*: He said, "God pervades everything. God is life, Truth and Light."
2. *Truth and Ahimsa* (Non-violence), According to Gandhiji, "Truth and Ahimsa are the two sides of a coin. They are interwined and it is practically impossible to separate them." *'Satyagraha'* implies holding of truth, through love and purity.
3. *Service of Humanity*: Gandhiji observed, "The immediate service of all human beings becomes a necessary part because it is the only way to see Him in his creation."
4. *Self-discipline and Self-purification*—Gandhi always held the high ideals of purity, sacrifice and service.
5. *Righteousness and truth as the highest religion*: Gandhiji was of the firm view that 'true religion and true morality are inseparably bound up with each other.'
6. *Ram Rajya as the Concept of a Society*: He wanted to establish Ram Rajya which he identified with justice, peace, happiness and welfare of all.

## 8.5 FACTORS THAT INFLUENCED GANDHIJI'S PHILOSOPHY OF LIFE AND PHILOSOPHY OF EDUCATION

Following were the chief influences which had a great effect on Gandhiji's philosophy of life and philosophy of education.

1. *Mother's Influence*: Gandhiji's mother taught him the lessons of simplicity and piety.
2. *Three Great Thinkers*: (i) Rayachand Bhai Patel who taught Gandhiji the first lesson in non-violence.
   (ii) Ruskin, through his book *'Unto the Last'* drew his attention to the principle of dignity of labour.
   (iii) Leo Tolstoy's *'The Kingdom of the God is within you'*, greatly influenced his spiritual outlook.
3. *The Phoenix Settlement (South Africa)*: Gandhiji conducted experiments here.
4. *The Tolstoy Farm*: In 1911, Gandhiji started an Ashram in Transwal. It was here that Gandhiji helped children in their all round development. He taught vocations such as cooking, digging and massage work. The medium of instruction was mother-tongue. English was also taught. Children learnt by doing. Textbooks were not used. No punishment was administered. Creed of non-violence was put into practice in letter and spirit.
5. *The Sabarmati Ashram*: After returning to India in 1914, Gandhiji started the Sabarmati Ashram. A school was attached with the *Ashram* which Gandhiji wanted it to make a model school.
6. *The Sevagram Ashram and the Evolution of Basic Education*: In April 1935, Gandhiji founded the Sevagram, a village with an ideal, near Wardha. Gandhiji had earlier written a few articles on education in *'Harijan'* a paper started by Gandhiji. Here, Gandhiji convened a conference in October 1937 which was attended by the leading educationists of the country. Gandhiji's views on education were considered and a Committee under the Chairmanship of Dr. Zakir Hussain was appointed. The Committee gave a concrete shape and finalised the programme of Basic Education or *Bunyadi Shiksha* or *Nai Talim*. This Scheme is also known as Wardha Scheme.

## 8.6 GANDHIJI'S VIEWS ON DIFFERENT ASPECTS OF EDUCATION

1. *Concept of Education*: Gandhiji summed up his ideas on education in these words, "By education I mean an all-round drawing out of the best in child and man—body, mind and spirit."
   'All round' implies the harmonious development of the individual. Man is neither mere the gross animal body, nor intellectual and nor the heart and soul alone. A proper and harmonious combination of all these three is required for making the whole man. Any programme on education which puts exclusive emphasis on one of

these aspects of the human personality is against the principle of education.

2. *Objective of Education*: "The ultimate objective of education is not only a balanced and harmonious individual but also a balanced and harmonious society—a just social order in which there is no unnatural dividing line between the havens and have-nots and everybody is assured of a living wage and right to freedom."
3. *Education and Character*: Gandhiji said, "What is education without character and what is character without elementary purity?"
4. *Learning by Earning*: According to Gandhiji, students should learn and side by side earn by doing some work in the school.
5. *Craft Centred Education*: Craft should become the source and centre of learning. Gandhiji suggested crafts like weaving and spinning etc. About spinning Gandhiji said, "Just as we cannot live without eating, so it is impossible for us to attain economic independence and banish pauperism."
6. *Self-sufficient Education*: Education should be imparted in such a way through crafts that their products/manufactured articles by the students should meet some expenditure in running the school.
7. *Dignity of Labour*: Love for work with hands should be developed in the students.
8. *Medium of Instruction*: Mother-tongue should be the medium of instruction. The foreign medium has made our children practically foreigners in our own land.
9. *Freedom but under Discipline*: The highest form of freedom comes through humility and self-control.
10. *Women Education*: Gandhiji advocated same facilities for women as for men and special facilities where necessary.
11. *Ideal Teacher*: According to him a teacher has to be both father and mother to his pupils. He stated, "Woe to the teacher who teaches one thing with the lips and carries another in the heart."

## 8.7 GANDHIJI AS AN IDEALIST, NATURALIST AND PRAGMATIC EDUCATIONIST

*Idealism*: Gandhiji emphasis on truth, non-violence and character development clearly indicates that he was an idealist.

*Naturalism*: Gandhiji views of making mother-tongue as the medium of instruction and providing freedom to the child reflect his naturalism.

*Pragmatism*: Gandhiji had an experimental approach to educational and other issues. He also emphasized learning through real life activities.

## 8.8 CRITICISM OF GANDHIAN APPROACH TO EDUCATION

1. *Based on Unsound Psychological Foundations*: It ignores cognitive (intellectual) and affective (feelings etc.) aspects of child's development.

2. *Cruelty on the Child*: It is nothing short of cruelty to make the child learn when he ought to be playing and enjoying himself.
3. *Craft as the only Basis of Correlation*: It is absurd to hang all knowledge from the peg of a single craft.
4. *Not Suited to the Age of Industrialisation*: With industrialization of India, knowledge of science and technology assumes far more importance than the skills in crafts.
5. *Self-sufficiency Aspect not Practicable*: Education imparted in schools cannot meet the expenditure on it. Now the policy is to provide free and compulsory education to all children upto the age of 14 years.

## 8.9 CONTRIBUTION AND RELEVANCE OF GANDHIJI'S VIEWS ON EDUCATION IN MODERN TIMES

1. The most important point in Gandhi's scheme of education is its emphasis on relating school education to the needs of the society. He wanted to achieve this objective through a system of 'Learning while earning'. He gave an important place to the learning of craft. It will be seen from the curriculum of the present day schools that work experience and socially useful productive work find an important place.
2. His emphasis on education through the mother-tongue is the accepted principle by all thinkers.
3. Gandhiji stress on inculcating dignity of labour is the need of the hour.
4. There is the dire need to develop elements of spirituality in our life which is dominated by materialism.

(*See also Chapter 14*)

# 9

# Zakir Hussain (1897-1969)

## 9.1 BRIEF LIFE SKETCH

*Family Background*: Zakir Hussain was born at Hyderabad (now in Andhra Pradesh) on February 8, 1897. His father practised as a lawyer. His father died when Zakir Hussain was barely nine years of age. At that time he was studying at the Sultan Bazar Government High School in Hyderabad. After the death of his father, the family shifted to Qaimganj (U.P.) at the ancestral home. His mother greatly influenced him.

*Education*: In 1908, Zakir Hussain was sent to Islamia High School—a residential school at Etawah. At school, he showed a keen interest in current affairs. During his school days, he came into contact with nationalist leaders. He also came under the influence of a sufi saint.

After passing the Matriculation Examination in 1913, he joined the Mohammadan Anglo Oriental College, Aligarh. He passed the B.A. examination with Philosophy, English Literature and Economics. As a post-graduate student, he took up Economics and Law.

Zakir Hussain left the college at the call of the Non-cooperation Movement by Gandhiji. Along with other students, he founded Jamia Millia Islamia (National Muslim University) in 1920 at Aligarh.

In 1922, he went to Germany to join the University of Berlin for his Ph.D. degree. He got his Ph.D. degree in 1926. His thesis was *'The Agricultural Economy of India'*.

*Positions Held*: On his return to India in 1926, he was made the Vice-Chancellor of Jamia Millia Islamia, Delhi at the age of 29 only. He stayed here for about 22 years and developed the institution into an important centre of learning.

In 1937 as desired by Gandhiji, he presided over the National Committee on Basic Education. The Committee prepared the details of the scheme of Basic Education.

In 1948, he was made the Vice-Chancellor of the Aligarh Muslim University. He remained in the post for about 8 years. He served as a member of the University Education Commission (1948-1949).

In 1952, he was nominated to the Rajya Sabha. In 1957, he became the Governor of Bihar.

In 1962, he was elected to the office of the Vice-President of India.

In 1967, he become the President of India and remained at this post till his death in 1969.

**Publications on Education and Allied Subjects**

1. *'Shiksha'* (Hindi)
2. *'Educational Discourses'* (Urdu)
3. *'Dynamic University'*
4. *'Educational Reconstruction in India'*
5. *'Abukhan ki Bakri Aur Chandha Aur Kahaniyan'* (Urdu)
6. *'Kuchhwa Aur Khargosh'* (Urdu)
7. Speeches, Articles and Addresses on Education

## 9.2 DR. ZAKIR HUSSAIN'S VIEWS ON VARIOUS ASPECTS OF EDUCATION

1. *Importance of Education*: In his speech after being sworn as the President of India, he said, "I maintain that education is a prime instrument of national purpose and that the quality of its education is inescapably involved in the quality of the nation."

2. *Aims of Education*: Dr. Zakir Hussain laid stress on the following aims of education:

(i) Education should develop a sense of common national ethos.
(ii) Education should develop higher values of life.
(iii) Education should develop qualities of citizenship.
(iv) Education traditional knowledge and real work experience skills.
(v) Education should develop positive attitude.
(vi) Education should develop a sense of social responsibility.
(vii) Education should develop vocational efficiency.

3. *Education and Politics*: Education is the master and politics its servant.

4. *Education, Morality Science and Technology*: It is necessary to combine power with morality and science with ethics. The scientists and technologists must keep in view social welfare. Education thus should develop the totality of the child.

5. *What Education is Not?* Education is not putting information into the mind and the head of the child.

6. *What is Lacking in Indian Education?* Zakir Hussain pointed out the following major drawbacks. (i) Indian education is like a stagnant pool for quite a while. (ii) Indian education ignores new ideas and fresh thinking in educational matters.

7. *Methods of Instruction*: (i) Instruction should be in accordance with the aptitude of the child. (ii) Child should be closely observed. (iii) Self-activity on the part of the child should be given due importance. (iv) Instruction should be work based.

8. *Concept of Work Education*: (i) Productive work must be related to

mental work. (ii) Following is the chain in work education. 'Thinking and Doing' and 'Doing and Thinking'. (iii) All work is not educative. It is educated only when it is preceded by mental effort. (iv) Only that work is educative which serves value. (v) The real school work trains children to think before they take up an activity. (vi) Work should be properly planned and executed. Its 'why' and 'how' must be carefully considered. (vii) Work should be treated as worship.

9. *True Nature of Freedom, Discipline and Authority*: Running of the school without proper direction would be a fruitless venture. Freedom and authority in education are not opposites. There is no authority in education without the inner freedom. There is no freedom without creative work and orderly environment. The individual is helped by the school to go through certain stages. In the beginning the authority of the teachers is of age, experience and maturity. At the end, the authority is of the values developed by the child. Responsibility freedom and discipline go together and education should train a student in each of these.

10. *The Teacher's Role*: The teacher must make efforts to lead his pupils to acquire higher values of life. This he should do through his personal conduct.

The teacher is not to dictate or dominate. He is to help and serve the student.

The teacher must understand that the pupil has his own personality and the personality must be well looked after and nourished. He has to help the bird into full bloom.

The teacher should possess limitless love and patience in dealing with children.

## 9.3 CHARACTERISTICS OF A GOOD SCHOOL

In his speech on the Founder's Day Celebration of Modern School, New Delhi, on November 25, 1962, Zakir Hussain stated the following Characteristics of a good school:

1. *Understanding of the Individuality of Each Pupil*: A true understanding of the individuality of the pupil is the first concern of the school and the teacher.

2. *Understanding of the Stages of Development*: The second concern of the school is that it always keeps in view the stages of development of the individuality of the pupil.

3. *All-Round Development*: The third concern of the school is that it devotes its efforts to the growth and development of the head, the heart and the hand of the pupil i.e. development of the intellectual, moral and the physical side of the pupil's like.

4. *Provision for Purposeful Activities*: The fourth concern of the school is to provide purposeful activities of educationally productive work.

5. *Balanced Individual and Social Development*: The fifth concern of the school is to relate individual development of the pupil with a sense of social responsibility.

6. *Self-Education*: The sixth concern of the school is to initiate in the pupils the process of self-education.

## 9.4 CONTRIBUTION OF DR. ZAKIR HUSSAIN TO EDUCATION

1. Establishment of the Jamia Milia Islamia, Okhla, New Delhi.
2. Formulation of the Wardha Scheme or Basic Education.

In July 1937, Gandhiji expressed his views on education in the *'Harijan'* a paper started by him. He stated, "Literacy itself is no education. I would, therefore, begin the child's education by teaching it a useful handicraft and enabling it to produce from the moment it begins its training."

The same year, in October, a Conference of National Workers was held at Wardha under the Presidentship of Gandhiji. The conference appointed a committee of eminent educationists under the Chairmanship of Dr. Zakir Hussain to prepare a detailed syllabus. The report of the Committee on education published in March 1938 came to be known as the Wardha Scheme of Education. Dr. Zakir Hussain played a notable role in the preparation of the report. It is also known as *'Report of the Zakir Hussain Committee and the Detailed Syllabus'* (1938).

## 9.5 MAIN OUTLINE OF THE SEVEN YEARS COURSE OF BASIC EDUCATION AS SUGGESTED BY THE COMMITTEE

1. *The Basic Craft*: It is to be chosen from the following:
   (a) Spinning and Weaving
   (b) Carpentry
   (c) Agriculture
   (d) Fruit and Vegetable Gardening
   (e) Leather Work
   (f) Any other craft for which local and geographical conditions permit.
2. *Mother-tongue*: This is the foundation of all education.
3. *Other subjects*: (i) Social studies, (ii) General Science, (iii) Drawing, (iv) Music, (v) Hindustani
4. *Total Duration of Elementary Education* : 7 years
5. *Distribution of Work in the Curriculum*

| | *Item/Subject/Activity* | *Daily Time to be Developed* |
|---|---|---|
| 1. | The Basic Craft | 3 hours 20 minutes |
| 2. | Music, Drawing and Arithmetic | 40 minutes |
| 3. | Mother-Tongue | 40 minutes |
| 4. | Social Studies and General Science | 30 minutes |
| 5. | Physical Training | 10 minutes |
| 6. | Recess | 10 minutes |
| | Total | 5 hours 30 minutes |

6. *Working Day in the School* — 228 days.

# 10

# Idealism

## 10.1 MEANING OF IDEALISM

Idealism contends that spiritual aspects are the chief aspects of human life. Natural or scientific facets of life are subordinate to spiritual ones. When the emphasis is on the spiritual aspect, it is called idealism or philosophy of idealism. The idealist 'idolise' the mind beyond everything. Idealism exalts human personality.

Idealism in India is as old as the Vedas. The Vedic seers were great idealists. The Upanishads and the *Bhagwad Gita* made a very comprehensive analysis of idealism. In the West, Plato—a Greek philosopher (427-347 B.C.) was a great idealist.

According to *Kathopanishad*, an idealist is one who possess supreme knowledge by concentration of mind.

Brubacher states, "It is the mind that is central in understanding the world"

## 10.2 CHIEF EXPONENTS OF IDEALISM

1. *Eastern Idealists*: (i) Vedic seers, (ii) The Upanishads and *Gita*, (iii) Swami Dayanand, (iv) Swami Vivekananda, (v) Mahatma Gandhi, (vi) Rabindranath Tagore, (vii) Sri Aurobindo.
2. *Western Idealists*: (i) Plato—a Greek philosopher (427-347 B.C.), (ii) Kant—a German philosopher (1724-1804 A.D.), (iii) Froebel—a German philosopher (1772-1852 A.D.), (iv) William T. Haris—an American philosopher (1835-1909 A.D.)

## 10.3 MAIN PRINCIPLES OF IDEALISM

Following are the main principles of idealism:

1. God is the source of all creation.
2. God is the source of all knowledge.
3. Spirit and mind constitute reality.
4. Material and physical universe is not a complete expression.
5. The universe of ideas and values i.e. spiritual universe is superior to material and physical universe.
6. Spiritual aspect is more important than material aspect.
7. Values are absolute, eternal and unchanging.

8. What is ultimately real, is not the object itself, but the ideal or idea behind it.
9. Man being spiritual is a supreme creation.
10. Man needs some encouragement and light in the face of darkness.
11. They are intrinsic moral and spiritual values.
12. Reality is to be found in man's mind rather than in material nature.
13. Study of man's mind and his nature is more important than the study of material universe.
14. Man has a superior nature and it is expressed in the form of intellectual culture, morality and religion.

## 10.4 IDEALISM AND VARIOUS ASPECTS OF EDUCATION

1. *Idealism and Aims of Education*: Idealism provides us clear aims of education and this is considered to be the most important contribution of idealism to education.

According to Froebel, "The object of education is the realisation of a faithful, pure, inviolable and hence holy life. Education should lead man to unity with God." Sri Aurobindo in this context has observed, "The central aim of education is the building of the powers of the human mind and spirit."

R.W. Emerson has expressed this view in the following verse.

*Not gold but only men can make a people great and strong*
*Men who for truth and honour's sake stand fast and suffer long.*

The aim of education has been very beautifully stated by the University Education Commission in these words, "If we with to bring about a savage upheaval in our society, a *'Rakshasa Raj'*, all that we need to do is to give vocational and technical education and starve the spirit. We will have a member of saintists without conscience."

According to Rusk, "Education must enable mankind to enter into the spiritual realism."

According to idealism, following are the aims of education:

1. Unfolding the Divine in man.
2. Universal education with universal individual.
3. Self-realisation.
4. Transmission of cultural and spiritual heritage.
5. Development of moral values which falls into two categories:
   (i) Duties to self which include industriousness, self culture etc.
   (ii) Duties to others i.e. respect for and appreciation of the opinion of others, co-operativeness generosity etc.
6. Development of rational attitude.

While discussing aims of education, it must be kept in view that idealism does not ignore the vocational aim of education. If simply gives it secondary importance.

2. *Curriculum and Idealism*: Idealism stresses three values of 'truth', 'goodness' and 'beauty'. These three values determine three types of human

activities—intellectual, moral and aesthetic. Each type of activity is represented by studies or subjects that should form a part of the curriculum. The following arrangement of the curriculum is recommended by idealism.

| *Value* | *Subject/Activity* |
|---|---|
| 1. Truth | 1. It is represented by intellectual subjects or activities. This includes subjects like humanities, languages, social sciences and physical sciences. |
| 2. Goodness | 2. This includes subjects like ethics, metaphysics and religion etc. |
| 3. Beauty | 3. Aesthetic subjects or activities like art and poetry etc. relate to this part of the curriculum. |

Ross's scheme for a complete curriculum in the light of idealism is as under:

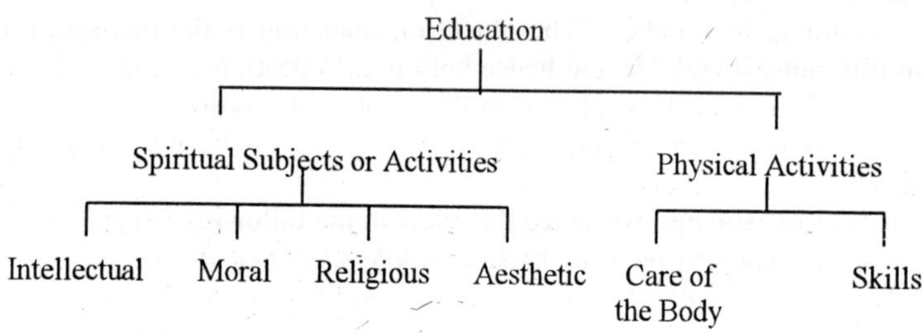


*Fig. 10.1: Complete Ideal curriculum*

3. *Idealism and Methods of Teaching*: The idealist suggests the following techniques and methods of teaching:

(i) Narration
(ii) Explanation
(iii) Exposition
(iv) Questioning
(v) Discussion
(vi) Practice and Repetition

4. *Idealism and Discipline*: While 'freedom' is the slogan of the naturalists, 'discipline' is that of idealists. Disciplining the mind and body of the child are the watchwords of the idealists. An idealist attaches great importance to the guidance of the teacher to the child for realising his 'self'. Suggested features of discipline according to idealists are:

(i) Idealism believes in inner discipline.
(ii) Inner discipline can be obtained through guidance as well as restrain—inner as well as outer or external.
(iii) There is need for restricting freedom of the child. A child cannot be given a long rope with which he may hang himself.
(iv) The teacher should win over the child through 'impression' i.e.

good personal examples of behaviour and conduct. The child especially in the plastic period of his early life considers the teacher to be an ideal person to be emulated by the pupils.

(v) Participation in social service activities develops spirit of sacrifice—an important feature of the life of an ideal person.

5. *Idealism and the Teacher*: Teacher assumes an importance place idealism. He is the key figure in the educative process. His personality is the most vital influence on the education of the child. A child is greatly influenced by his conduct, his way of speech, his etiquette etc.

Idealism considers the teacher a friend, philosopher and guide to his pupils. He guides them in such a way as they may attain 'self-realisation'. Character development and value development are the most important concerns of the teacher.

Froechel's metaphor of the 'Kindergarten' perhaps, explains best the role of the teacher in idealism. The school is regarded as a garden, the child as the plant and the teacher as the gardener. The gardener i.e. the teacher tends the little plants (human plants) in his charge carefully and helps them to grow to perfection. The gardener makes all efforts to ensure that the plant attains its finest form in all respects.

The main functions of the teacher are:

1. To understand the pupil thoroughly.
2. To have a deep knowledge of his subject.
3. To inculcate the students an attitude of hard work.
4. To use thought provoking questions and other techniques to encourage his pupils to think for themselves.
5. To develop in the students the habit of self-study.
6. To present high standards of moral behaviour.
7. To influence the pupils with his ideal behaviour and conduct.
8. To inculcate in the students higher values of life.
9. Above all to be a personal friend, guide and philosopher to his students.

## 10.5 LIMITATIONS AND WEAKNESSES OF IDEALISM IN EDUCATION

1. Undue stress on gaining knowledge is likely to turn educational institutions into 'information mongers' workshops.
2. Under the impact of idealism in education, curriculum is likely to be overloaded.
3. Obsolete knowledge may create hindrance in infusing new spirit in the curriculum.
4. For the classroom teacher, 'mind', 'soul' and spirit have little relevance.
5. The modern scientific view, by and large, does not support the concept of spiritual universe.
6. The idealist in education stresses the imitation of the teacher's model behaviour. Such a model behaviour is quite often not

available in our educational institutions.

7. The present generation prefers to experiment and innovate rather than to imitate.
8. In general, the idealist view in education pays less attention to the present environment dominated by electronic development.

## 10.6 CONTRIBUTION OF IDEALISM TO EDUCATIONAL THEORY AND PRACTICE

1. The present world is threatened by materialism which ignores higher values of life. Idealism aims to restore man to his proper place.
2. Idealism holds that the past culture must be given its due place in any scheme of educational reconstruction.
3. The present machine and electronic age treats the human being as a machine. Idealism warms against this type of approach.
4. Idealism assigns an important place to the teacher in the educative process.
5. Idealism insists that for the realisation of the 'self', every human being must receive a chance to be educated. Thus the goal of the idealist in this context is universal education.
6. Emphasis of the idealist on personality development has provided a fresh look at human relations in teaching.
7. Idealism provides clear guidelines for determining aims in education, curricular, teacher's role and methods of teaching-learning.

## 10.7 SUMMING UP

In a world threatened by materialism the philosophy of idealism provides light and direction to man for restoring his proper place. The need of the hour is to develop higher values among students. This lead must come from leaders—political, religious and all those who occupy high places in different walks of life. They must set good examples. Educational institutions alone cannot develop higher values of life.

# 11

# Naturalism

## 11.1 MEANING OF NATURALISM

'Return to nature', 'break the chains of society' are the important slogans raised by the naturalists. Following are the important definitions of naturalism which thrown adequate light on the concept of naturalism:

In the words of George Haward, "Naturalism is the exclusion of whatever is spiritual."

Hocking states, "Naturalism considers nature as the whole of reality."

James Wards writes, "Naturalism separates nature from God."

## 11.2 CHIEF CHARACTERISTICS OF NATURALISM

1. Nature alone is the source of all knowledge.
2. Mind is subordinate to nature.
3. Material world is the real world.
4. There is nothing like 'supernatural'.
5. All values exist in nature.
6. Scientific knowledge is final.
7. Values are created in terms of specific needs.
8. Senses are the gateways of knowledge.
9. In the natural order of things all human-beings are equal.
10. Everything that comes to us from nature is good but it generates in the hands of man.
11. Man creates societies to meet some of his needs.
12. Moral instinct, innate conscience, providence, power of prayer and freedom of will etc. are all illusions.

**Types of Naturalism**

| (1) | (2) | (3) |
|---|---|---|
| *Biological Naturalism* | *Mechanical Naturalism* | *Physical Sciences Naturalism* |
| This type of naturalism assumes man as a product of evolution. | According to it, man is like a machine. | It lays stress on external nature. |

## 11.3 PROMINENT NATURALIST PHILOSOPHERS

1. Bacon, Francis (1561-1626 A.D.), English philosopher
2. Comenius, John (1529-1670 A.D.), Czecheslovacian philosopher
3. Demoritius (460-370 B.C.), Greek philosopher
4. Rousseau, Jean Jacques (1712-1877), French (Swiss born) philosopher
5. Spencer, Herbert (1820-1903 A.D.), English philosopher
6. Tagore, Rabindra Nath (1861-1941), Indian philosopher

## 11.4 NATURALISM AND ITS VARIOUS DIMENSIONS IN EDUCATION

### 1. Principles of Education according to Naturalism

1. Naturalism accords an importance place to the child in the educative process.
2. Naturalism advocates education in accordance with the nature of the child.
3. Naturalism considers natural environment as an important source of education.
4. Naturalism gives an important place to the present life of the child and makes it the basis of education.
5. Naturalism states that adequate freedom should be given to the child in the educative process.
6. Naturalism has an insignificant place for acquiring knowledge from books.

### 2. Naturalism and Aims of Education

It is generally accepted that naturalism has very little to offer as regards aims of education. Naturalists differ in this respect. However, following aims of education can be deduced from the writings of the naturalist philosophers.

1. Developing the child in accordance with his nature.
2. Sublimating of redirecting and co-ordinating the natural tendencies of the child.
3. Equipping the child for the struggle of existence and ensuring his survival.
4. Enabling the child to live in harmony with his surroundings and environment.
5. Laying stress on the autonomous development of the individuality of the child.

### 3. Naturalism and Curriculum

Although there are divergent views of the naturalists on curriculum contents, they agree on the following points:

1. Curriculum should cater to the aptitudes, interests and needs of the child.

2. Curriculum should be constructed to meet the needs of the child according to the nature of development at each stage.

Rousseau, the prominent exponent of idealism in education recommended the following curriculum at four stages of the development of the child.

| *Stage* | *Years of Duration* | *Aim* | *Curriculum* |
|---|---|---|---|
| 1. Infancy | From birth to 5 years of age | Physical development | Physical education in a natural way. No set curriculum. |
| 2. Childhood | 5 to 12 years of age | Providing strength to the child with which he may prepare himself for freedom. | Negative education (Explained below) |
| 3. Boyhood or pre-adolescent period | 12 to 15 years | To make the child functionally useful. | Period of intellectual development. Curriculum to includes astronomy, science and art. Learning of manual and industrial arts. |
| 4. Adolescence period | 15 to 18 years of age develop | To enable the students. complex social relationships. | 1. Study of economics, history, politics and society<br>2. Moral education through activities and occupations |
| 5. Education of Woman | | 1. Since woman is made to please the man, her education would be quite different. | 1. Teaching details of house keeping. |
| | | 2. Preparing her for pleasing the man and for household work. | 2. Cooking |
| | | | 3. Cleaning<br>4. Maintaining accounts<br>5. Cleanliness<br>6. Moral education through examples so that she remains chaste. |

The chief characteristics of curriculum according to naturalism in general are:

1. Curriculum is based on the nature of the child, his interests etc.
2. It lays stress on the subjects which are helpful in the self-preservation of man.

3. It stresses basic sciences.
4. It gives importance to physical and health sciences.

**5. Naturalism and Methods of Teaching**

1. *Experience is the Best Teacher*: Rousseau advises, "Give your scholar no verbal lessons; he should be taught by experience."
2. *Observation method*: The child should observe things and discover for himself.
3. *Individualised Instruction*: According to a naturalist, every child's ability to acquire knowledge and to benefit the individual. Hence the method of class teaching is not useful.
4. *Self Education*: The naturalist advocates that the child is expected to acquire information, knowledge and ideas by himself.
5. *Things rather than Words*: Rousseau says, "Teach by doing whatever you can, and only fall back upon words when doing is out of question."
6. *Social Learning through Participation*: A child acquires social learning when he takes part in the social activities.

**6. Naturalism and Discipline**

1. *Discipline by Natural Consequences*: The concept of discipline, according to idealists may be expressed in four words, "Discipline by natural consequences." Natural consequences are those experiences which the child receives by following an activity. When the child runs its head against the table, it feels pain. The remembrance of pain makes the child disciplined.
2. *No Punishments*: Rousseau states, "Children should never receive punishment as such, it should always come as the natural conseques of his action." If a child is late for a picnic party, let him learn from this experience of being late.
3. *Full Freedom to the Child*: A naturalist starts with the assumption that the nature of child is essentially good. Therefore, he should be given freedom of expression and development.

**7. Naturalism and the Teacher**

Naturalists make the following observations regarding the role of the teacher:

1. *Art of Observing*: Rousseau states, "I wish some discreet person would give us a treatise on the art of observing children."
2. *Art of Suggesting*: Rousseau writes, "To know how to suggest is the art of teaching."
3. *Art of Stimulating*: Rousseau says, "The highest function of the teacher consists not so much is imparting knowledge as on stimulating the pupil in its love and pursuit."

4. *Free development of the child*: The teacher should not impose himself on children. He should provide an environment full of freedom.

**8. Idealism and the Child**

A naturalist accepts the child as a 'hero' or 'star' in the drama of education. Tender regard for the child is very essential in his education.

## 11.5 NEGATIVE EDUCATION ACCORDING TO ROUSSEAU — A PROMINENT NATURALIST

1. *No Book Learning*: Rousseau said, "I hate books because they are curse to children."
2. *No Habit Formation*: According to Rousseau, habits make children 'slaves'.
3. *No Direct moral Instruction*: "A child should be left free to act and learn what is right or wrong."
4. *No formal discipline*: A child should learn from the "natural consequences of his actions."
5. *No Sticking to Traditional Procedure of Education*: Rousseau said, "Follow the reverse of the current procedure and you will almost do right."
6. *Nature a Great Teacher*: According to Rousseau, the nature of the child is good. Hence he should have the freedom to learn from nature and natural surroundings.

## 11.6 LIMITATIONS OF NATURALISM IN EDUCATION

1. *No Clear Cut Goals*: Naturalism does not offer definite aims of education.
2. *Neglect of Books*: There is a very minor place for books. We cannot neglect the treasure of knowledge contained in the pointed materials.
3. *Negligible Importance to Higher Values*: Naturalism by and large, ignores the higher ends in the process of education.
4. *Undue Emphasis on Education through Nature*: It is certain that physical nature alone cannot be considered adequate for providing all education.
5. *Absolute Freedom a Myth*: Absolute freedom does not exist. It never existed. It will never exist in a civilised society. "Child cannot be given the long rope to hang himself."
6. *Very Little Role for the Teacher*: Naturalism minimizes the role of the teacher in the educative process. Even in the electronic age, a teacher occupies an important place in the teaching-learning process.
7. *Neglect of Moral and Spiritual Values*: Naturalism ignores the moral and spiritual development of the child.

## 11.7 CONTRIBUTION OF NATURALISM TO EDUCATION

1. Naturalism has brought to the forefront the importance of the recognition of child in the process of education.
2. Naturalism has very clearly drawn the attention of the educators to study child carefully and provide education accordingly. It advocates that education, should be 'child centred'.
3. Naturalism has stressed that the educative process should be made pleasurable and enjoyable.
4. Naturalism indicates that educational institutions should be set up in natural surroundings.
5. Naturalism brings to light the significance, of progressive methods of teaching like 'learning by doing', 'learning by observing' and 'learning by inductive approach'.
6. Naturalism has given birth to new movements and new types of educational institutions like A.S. Neill's Summer School and Visvabharati.

# 12

# Pragmatism

## 12.1 MEANING OF PRAGMATISM

Pragmatism is also known as 'Practical Philosophy', 'Worldly-wise Philosophy', Utilitarian Philosophy, 'Down to Earth Philosophy' and 'Cash Philosophy' on account of its emphasis on 'utility' aspect.

The word 'pragmatism' is derived from a Greek word *'Pragma'* which means 'to do', 'to make', and to 'accomplish'. Therefore words 'doing', 'making', 'accomplishing' etc. are used while referring to pragmatism. Expressions like 'action', 'practice' and 'activity' have become popular in education in account of pragmatism.

Pragmatism stands between idealism and naturalism.

### Chief Promoters of Pragmatism

C.S. Pierce (1839-1914 A.D.) was the first to use the word pragmatism in philosophical thought. Pragmatism, first appeared in 1878 in the essay, '*How to Make Our Ideas Clear*', written by Pierce. Pragmatism was popularised by William James (1842-1910) and John Dewey (1859-1959), both American philosophers.

### Origin of Pragmatism

Pragmatism represents the American way of life and thinking. The (Puritans) foreigners who came to the U.S.A. from Europe had to face several new problems. They had no ready made solutions of their problems. The application of the well-known ideals of Europe would not serve the purpose. Consequently they built up a philosophy of life through 'experience'. This philosophy of experience became popular as pragmatism.

## 12.2 FUNDAMENTAL PRINCIPLES OF PRAGMATISM

1. Experience is the central idea in pragmatism. According to John Dewey, "Truth is made just as health, wealth and strength are made in the course of experience."
2. William James sees no difference between 'pragmatism' and 'practicalism'. Truth is that which works in institutions. It changes with times.
3. There are no absolute values of life.

4. Action is real and ideas are tools.
5. Man is an active being.
6. Man has the ability to solve his problems.
7. Man solves his problems though the logic of experiments and scientific methods.
8. Knowledge is functional and tentative.
9. Utilitarian aspect is supreme.
10. Past has little value.
11. Present and future are more important.
12. Spiritual character of existence has little significance.
13. Pragmatism rejects all types of authoritarianism whether in government or religion or education.

## 12.3 BROAD FEATURES OF PRAGMATISM IN EDUCATION

1. Educational practices have to be experimental.
2. Values are created through experimentation.
3. Child learns by doing more than by reflection.
4. Education is a continuous process. Education is a constant reorganising or reconstructing of experience.
5. Education should enable the child to learn new techniques to cope with new situations.
6. Curriculum is activity centred.
7. Curriculum is integrated.
8. Moral values cannot be imposed by the elders upon the younger generation.
9. Life situations should be made the basis of education.
10. Education is a social necessity. It is the means by which it renews itself.
11. Suitable environment is needed for the development of the personality of the child.
12. Freedom should be given to the child for the development of his all round personality.
13. Educational experiments lead to the development of philosophy of education.

### A. Pragmatism and Aims of Education

1. There are no pre-conceived aims of education.
2. Aims of education are not final and fixed.
3. Aims of education arise out of situations
4. Education is its own end.
5. Education should enable an individual to adapt to the environment.
6. Education should provide more and more purposeful experience.
7. Dewey lays on emphasis in preparing a socially efficient individual.

### B. Pragmatism and Curriculum

Pragmatism points out the following criteria for curriculum construction.

1. *Principle of Utility*: This is the first concern. The school must provide those experiences that are useful to the child. The utility aspect requires direct training for the later stage of the school.
2. *Principle of Child's Natural Instincts*: The curriculum should be based on the natural instincts of the child.
3. *Principle of Graded Curriculum*: The curriculum should take into account the successive stages of child's development.
4. *Principle of Child's Occupations and Activities*: Curriculum attaches limited importance to book learning. Besides the subjects, the curriculum includes purposive, productive and socialised activities.
5. *Principle of Integration*: Subjects are not treated water-light compartments. Subjects are presented as modes of activities. Integration, for the pragmatist is of life, with activity of the learner.
6. *Principle of Social Worth*: A pragmatist also recognises that the subjects and experiences provided to the child must make him socially useful.
7. *Principle of Dynamism*: The pragmatist does not believe in the rigidity of the curriculum. So the curriculum is not static. Curriculum changes according to the needs of the pupils and the society. The main aim of knowledge i.e. human progress should not be overlooked.

Curriculum includes tools of knowledge as reading, writing, counting, nature study, drawing, handwork, hygiene, physical training, history, geography, science—domestic science for girls and agricultural science for boys. Vocational training is an indispensable part of the curriculum.

### C. Pragmatism and Methods of Teaching

1. *Learning by doing*: The pragmatists regard learning as a by-product of activity. This is explained as:

   *Child's activities are:*

   —Spontaneous activities.

   —Purposeful activities.

   —Socialised activities

   *The teacher's job is to keep him alive to:*

   —His purposes.

   —His capacities.

   —His limitations.

   *So that the child evolves:*

   —His own discipline.

   —Makes his own adjustment.

   —And thus realizes himself.
2. *Project Method*: William Kilpatric, an ardent follower of Dewey,

the most prominent pragmatist, originated the Project Method of Teaching. According to him a project is a whole-hearted, purposeful activity, preceding in a social environment.

The Project Method considers the school, the curriculum and the contents of studies from the point of view of the child. Subjects and activities are integrated round a project which relates to a real situation.

The teacher provides suitable and interesting situations, preferably social ones. Children many subjects while undertaking the project. For instance a project on 'know your country' involves several activities and experiences relating to many subjects. Likewise a project on 'Village Survey' provides lots of information and experiences.

### D. Pragmatism and Discipline

The pragmatism holds that discipline should be social through and through. Free, purposeful and co-operative activities organised in the school lead to social discipline. These activities inculcate attitudes of co-operation and consideration. Besides, these keep the students busy in worthwhile tasks. Moral development taken place through such activities. Students develop a sense of self-control.

### E. Pragmatism and the Teacher

Pragmatism regards the teacher as a helper and guide. The teacher assumes the role of an 'arranger of experience.' According to Dewey, "The teacher is a guide and director, he steers the boat, but the energy that propels it must come from those who are learning."

## 12.4 LIMITATIONS OF PRAGMATISM

1. Pragmatism, by and large, ignores eternal values.
2. Pragmatism pays little attention to spiritual values.
3. Pragmatism lays too much emphasis on material things.
4. Pragmatism advocates a utilitarian approach only.
5. Pragmatism provides very insignificant place to cultural values.
6. Pragmatism believes that experience is all in all. It ignores the knowledge accumulated through the ages.
7. Pragmatism does not give due importance to regular and systematic instruction.
8. The entire knowledge and experience needed by the child cannot be obtained through projects.
9. Pragmatism places heavy demands on the teacher.
10. Pragmatism does not indicate fixed educational goals.

## 12.5 CONTRIBUTION OF PRAGMATISM TO EDUCATION

1. Pragmatism saves the child from the burden of education which is too much centred on books.
2. Pragmatism helps us in realizing the value of to-day' life by experiencing it.

3. Pragmatism advises us to have a balanced approach towards the past, present and future. The past may be glorious and rich but it must guide for living a glorious and rich life in the present. Thus too much emphasis on cultural heritage should not be laid.
4. Pragmatism rightly advocates that the present experiences of the child should not be sacrificed for the future which is very uncertain.
5. Pragmatism contributors to the development of a system which is vocation-centred. In India this aspect remained ignored for a long time.
6. Pragmatism recognises that an individual should be socially efficient and productive. The curriculum duly takes note of it.
7. Another important principle which has been given by the pragmatism in the curriculum is that of integration of knowledge.
8. The pragmatism's contribution to the method of teaching is commendable. Project method can serve several educational tasks.
9. The pragmatic approach is neither teacher-centred, nor examination centred, nor curriculum centred but pupil-centred. Of course, this approach considers the teacher a friend and guide of the child.

# 13

# Humanism: Comparative Study of Idealism, Naturalism and Pragmatism

## 13.1 MEANING OF HUMANISM

Humanism is a very old philosophy but it emerged as a modern philosophy in the sixteenth century A.D. Scholars and writers during Renaissance in Europe brought to focus the main features of humanism. Humanism is an 'ism' that gives prominence to the human being.

The word humanism is derived from the Latin word 'Homo', meaning human being.

Humanism has been interpreted in the following ways:

1. Humanism is a reasonable balance in life.
2. Humanism takes vivid interests in all sides of life.
3. Humanism is free from religious bigotry.
4. Humanism is responsive to all passions.
5. Humanism regards man or the human being as the centre and measure of all activities.

## 13.2 PRINCIPLES OF HUMANISM

Following are the main principles of humanism:

1. Man is the maker and master of his own destiny.
2. Man is competent to solve all his problems.
3. Man's happiness lies in this world.
4. Man should be made free in this world for the achievement of his happiness.
5. Humanism believes in the interests and welfare of all human beings.
6. Humanism stands for brotherhood of man.
7. Humanism stands for international friendship.
8. Humanism does not believe in supernaturalism.

## 13.3 HUMANISM AND MODIFICATION OF HUMAN NATURE

Humanism believes that human nature is flexible. Human nature may have to be reconditioned and reshaped to face the new challenges. Humanism does not believe in the dictum, "You cannot change human nature". This task of reconditioning, reshaping and transforming human nature has to be directed towards the good of the individual and society. Humanism wants to check the egoistic nature of man.

Humanism wants that the life of the human being should be so transformed that welfare of all should become the goal. Humanism states that for this achievement of this goal, an individual may have to renounce some of his desires. He must have strict control over himself in the interest of human happiness on this earth.

## 13.4 HUMANISM AND DEMOCRACY

Humanism accepts that the growth of the human being must always be seen in the context of social welfare. Humanism believes that democracy has a permanent value and validity for mankind.

## 13.5 EDUCATIONAL IMPLICATIONS OF HUMANISM

The humanistic approach is based on understanding the needs of the learners. This is the first step towards the fulfilment of learning objectives. The learner is competent to solve his problems provided he is properly guided. A suitable environment has to be created for this. Watchwords of humanism in education are: 'better learner', a 'better human being' and a 'well adjusted personality'.

Following are the main educational implications of humanism:

1. Betterment of each learner or all learners is the chief concern of education.
2. Learning becomes effective when it is need-based.
3. It aims at increasing the learner's self-direction.
4. Its focus is on learning at a higher level i.e. self-actualisation.
5. It stresses self-discipline and self-control.
6. It points out that education should develop values so that the learners become broad-minded.
7. It advocates co-operation, mutual toleration and social understanding.
8. It points out that the qualities of brotherhood and international understanding must be given their due attention.
9. Teacher is considered as a guide and helper to the students.

## 13.6 HUMANISM AND CURRICULUM

Following are the chief characteristics of curriculum in humanism:

*Due Regard for Ancient Cultures*: Educational programmes should foster an admiration and love for ancient cultures. Ancient cultures are important sources for the growth of humanistic values.

*Respect for Scholars.* The younger generation must be taught to learn to respect the wisdom of scholars as it relates to important human values.

*Group Work*: Adequate opportunities should be provided to the learners for group work so that they develop an attitude of tolerance.

## 13.7 COMPARATIVE IMPACT OF IDEALISM, NATURALISM AND PRAGMATISM ON EDUCATIONAL THEORY AND PRACTICE

| *Idealism* | *Naturalism* | *Pragmatism* |
|---|---|---|
| *1. Basic Philosophical Features* | | |
| 1. Idealism believes in the existence of God. | Naturalism has no belief in the existence of God. | Pragmatism has some belief in the existence of God. |
| 2. Ultimate reality is spiritual. | Ultimate reality is physical. | Ultimate reality is utility. |
| 3. Universe is God's creation. | Universe is man's creation. | Universe is natural creation. |
| 4. Eternal spiritual values never change. | Values are not eternal. | Values are changeable. |
| 5. Truth, beauty and goodness are eternal values. | There are no such values. | The nature of these values undergoes changes. |
| 6. Spiritual laws are Universal. | Physical and natural laws are Universal. | No law is universal. |
| *2. Aims of Education* | | |
| 1. Self-realization aim. | 1. Self-expression aim. | 1. Social efficiency aim. |
| 2. Spiritual development aim. | 2. Autonomous development of the individuality aim. | 2. Adjustment with present aim. |
| 3. Character development aim. | 3. Adjustment to environment aim. | |
| *3. Curriculum* | | |
| 1. Emphasis on ethics and humanities. | 1. Emphasis on sciences. | 1. Stress on utilitarian subjects and vocational subjects. |
| 2. Study of cultural heritage. | 2. Curriculum band on the need, ability and aptitude of the individual nature. | 2. Life experiences.<br>3. Integrated curriculum. |
| *4. Methods of Teaching* | | |
| 1. Lecture method. | 1. Direct observation. | 1. Learning by doing. |
| 2. Question answer method. | 2. Heuristic method. | 2. Project method. |
| *5. Discipline* | | |
| 1. Emphasis on regulated freedom. | Uncontrolled freedom. | Social discipline. |
| 2. Self discipline. | Discipline through natural | Discipline through co- |

*6. Teacher's Role*

| | | |
|---|---|---|
| 1. Important role of the teacher. | Limited role of the teacher. | Teacher as a guide. |
| 2. Importance of teacher's personality. | Very little importance to teacher's personality. | Limited importance. |
| 3. Teacher as an ideal person. | Teacher as an observer. | Teacher as a friend and philosopher. |

*Summing up*: We cannot remain wedded to a particular philosophy. Each philosophy contributes something to educational theory and practice. We must make a balanced and rational use of each type of philosophy according to needs.

# 14

# Practical Work: Diverse Issues

## 14.1 LIFE SKETCH AND CONTRIBUTION OF MAHATMA GANDHI

### Life Sketch of Mahatma Gandhi

(*Note* : Life sketch as given in chapter eight to be supplemented.)

*Gandhiji's Role in Freedom Struggle: Gandhiji as the Messiah of Indian Nationalist Movement*: Gandhiji emerged as the Messiah of the Indian Nationalist movement in 1919 and there after he completely dominated Indian political struggle down to 1947. There was hardly a non-violent movement for the freedom of India which Gandhiji did not lead.

Gandhiji was a saint-politician-statesman who always used 'soul force' against brutal force of the British rulers.

Gandhiji had an implicit faith in the united power of the masses of India. He inculcated a spirit of self-sacrifice among the people of India to face the mighty power of the British. He made the struggle of freedom a mass movement. He won the co-operation of the peasants and workers. He worked had to forge Hindu-Muslim Unity. He exhorted students and women to rise against the British. Businessmen, engineers, doctors, lawyers and teachers etc. took part in the peaceful movements launched by him.

### Important Political Movements and Events Associated with Gandhiji in the Freedom Struggle

1. Champaran Satyagraha (1917)
2. Ahmedabad Mill Strike (1918)
3. Kheda or Kaira Satyagraha (1918)
4. Non-Co-operation Movement (1920-22)
5. Khilafat Movement (1920-22)
6. President of the Indian National Congress (1924)
7. Movement of Purna Swaraj (1929)
8. Civil Disobedience Movement (1930)
9. Gandhi-Irwin Pact (1931)
10. Gandhi-Ambedkar Pact or Poona Pact (1932)
11. Round Table Conferences (1930-32)
12. Quit India Movement (1942)

13. Pilgrimage to Noakhali (West Bengal) to check Hindu-Muslim Riots (1946)
14. Fasts for Self-purification (1924, 1932, 1933, 1934 and 1947)

**Important Movements Started by Gandhiji for National Development**

1. National awakening through Ahimsa and Satyagraha.
2. Rural uplift
3. Promotion of Khadi
4. Uplift of the Harijans
5. Prohibition
6. Basic Education
7. Hindu Muslim Unity

**Thoughts of Gandhiji on Education in His Own Words**

*Meaning of Education*

Real Education has to draw out the best from the boys and girls to be educated. This can never be done by packing ill-assorted and unwanted information into the heads of the students. It becomes a dead weight crushing all originality in them and turning them into mere automata.

(*Harijan*, December 1, 1933)

By education I mean an all-round drawing out of the best in child and man—body, mind and spirit. (*'Harijan'*, July 31, 1937)

Literacy is not the end of education, not even the beginning. It is only one of the means whereby man and women can be educated. Literacy in itself is no education. (*'Harijan'*, July 31, 1937)

I would develop in the child his hands, his brain and his soul.

(*'Basic Education'*, p. 23)

Purity of personal life is the one indispensable condition for building a sound education (*'Towards New Education'*, p. 31)

I hold that true education of the intellect can only come through a proper exercise and training of the bodily organs, e.g., hands, feet, eyes, ears, nose, etc. (*'Basic Education'*, p. 123)

True education is that which draws out and stimulates the spiritual, the intellectual and physical faculties of the children.

(Tendulkar, *'Mahatma'*, Vol. IV, p. 187)

**Education and Character**

The end of all knowledge must be building up character. What is education without character and what is character without elementary purity?

(*'Towards New Education'*, p. 301)

All our learning of recitation of the Vedas, correct knowledge of Sanskrit, Latin and Greek and what not will avail as nothing of they do not enable us to cultivate purity of heart. The end of all knowledge may be the building of character. (*'True Education'*, p. 229)

### The Teacher

Woe to the teacher who teaches one thing with the lips and carries another in the heart. (*'To the Students'*, p. 16)

The politician may succeed in his purpose even though he lacks character, but a pupils' teacher cannot do without character. If he lacks, he will be like salt without its savour. (*'True Education'*, p. 161)

I always felt that the true textbook for the pupils is his teacher. (*'Autobiography'*, p. 41)

It is possible for a teacher living miles away to affect the spirit of the pupils by his way of living. (*'Towards New Education'*, p. 44)

### Education Through Craft

I want the whole process of education to be imparted through some handicraft or industry. (*Basic Education'*, p. 191)

My idea is not to teach a particular profession or occupation to the children, but to develop the full man through teaching that occupation. (Tendulkar, *'Mahatma'*, Vol. IV, p. 200)

The brain must be educated through hand. (*'Basic Education'*, p. 190)

The old idea was to add a craft to the ordinary curriculum of education followed in the schools. That is to say, the craft was to be taken in hand wholly separate from education. To me that seems a fatal mistake. The teacher must learn the craft and correlate his knowledge to the craft, so that he will impart all that knowledge to his pupils through the medium of the particular craft that he chooses.

Take the instance of spinning. Unless I know arithmatic I cannot report how many yards of yarn I have produced on the *'takli'*. I must learn addition and substraction and multiplication and division. In dealing with complicated sums, I shall have to use symbols and so I get my algebra. Even here, I would insist on the use of Hindustani letters instead of Roman.

*Takli*-spinning leads me into the History of East India Company.

There is no limit to the possibilities of knowledge that can be imparted through this medium. (*'Harijan'*, February 18, 1939)

### Methods of Teaching

It is not by making our brains a store-house for cramming facts that our understanding is opened. An intelligent approach to an industrial training is often a more valuable aid to the intellect than an indifferent reading of literature. (*'Towards New Education'*, p. 25)

Pupils should know to discriminate between what should be received and what rejected. It is the duty of the teacher to teach his pupils discrimination. (*'Towards New Education'*, p. 34)

The utterly false idea that intelligence can be developed only through book-reading should give place to the truth that the quickest development of the mind can be achieved by artisan's work being learnt in a scientific way. (Bose, Nirmal Kumar, *'Selections from Gandhiji'*, p. 288)

The brain must be educated through the hand. (*'Harijan'*, Feb. 29, 1939)

The core of my suggestion is that handicrafts are to be taught not merely for production work but for developing the intellect.

(*'Basic Education'*, p. 44)

I want to teach through hand-work all the subjects like History Geography, Arithmetic, Science, Language, Panting etc.

(Tendulkar, *'Mahatma'*, Vol. IV, p. 196)

**Freedom and Discipline**

The student's mind must not be caged. This does not mean that they are not subject to discipline. No school can be run without it. But discipline has nothing to do with artificial restraint upon students' all round growth.

(*'True Education'*, p. 57)

I have always been opposed to corporal punishment.

(*'Towards New Education'*, p. 19)

The worst thing that can happen to boys in school is to have to render blind obedience to everything that the teacher says.

(*'True Education'*, p. 88)

If the boys and girls do not learn discipline in their school days, money and time spent on their education is a national loss.

(*'Harijan'*, Feb. 17, 1946)

Ahimsa in education must have an obvious bearing on the mutual relations of the students. (*'To the Students'*, p. 67)

**Self-Sufficiency in Education**

Self-sufficiency is not a prior condition, but to me it is the acid test. This does not mean that Basic Education will be self-supporting from the very start. But taking the entire period of seven years' income and expenditure must balance each other. (*'Basic Education'*, p. 108)

*'Nai Talim'* without the self-support basis would be like a lifeless boy.

(*'Basic Education'*, p. 108)

When I used the word self-supporting, I did not mean that all the capital expenditure would be defrayed from it, but at least the salary of the teacher would be found out of the proceeds of the articles made by our pupils. The economic aspect of the basic system of education is thus self-evident.

(*Basic Education'*, p. 10)

I can very keen on finding the expenses of a teacher through the product of the manual labour of his pupils because I am convinced that there is no other way to carry education to crores of our children.

(*'Basic Education'*, p. 192)

My *'Nai Talim'* is not dependent on money. The running expenses of this education should come from the educational proceeds itself.

(*'Harijan'*, March 2, 1947)

**Dignity of Labour**

Manual work will have to be very centre of the whole thing.

(*'India of my Dreams'*, p. 72)

The introduction of manual training will serve as a double purpose in a poor country like ours. It will pay for the education of our children and teach them an occupation which they fall back in later life. Such a system must make our children self-reliant. (*'Towards New Education'*, p. 42)

Useful manual labour, intelligently performed, is the means par excellence for developing the intellect. (*'Basic Education'*, p. 106)

**Medium of Instruction**

The foreign medium has made our children practically foreigners in their own land. It is the greatest tragedy of the existing system.

(*'Towards New Education'*, p. 48)

As a result of English being medium of instruction we have last all originality. We have become birds without wings. (*'To the Students'*, p. 89)

The baby takes its lesson from its mother. I therefore regard it a sin against the motherland to inflict upon her children a tongue other than their mother's for their mental development. (*'Medium of Instruction'*, p. 8)

The medium of instruction must be altered at any cost, the provincial languages being given this rightful place. I would prefer temporary chaos in higher education to the criminal waste that is daily accumulating.

(*'Towards New Education'*, p. 89)

(*see Chapter 8 also*)

**Select Bibliography**

Aggarwal, J.C. *'Thoughts of Gandhiji on Education'*: Extension Services Department, Teacher's College, Jamia Millia Islamia, New Delhi, 1966.

Gandhi, M.K., *'Towards New Education'* (edited by Bharatan Kumarappa), Navajivan Trust, Ahmedabad, 1953.

Gandhi, M.K., *'Basic Education'*, Navajivan Trust, Ahmedabad, 1956.

Gandhi, M.K., *'The Problem of Education'* Navajivan Trust, Ahmedabad, 1962

Gandhi, M.K., *'True Education'*, Navajivan Trust, Ahmedabad, 1962.

Gandhi, M.K., *'Harijan'*, July 31, 1937, Feb. 18 and 29, 1939, Feb. 17, 1946.

NCERT, *'Gandhi on Education'* (compilation of an anthology of Gandhiji's writing on Education), NCERT, New Delhi, 1998.

## 14.2 CRITICAL ANALYSIS OF PRIMARY SYSTEM OF EDUCATION IN INDIA

**Constitutional Commitment on Universal Elementary Education (UEE)**

The universalisation of primary education has been one of the most important goals of educational development in since Independence. It found expression in Article 45 of the Constitution of India as a Directive Principle of State Policy. It states, "The State (here State implies the Central Government and State Governments) shall endeavour, to provide, within a period of ten years from the commencement of this Constitution, for free and compulsory education for all children until they complete the age of fourteen years."

*Concept of Primary Education*: It is observed that the term "compulsory education' used in the Article 45 makes no reference to the duration of the compulsory education and the age group to which it caters.

Article 45 of the Constitution uses neither the term primary education nor elementary education.

It is also not clear whether the compulsory education includes nursery/pre-primary education also.

According to Gandhiji, "The course of primary education should be extended at least to seven years." (*'Harijan'*, July 31, 1937)

The Education Commission (1964-66) uses the term 'Primary' as given below:

(a) Lower Primary: Classes I to IV or I to V
(b) High Primary: Classes V to VII or VI to VIII
(c) Lower Secondary Classes : Classes VIII to X or IX to X

*'National Curriculum for Primary and Secondary Education: A Frame Work'*, (1985), a publication of NCERT has observed, "primary as referred to here is a substitute for 'Elementary', a terminology used in earlier documents."

The National Policy on Education 1986 and as amended in 1992 has used the term elementary education. In part V it states, "The new thrust in elementary education will emphasise two aspects : (i) Universal enrolment and universal retention of children upto 14 years of age, and (ii) a substantial improvement in the quality of education."

The Government of India, Ministry of Human Resource Development, Department of Education, in its Annual Reports includes Class I to VIII under elementary education (Primary I to V and Middle VI to VIII).

There are great variations in the structure of school education in India.

*Summing up*: Without going into details, it is accepted that compulsory education implies 8 years of education, (Classes I to VIII), catering to the age group 6 to 14.

### Implementation of the Constitutional Provisions

According to the Article 45, the objective regarding free and compulsory education should have been achieved by 1960. However, this could not be implemented on account of several reasons. The target date had to be revised first to 1970, then to 1976 and later on to 1990. The National Policy on Education (NPE) fixed 1995 as the target date. Under in the *'Sarva Shiksha Abhiyan' (SSA)* or 'Education for All', launched in 2001, it is envisaged that elementary education of satisfactory quality for all would be be provided by 2010. In 2002, Article 45 was amended and Article 21A. '*Right to Education*' for free universal primary education was inserted in the constitution, and in August 2009, RTE Act was passed by Parliament.

**Table 14.1: Gross Enrolment Ratios at the Elementary Stage (1950-51 to 2009-10)**

| *Year* | *I-V Classes Primary* | *VI to VIII Classes Upper Primary* | *I to VIII Total* |
|---|---|---|---|
| 1950-51 | 42.6% | 12.7% | 32.1% |
| 1960-61 | 62.4% | 22.5% | 48.7% |
| 1970-71 | 78.6% | 33.4% | 61.9% |
| 1980-81 | 80.5% | 41.9% | 67.5% |
| 1990-91 | 100.1% | 62.1% | 86.0% |
| 2004-2005 | 107.8% | 69.9% | 93.5% |
| 2009-2010 | 115.63% | 75.80% | 104.7% |

*Note*: Gross Enrolment Ratio (GER) is defined as the percentage of the enrolment in classes I-V and VI-VIII and/or I-VIII to the estimated child population in the age groups 6 to 11 and 11 to 14 or 6 to 14 years respectively. Enrolment in these stages includes under-age or over-age children. Hence the percentage may be more than 100% in some cases.

*Source*: *'Selected Educational Statistics'*, Ministry of HRD and DISE 2009-10: Flash Stistics April '12.

**Table 14.2: Elementary Education Progess since 2005-06**

| | 2005-06 | 2009-10 |
|---|---|---|
| Primary schools | 7.38 lakh | 8.10 lakh |
| Upper Primary schools | 3.85 lakh | 4.94 lakh |
| Primary Enrolment | 125 million | 133 million |
| Upper Primary Enrolment | 43.7 million | 54.5 million |
| Elementary Enrolment | 169 million | 188 million |
| GER Primary | 104 | 115 |
| GER Upper Primary | 59 | 75.8 |
| Teachers in Govt. Schools | 3.4 million | 3.9 million |

Enrolments at elementary level increased from 169 million in 2005-06 to 188 million in 2009-10. In 2005-06, 125.7 million children were enrolled in government schools. This figure increased to 131 million in 2009-10. In addition, another 17 million are enrolled in government aided schools, and 40 million are attending private unaided schools.

**Causes and Problems for Non-fulfilment of Constitutional Provisions Regarding UEE**

Following are the causes and problems pointed out by experts and various committee and commissions:

1. Lack of priority to elementary and secondary education.
2. Lack of finance.
3. Population explosion.
4. Problems resulting from the poverty of the parents.
5. Adult illiteracy.
6. Wastage and stagnation.
7. Problem of girls status.
8. Problems of states with low enrolment.
9. Problem of education of the Backward sections and classes.
10. Problem of unattractive schools.
11. Problem of unsuitable contents of education.
12. Problem of small habitations.
13. Problem of single teacher schools.
14. Problem of the education of the handicapped.
15. Uninspiring teaching-learning environment.
16. Problem of enforcing compulsory Primary Education Acts.

**Wastage and Stagnation at the Elementary Stage**

One of the most important problems of the elementary education is the enormous wastage and stagnation.

Wastage implies dropping out of pupils from school i.e. leaving school before the completion of class 8.

Stagnation means as the retention of a child in the same class for more than one year or failure of a child in a class.

The following table points out the seriousness of the problem of drop-outs in India.

**Table 14.3: Drop out Rates**

| *Class/Year* | *1970-71* | *1980-81* | *1990-91* | *1992-93* | *2004-05* | *2009-10* |
|---|---|---|---|---|---|---|
| *Classes I to V* | | | | | | |
| Boys | 64.5 | 56.2 | 40.1 | 43.8 | 31.8 | 30.25 |
| Girls | 70.9 | 62.5 | 46.0 | 46.7 | 25.4 | 27.25 |
| Total | 70.0 | 58.7 | 42.6 | 45.0 | 29.0 | 28.86 |
| *Classes I to VIII* | | | | | | |
| Boys | 74.6 | 68.0 | 59.1 | 58.23 | 50.5 | 40.59 |
| Girls | 83.4 | 79.4 | 65.1 | 65.2 | 51.3 | 44.39 |
| Total | 77.9 | 72.7 | 60.9 | 61.10 | 50.8 | 42.39 |

**Table 14.4: Percentage of Girls' Enrolment to Total Enrolment at the Elementary Stage**

| *Year* | *Primary (I-V)* | *Middle (VI-VIII)* |
|---|---|---|
| 1950-51 | 28.1% | 16.1% |
| 1960-61 | 32.6% | 23.9% |
| 1970-71 | 37.4% | 29.3% |
| 1980-81 | 38.6% | 32.9% |
| 1990-91 | 41.5% | 36.7% |
| 2004-05 | 46.7% | 44.4% |
| 2009-10 | 48.5% | 48.1% |

It will be observed from the above table that substantial progress has been achieved in the enrolment of girls. Nevertheless, it is far below the enrolment of boys.

**Table 14.5: Teacher-Pupil Ratio**

| *Year* | *Primary* | *Upper Primary* | *High/Hr. Secondary* |
|---|---|---|---|
| 1950-51 | 1:24 | 1>20 | 1:21 |
| 1960-61 | 1:36 | 1:31 | 1:25 |
| 1970-71 | 1:39 | 1:32 | 1:25 |
| 1980-81 | 1:38 | 1:33 | 1:27 |
| 1990-91 | 1:43 | 1:37 | 1:31 |
| 2002-03 | 1:42 | 1:34 | 1:30 |
| 2009-10 | 1:33 | 1:31 | 1:30 |

**Table 14.6: Gross Enrolment Ratio in Classes I-VIII (2009-10)**

| *S. No.* | *States/UTs* | *All Categories of Students* | | | | | | | | |
|---|---|---|---|---|---|---|---|---|---|---|
| | | *Classes I-V (6-10 years)* | | | *Classes VI-VIII (11-13 yrs)* | | | *Classes I-VIII (6-13 yrs)* | | |
| | | *Boys* | *Girls* | *Total* | *Boys* | *Girls* | *Total* | *Boys* | *Girls* | *Total* |
| 1. | Andhra Pradesh | 98.02 | 98.29 | 98.16 | 77.92 | 77.37 | 77.65 | 90.18 | 90.11 | 90.15 |
| 2. | Arunachal Pradesh | 169.99 | 163.42 | 166.77 | 106.14 | 96.21 | 101.20 | 146.31 | 138.10 | 142.26 |
| 3. | Assam | 91.67 | 94.15 | 92.89 | 67.32 | 70.32 | 68.80 | 82.21 | 84.90 | 83.54 |
| 4. | Bihar | 125.71 | 109.20 | 117.83 | 60.84 | 49.70 | 55.46 | 100.79 | 86.03 | 93.72 |
| 5. | Chhattisgarh | 126.32 | 120.52 | 123.46 | 87.16 | 81.08 | 84.15 | 111.57 | 105.60 | 108.62 |
| 6. | Goa | 93.44 | 91.67 | 92.59 | 81.18 | 77.11 | 79.24 | 88.75 | 86.13 | 87.50 |
| 7. | Gujarat | 119.95 | 120.97 | 120.42 | 90.52 | 82.01 | 86.51 | 108.88 | 106.04 | 107.56 |
| 8. | Haryana | 88.56 | 92.00 | 90.10 | 77.34 | 80.64 | 78.86 | 84.31 | 87.58 | 85.79 |
| 9. | Himachal Pradesh | 107.71 | 107.67 | 107.69 | 114.62 | 112.08 | 113.41 | 110.37 | 109.38 | 109.90 |
| 10. | Jammu & Kashmir | 110.34 | 112.60 | 111.41 | 95.34 | 90.87 | 93.20 | 104.67 | 104.27 | 104.48 |
| 11. | Jharkhand | 157.46 | 158.21 | 157.83 | 71.22 | 49.71 | 60.65 | 123.82 | 115.62 | 119.80 |
| 12. | Karnataka | 105.39 | 104.00 | 104.71 | 90.92 | 87.69 | 89.34 | 99.81 | 97.66 | 98.76 |
| 13. | Kerala | 93.42 | 93.88 | 93.65 | 107.13 | 102.35 | 104.77 | 98.58 | 97.11 | 97.86 |
| 14. | Madhya Pradesh | 149.34 | 150.03 | 149.67 | 106.08 | 97.42 | 101.87 | 133.32 | 130.18 | 131.81 |
| 15. | Maharashtra | 104.90 | 102.30 | 103.66 | 91.54 | 86.93 | 89.32 | 99.82 | 96.40 | 98.18 |
| 16. | Manipur | 189.66 | 182.26 | 186.01 | 107.21 | 99.19 | 103.25 | 155.44 | 147.73 | 151.64 |
| 17. | Meghalaya | 169.95 | 174.09 | 172.01 | 80.45 | 91.44 | 85.92 | 135.15 | 141.86 | 138.49 |
| 18. | Mizoram | 173.95 | 162.20 | 168.15 | 100.83 | 94.98 | 97.93 | 142.98 | 133.58 | 138.33 |
| 19. | Nagaland | 99.63 | 98.89 | 99.27 | 59.13 | 60.70 | 59.89 | 83.20 | 83.45 | 83.32 |

| | | | | | | | | | |
|---|---|---|---|---|---|---|---|---|---|
| 20. Odisha | 118.42 | 119.28 | 118.84 | 85.39 | 82.01 | 83.74 | 105.62 | 104.68 | 105.16 |
| 21. Punjab | 108.56 | 107.50 | 108.09 | 93.59 | 89.73 | 91.84 | 102.84 | 100.60 | 101.83 |
| 22. Rajasthan | 119.10 | 115.05 | 117.19 | 95.05 | 72.75 | 84.38 | 109.97 | 98.71 | 104.63 |
| 23. Sikkim | 157.91 | 152.75 | 155.34 | 70.89 | 86.59 | 78.64 | 118.82 | 123.37 | 121.08 |
| 24. Tamil Nadu | 114.33 | 115.29 | 114.79 | 114.30 | 112.09 | 113.22 | 114.32 | 114.07 | 114.20 |
| 25. Tripura | 146.81 | 143.72 | 145.29 | 93.33 | 93.14 | 93.24 | 123.56 | 121.74 | 122.66 |
| 26. Uttar Pradesh | 106.59 | 114.70 | 110.42 | 74.29 | 65.88 | 70.25 | 94.65 | 96.27 | 95.42 |
| 27. Uttarakhand | 108.63 | 111.77 | 110.12 | 101.04 | 107.93 | 104.33 | 105.79 | 110.32 | 107.95 |
| 28. West Bengal | 124.79 | 126.42 | 125.59 | 80.27 | 87.00 | 83.59 | 107.16 | 110.74 | 108.92 |
| 29. A&N Islands | 74.69 | 72.61 | 73.67 | 77.05 | 73.71 | 75.41 | 75.62 | 73.04 | 74.34 |
| 30. Chandigarh | 61.12 | 64.80 | 62.75 | 65.30 | 64.54 | 64.96 | 62.62 | 64.71 | 63.55 |
| 31. D&N Haveli | 107.37 | 107.53 | 107.45 | 101.08 | 90.46 | 96.16 | 105.24 | 101.98 | 103.69 |
| 32. Daman & Diu | 75.09 | 84.84 | 79.28 | 67.46 | 80.98 | 73.17 | 72.35 | 83.48 | 77.10 |
| 33. Delhi | 119.86 | 122.54 | 121.10 | 110.82 | 106.95 | 109.01 | 116.31 | 116.35 | 116.33 |
| 34. Lakshadweep | 82.34 | 82.30 | 82.32 | 61.85 | 65.58 | 63.67 | 73.99 | 75.68 | 74.83 |
| 35. Puducherry | 96.01 | 101.97 | 98.83 | 94.96 | 97.98 | 96.40 | 95.60 | 100.39 | 97.87 |
| **India** | **115.55** | **115.39** | **115.47** | **84.53** | **78.30** | **81.52** | **103.75** | **101.09** | **102.47** |

**Table 14.7: Enrolment in School Education (All Categories of Students)**

| *S. No.* *States/UTs* | *Total - VI-VIII* | | | *Total - I-VIII* | | |
|---|---|---|---|---|---|---|
| | *Boys* | *Girls* | *Total* | *Boys* | *Girls* | *Total* |
| (1) | (2) | (3) | (4) | (5) | (6) | (7) |
| 1. Andhra Pradesh | 1842980 | 1775783 | 3618763 | 5469574 | 5286480 | 10756054 |
| 2. Arunachal Pradesh | 41397 | 37152 | 78549 | 153870 | 141524 | 295394 |
| 3. Assam | 682371 | 691846 | 1374217 | 2145011 | 2151920 | 4296931 |
| 4. Bihar | 2341538 | 1785127 | 4126665 | 10097743 | 7936720 | 18034463 |
| 5. Chhattisgarh | 699921 | 637035 | 1336956 | 2378147 | 2193719 | 4571866 |
| 6. Goa | 36024 | 31163 | 67187 | 102993 | 91475 | 194468 |
| 7. Gujarat | 1599409 | 1291357 | 2890766 | 5114802 | 4358103 | 9472905 |
| 8. Haryana | 630566 | 559497 | 1190063 | 1814130 | 1562312 | 3376442 |
| 9. Himachal Pradesh | 217996 | 194923 | 412919 | 545268 | 490849 | 1036117 |
| 10. Jammu & Kashmir | 348641 | 306791 | 655432 | 1011548 | 918758 | 1930306 |
| 11. Jharkhand | 805909 | 543814 | 1349723 | 3591542 | 3222449 | 6813991 |
| 12. Karnataka | 1528585 | 1416574 | 2945159 | 4349073 | 4056129 | 8405202 |
| 13. Kerala | 854766 | 798260 | 1653026 | 2090052 | 1988052 | 4078104 |
| 14. Madhya Pradesh | 2559644 | 2224059 | 4783703 | 8687306 | 7876529 | 16563835 |
| 15. Maharashtra | 2931620 | 2585409 | 5517029 | 8415779 | 7466081 | 15881860 |
| 16. Manipur | 77081 | 69478 | 146559 | 269234 | 248984 | 518218 |
| 17. Meghalaya | 70805 | 79763 | 150568 | 305848 | 317373 | 623221 |
| 18. Mizoram | 31589 | 29299 | 60888 | 105780 | 96771 | 202551 |
| 19. Nagaland | 46104 | 44122 | 90226 | 159905 | 150125 | 310030 |
| 20. Odisha | 1054038 | 966858 | 2020896 | 3362995 | 3151200 | 6514195 |
| 21. Punjab | 743764 | 588276 | 1332040 | 2138723 | 1697156 | 3835879 |
| 22. Rajasthan | 2308038 | 1620005 | 3928043 | 7035347 | 5691652 | 12726999 |
| 23. Sikkim | 15150 | 18025 | 33175 | 56514 | 57833 | 114347 |
| 24. Tamil Nadu | 1935096 | 1800072 | 3735168 | 5125286 | 4810338 | 9935624 |
| 25. Tripura | 111489 | 107814 | 219303 | 339614 | 324205 | 663819 |
| 26. Uttar Pradesh | 5219366 | 4280860 | 9500226 | 17998920 | 16575211 | 34574131 |
| 27. Uttarakhand | 316359 | 309857 | 626216 | 884281 | 842074 | 1726355 |
| 28. West Bengal | 2145368 | 2262454 | 4407822 | 7233007 | 7240919 | 14473926 |
| 29. A&N Islands | 11618 | 10705 | 22323 | 29171 | 27394 | 56565 |
| 30. Chandigarh | 27320 | 21839 | 49159 | 72727 | 60191 | 132918 |

| (1) | (2) | (3) | (4) | (5) | (6) | (7) |
|---|---|---|---|---|---|---|
| 31. D&N Haveli | 10007 | 7730 | 17737 | 30746 | 26771 | 57517 |
| 32. Daman & Diu | 4855 | 4263 | 9118 | 14492 | 12455 | 26947 |
| 33. Delhi | 540708 | 456572 | 997280 | 1445359 | 1251860 | 2697219 |
| 34. Lakshadweep | 1746 | 1764 | 3510 | 5127 | 5144 | 10271 |
| 35. Puducherry | 36313 | 34275 | 70588 | 93369 | 88806 | 182175 |
| **India** | **31828181** | **27592821** | **59421002** | **102673283** | **92417562** | **195090845** |

## Table 14.8: Statewise and Sexwise Dropout Rates of Students (2009-2010)

| *Sl. No.* *State/UTs* | *(All Categories of Students)* | | | | | | | | |
|---|---|---|---|---|---|---|---|---|---|
| | *Classes I- V* | | | *Classes I- VIII* | | | *Classes I- X* | | |
| | *Boys* | *Girls* | *Total* | *Boys* | *Girls* | *Total* | *Boys* | *Girls* | *Total* |
| (1) | (2) | (3) | (4) | (5) | (6) | (7) | (8) | (9) | (10) |
| 1. Andhra Pradesh | 16.34 | 15.24 | 15.80 | 40.90 | 41.68 | 41.29 | 52.73 | 54.02 | 53.36 |
| 2. Arunachal Pradesh | 43.14 | 39.23 | 41.35 | 48.49 | 45.13 | 46.96 | 65.00 | 64.70 | 64.86 |
| 3. Assam | 38.99 | 32.67 | 35.89 | 59.94 | 62.55 | 61.21 | 77.41 | 77.82 | 77.60 |
| 4. Bihar | 43.51 | 40.97 | 42.45 | 64.98 | 67.33 | 66.02 | 78.46 | 76.06 | 77.56 |
| 5. Chhattisgarh* | 40.85 | 24.94 | 34.12 | 38.98 | 42.43 | 40.67 | — | — | — |
| 6. Goa | –12.44 | –4.29 | –8.54 | –25.08 | –10.07 | –17.86 | 35.85 | 32.63 | 34.30 |
| 7. Gujarat | 36.89 | 6.52 | 25.66 | 32.24 | 48.08 | 39.70 | 60.37 | 64.41 | 62.14 |
| 8. Haryana | –1.13 | –2.24 | –1.64 | 19.59 | 8.10 | 14.37 | 20.17 | 19.46 | 19.84 |
| 9. Himachal Pradesh | 0.35 | 1.17 | 0.74 | 1.42 | 3.41 | 2.38 | 22.28 | 18.93 | 20.65 |
| 10. J&K | 9.79 | 6.82 | 8.38 | 23.75 | 19.79 | 21.95 | 47.16 | 40.63 | 44.30 |
| 11. Jharkhand* | 27.61 | 26.41 | 27.05 | 56.26 | 68.44 | 61.87 | — | — | — |
| 12. Karanataka | 11.60 | 10.61 | 11.12 | 25.05 | 26.73 | 25.86 | 46.89 | 46.33 | 46.62 |
| 13. Kerala | –13.99 | –11.02 | –12.52 | –16.71 | –11.51 | –14.14 | –2.94 | –5.20 | –4.06 |
| 14. Madhya Pradesh | 21.77 | 20.49 | 21.16 | 19.71 | 23.36 | 21.44 | 60.98 | 71.32 | 65.71 |
| 15. Maharashtra | 20.19 | 22.54 | 21.31 | 24.36 | 27.55 | 25.88 | 38.63 | 42.62 | 40.54 |
| 16. Manipur | 33.05 | 40.08 | 36.48 | 57.65 | 56.59 | 57.13 | 57.82 | 55.71 | 56.79 |
| 17. Meghalaya | 60.52 | 54.51 | 57.60 | 74.25 | 70.33 | 72.29 | 79.31 | 76.46 | 77.89 |
| 18. Mizoram | 44.68 | 47.46 | 46.03 | 56.37 | 53.70 | 55.10 | 64.79 | 60.72 | 62.87 |
| 19. Nagaland | 40.10 | 39.78 | 39.95 | 32.55 | 30.52 | 31.58 | 75.69 | 73.97 | 74.86 |
| 20. Odisha | 26.71 | 26.18 | 26.45 | 53.13 | 55.56 | 54.30 | 69.98 | 65.91 | 68.19 |
| 21. Punjab | –24.59 | –10.67 | –18.07 | –24.04 | –13.43 | –19.12 | 41.23 | 39.45 | 40.42 |
| 22. Rajasthan | 49.11 | 52.11 | 50.51 | 41.19 | 59.68 | 50.32 | 70.52 | 73.42 | 71.64 |
| 23. Sikkim | 24.57 | 11.98 | 18.58 | 50.98 | 38.15 | 44.67 | 82.07 | 79.36 | 80.73 |
| 24. Tamil Nadu | 0.29 | 0.42 | 0.35 | 9.09 | 8.22 | 8.67 | 37.56 | 30.28 | 34.06 |
| 25. Tripura | 25.95 | 24.97 | 25.48 | 45.42 | 41.77 | 43.66 | 63.42 | 62.34 | 62.90 |
| 26. Uttar Pradesh | 42.38 | 41.70 | 42.06 | 50.66 | 55.23 | 52.78 | 29.19 | 15.09 | 23.83 |
| 27. Uttarakhand* | 33.82 | 31.33 | 32.62 | 32.69 | 28.72 | 30.77 | — | — | — |
| 28. West Bengal | 24.55 | 16.15 | 20.52 | 52.85 | 47.98 | 50.46 | 72.89 | 70.70 | 71.83 |
| 29. A&N Islands | 6.85 | 2.98 | 4.98 | 10.38 | 12.89 | 11.61 | 32.70 | 27.07 | 30.06 |
| 30. Chandigarh | –27.05 | –18.06 | –22.81 | –23.28 | –24.46 | –23.81 | 0.30 | 7.86 | 3.78 |
| 31. D&N Haveli | 15.18 | 19.95 | 17.52 | 33.44 | 53.42 | 43.31 | 54.78 | 63.48 | 58.83 |
| 32. Daman & Diu | 1.66 | 4.27 | 2.85 | 9.31 | 12.28 | 10.70 | 41.15 | 29.75 | 35.93 |
| 33. Delhi | 9.82 | 17.07 | 13.30 | –32.61 | –21.13 | –27.10 | –5.22 | 9.15 | 1.97 |
| 34. Lakshadweep | 14.31 | 8.06 | 11.11 | 13.32 | 3.81 | 9.01 | 27.58 | 22.67 | 25.13 |
| 35. Puducherry | –4.00 | –3.12 | –3.57 | –13.95 | –15.95 | –14.93 | 12.79 | 1.39 | 7.34 |
| **India** | **30.25** | **27.25** | **28.86** | **40.59** | **44.39** | **42.39** | **53.38** | **51.97** | **52.76** |

* Dropout rates for Classes I-X are shown combined with the respective parent state.

**Causes of Drop-outs and Stagnation**

Important causes are:

1. Irregular attendance of the pupils.
2. Book-centred environment.
3. Contents unrelated to life and environment.
4. Ineffective and uninspiring methods of teaching.
5. Faulty system of examination and evaluation.
6. Underfed and undernourished children.
7. Rigid school timing.
8. Poverty/migration of the parents and assistance from children in increasing income.
9. Lack of adequate awareness regarding education among parents.

**New Initiatives, Schemes and Projects undertaken Towards UEE**

Since the formulation of the National Policy on Education—NPE, several new programmes for improving the quality of primary education and its expansion have been started by the Government of India, Ministry of Human Resource Development, Department of Education. Some of the old schemes have been revised and strengthened. Assistance from various organisations like the UNICEF has also been secured. Following are the important programmes in this regard.

1. District Primary Education Programme (DPEP).
2. Lok Jumbish (People's Movement in Education) scheme in Rajasthan with the assistance of Swedish International Development Authority (SIDA)
3. Minimum Levels of Learning (MLLs)—a programme of reform in evaluation and examination at the elementary stage.
4. National Elementary Education Mission; to mobilise all resources—human, financial—necessary for achieving the goal of UEE.
5. Non-formal education for those children who cannot attend full day school.
6. National Programme of Nutritional Support to Primary Education (NP-NSPE), to provide wholesome food to school going children at the primary stage.
7. Operation Blackboard (OBB) to provide accommodation and teachers.
8. Shiksha Karmi Project (SKP) in Rajasthan with the help of Swedish International Development Agency (SIDA), to check drop-out rates and improve primary education.
9. Teacher Education Restructuring and Organisation for improving teacher education and training and setting up District Institutes of Education (DIETs) in each district.
10. Sarva Shiksha Abhiyan—SSA (Education for All):
    (i) Providing access to all children in the age group 6-14 by 2003.

(ii) Completion of five years of primary education by all children by 2007.

(iii) Completion of eight years of elementary education by all children by 2010.

(iv) Provision of elementary education of satisfactory quality for all children by 2010.

11. Making Elementary Education as a Fundamental Right—RTE Act 2009 implementated from 1 April 2010.

*Summing up*: The goal of UEE which was to be achieved by 1960 is likely to be achieved shortly. In this respect it is stated that almost all countries of Europe achieved this goal long back. Several countries of Asia like Japan have also made tremendous progress.

The USA could become one of the most powerful countries of the world on account of phenomenal expansion of educational facilities at all stages of education including primary stage. India can also achieve the objective of UEE provided a strong political will is forthcoming.

**Strategy Frame for Sarva Shiksha Abhiyan**

In order to achieve Universalisation of Elementary Education, in a holistic and convergent approach, the following key strategies have been worked out:

a) Emphasis to be laid on retention and achievement rather than on mere enrolment;

b) Adoption of incremental approach for creating school facilities-Education guarantee Centres in unserved habitations and "Back to school camps" for out of school children in the 10-14 age group.

c) Focus to be shifted from educationally backward states to educationally backward districts;

d) Adoption of desegregated approach with a focus on preparation of district specific and population specific plans;

e) Universal access to schooling facilities particularly to girls, desegregated groups and out of school children;

f) Making education relevant by curricular reforms to promote life skills.

g) Improvement in school effectiveness, teacher competence, training and motivation.

h) Decentralisation of planning and management through Panchayati Raj Institutions (PRLs)/Village Education Committees (VECs) and stress on participative processes;

i) Convergence of different schemes of elementary education and related services such as early childhood care and education, school health and nutrition programmes, etc.

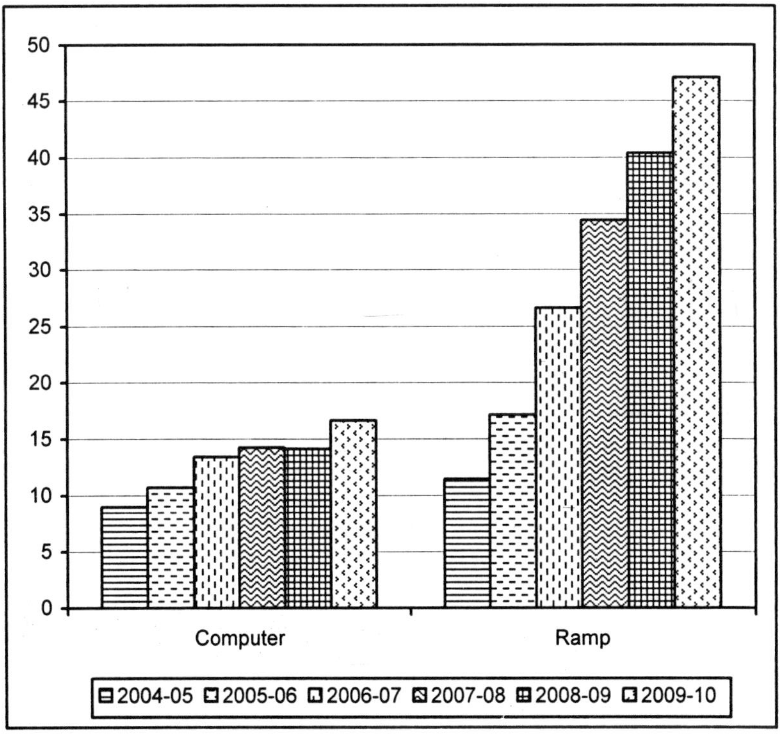


**Fig. 14.1**: *Percentage of Schools having Computer and Ramp Facilities—All Schools*

## Constitution (Eighty-Sixth Amendment/Act 2002)

In order to fulfil the goal of universal elementary education, Constitution (Eighty-sixth Amendment) Act, 2002 was passed. The Amendment includes the following changes:

1. *Article 45*: *Provision for Early Childhood Care and Education to Children below the Age of Six Years*: The State shall endeavour to provide early childhood care and education for all children until they complete the age of six years.
2. *Article 21 A*: *Right to Education*: The State shall provide free and compulsory education to all children of the age of six to fourteen years in such manner as the State may, by law determine.
3. *Article 51A*: Clause 'K' has been Added in 51A Fundamental Duties: It shall be the duty of every citizen of India "who is a parent or guardian to provide opportunities for education to his child or, as the case may be, ward between the age of six and fourteen years."

**Table 14.9: Select Facility Indicated in Percentage Schools (All) 2009-10**

| *State/UT* | *With Female Teachers* | *Having Drinking Wate* | *Having Common Toilet* | *Having Boundary Wall* | *Having Computer* | *Having Ramp* | *Having Electricity* |
|---|---|---|---|---|---|---|---|
| A & N Islands | 89.34 | 91.37 | 94.02 | 51.78 | 55.33 | 17.26 | 84.26 |
| Andhra Pradesh | 81.11 | 91.83 | 26.28a | 53.85 | 23.84 | 14.2 | 44.95 |
| Arunachal Pradesh | 83.63 | 85.39 | 54.43 | 27.77 | 14.22 | 3.3 | 19.67 |
| Assam | 67.79 | 81.33 | 71.52 | 27.55 | 4.96 | 42.65 | 11.67 |
| Bihar | 80.56 | 92.6 | 51.14 | 39.13 | 0.94 | 38.71 | 3.91 |
| Chandigarh | 99.43 | 100 | 98.25 | 99.43 | 90.34 | 43.18 | 100 |
| Chhattisgarh | 67.93 | 94.24 | 59.74 | 70.01 | 7.21 | 40.63 | 23.54 |
| Dadra & Nagar Haveli | 82.77 | 96.28 | 90.63 | 38.85 | 9.46 | 27.36 | 75.68 |
| Daman & Diu | 93.46 | 100 | 89.09 | 89.72 | 42.99 | 44.86 | 100 |
| Delhi | 92.3 | 100 | 94.95 | 97.94 | 82.41 | 70.52 | 98.65 |
| Goa | 98.34 | 99.24 | 81.08 | 69.04 | 30.75 | 34.49 | 95.98 |
| Gujarat | 84.29 | 96.74 | 81.22 | 86.74 | 42.82 | 79.62 | 94.8 |
| Haryana | 79.18 | 99.48 | 85.65 | 95.05 | 26.8 | 66.02 | 94.25 |
| Himachal Pradesh | 71.87 | 97.64 | 73.06 | 50.02 | 14.68 | 46.35 | 59.77 |
| Jammu & Kashmir | 73.41 | 86.31 | 61.54 | 30.17 | 12.73 | 11.85 | 18.3 |
| Jharkhand | 54.78 | 85.44 | 38.77 | 21.51 | 5.99 | 13.96 | 7.48 |
| Karnataka | 81.25 | 69.83 | 33.53 | 62.91 | 21.2 | 55.14 | 88.03 |
| Kerala | 99.45 | 98.99 | 85.2 | 76.91 | 86.86 | 61.84 | 88.59 |
| Lakshadweep | 90.91 | 100 | 92.31 | 56.82 | 93.18 | 70.45 | 100 |
| Madhya Pradesh | 67.13 | 94.03 | 82.86 | 43.02 | 10.48 | 53.55 | 20.07 |
| Maharashtra | 69.56 | 93.73 | 89.96 | 59.99 | 39.36 | 65.43 | 71.73 |
| Manipur | 81.23 | 92.05 | 83 | 31.81 | 15.66 | 6.04 | 21.57 |
| Meghalaya | 81.11 | 61.06 | 44.07 | 17.93 | 7.43 | 12.25 | 13.74 |
| Mizoram | 81.93 | 85.67 | 88.23 | 41.72 | 17.55 | 38.5 | 34.08 |
| Nagaland | 84.85 | 83.97 | 26.48 | 76.14 | 27.6 | 7.83 | 33.95 |
| Orissa | 66.74 | 89.07 | 31.78 | 57.61 | 7.28 | 36.19 | 15.75 |
| Puducherry | 97.83 | 100 | 88.46 | 85.69 | 79.91 | 52.31 | 99.86 |
| Punjab | 90.53 | 98.76 | 97.5 | 90.69 | 38.64 | 53.25 | 88.99 |
| Rajasthan | 64.49 | 96.44 | 85.29 | 71.95 | 14.99 | 51.09 | 33.74 |
| Sikkim | 88.05 | 96.69 | 91.95 | 26.69 | 35.85 | 5.51 | 57.12 |
| Tamil Nadu | 94.64 | 99.87 | 89.01 | 66.95 | 38.6 | 57.14 | 91.26 |
| Tripura | 54.17 | 79.41 | 66.99 | 12.92 | 9.04 | 55.96 | 13.15 |
| Uttar Pradesh | 77.81 | 98.18 | 61.32 | 51.65 | 4.72 | 58.98 | 25.54 |
| Uttarakhand | 74.24 | 89.61 | 72.67 | 77.62 | 24.13 | 35.02 | 36.23 |
| West Bengal | 72.99 | 96.02 | 80.9 | 0 | 7.45 | 49.6 | 26.5 |
| **All States** | **74.48** | **92.6** | **63.95** | **51.45** | **16.65** | **47.09** | **38.98** |

**Select Bibliography on Primary Education**

Aggarwal, J.C., *Documents on Primary Education in India*, Doaba House, Delhi, 1992.

Aggarwal, J.C., *Educational Reforms in India for the 21st Century*, Shipra Publications, Delhi, 2000.

*Annual Reports*, Government of India, Ministry of Human Resource Development, Department of Education, New Delhi, 1998, 1999 and 2000.

*Ministry of Law, Justice and Company Affairs, The Constitution of India*, Government of India, New Delhi, 2000.

*Selected Educational Statistics*, (2003-2004), Government of India, Ministry of Human Resource Development, Department of Education, New Delhi.

## 14.3 CHILD-CENTERED EDUCATION

*Introduction*: The National Policy on Education—NPE has laid great stress on developing a child-centred and activity based process of learning. This demands that the contents, modalities and environment in the schools must be carefully selected and provided for, especially at the nursery and elementary stages of education.

### Meaning of Child-Centred Education

Following definitions provide a comprehensive view of the various dimensions of child-centred education.

G.R. Hawes and L.L Hawes in the *Concise Dictionary of Education* (1932) define child-centred education as, "An educational theory or system that emphasises the pupil and his or her individual characteristics as central in conducting instruction instead of focussing on subject-matter, external authority, and educational requirements. Curriculum in constructed to the pupil's interests and needs." Here key words are: interests and needs of the individual pupil.

Derek Rowntree in *A Dictionary of Education* 1981 considers child-centred approach/education/teaching as, "...main point is made by the teacher who claims 'I teach children, not subjects'. Implies care for the 'whole child—his personality, needs and learning style and not just for his or her academic progress".

In their book *A Critical Dictionary of Education* (1986), Robin Barrow and Geoffrey Mitburn observe, "The essence of child-centred education is self-activity."

### Prominent Educators Who Stress Child-Centred Education

Following quotations of the great educators clearly indicate the importance of making education child-centred. The phrases like 'drawing out', 'innate powers', 'experiences and activity' used in the context of child education are pointers to make education child-centred.

The new teaching recognises the right of the pupil to do things in his own way, within reasonable limits. —*Adams*

Observation more than books, experience rather than person, are the prime educators. —*Alcott*

The first principle of true teaching is that nothing can be taught. The teacher is a helper and a guide. His business is to suggest and not to impose. —*Sri Aurobindo*

(a) Where there is experience, there is the living being.
(b) Action must precede knowledge.
(c) Education is by experience.
(d) The teacher is a guide and director, he steers the boat but the energy that propels it must come from those who are learning. —*Dewey*

The object of teaching is to bring more and more out rather than to put more and more in. —*Froebel*

Real education has to draw out the best from the boys and the girls to be educated. —*Mahatma Gandhi*

We have buried the tedious and stupid ABC primer side by side with the useless copy books. —*M. Montessori*

Nature invented play as a device for using that energy to prepare him (child) for serious business of life. —*Nunn, T.P.*

Education is the natural harmonious and progressive development of man's innate power. —*Pestalozzi*

Nature wills that children should be 'children' before they are men.

To know how to suggest is the art of teaching.

Childhood has ways of seeing, thinking, feeling peculiar to itself; nothing is more absurd than to wish to substitute ours in their place. —*Rousseau*

Teach the pupil not only to answer questions but also to question answers. —*Ruskin*

Children should be told as little as possible and induced to discover as much as possible. —*Spencer*

To the child, environment will provide an ever ready background for its spontaneous activity. —*Tagore*

And other's follies teach us not,
Not much their wisdom teaches;
And most, or sterling worth is, what
Our own experience teaches. —*Tennyson*

No one was really taught by anothers, each of us has to teach himself.

You cannot teach a child more than you can grow a plant. The plant develops its own nature. —*Vivekananda*

**Key Concepts of Child-Centred Education: Aim of Child-Centred Education**

It is the development of the total personality of the child.

*Programme*: Programme is to be activity-based with different teaching strategies.

*Pace of Learning*: It is to be based on the needs and abilities of children.

*Teaching-Learning*: It is interesting and inspiring. It is based on 'doing', 'questioning' and 'exploring'.

*Role of the Teacher*: The teacher assumes the role of an adviser and facilitator in learning and development. The teacher provides necessary help and guide.

*Role of the Child*: The child plays the role of a 'star' or 'hero' in the drama of education.

*Discipline*: It is achieved through the establishment of harmonious and positive human relations between teachers and pupils.

**Implications of Child-Centred Education**

Since the child is the focus, the activities must provide for his total growth. All essential areas of development—the aesthetic, the creative, the cultural, the emotional, the ethical, the lingural, the manual, the mathematical, the moral, the physical, the scientific, the social and the spiritual. However activities should cut across all these areas. In child-centred education, not only there will be an adequate number of activities but also enough variety in them.

Child-Centred requires 'individualised' instruction coupled with group work where needed so that the teacher may study each child carefully and intensively. He may observe him over a period of time and take steps in the light of the requirements of the child.

**Why Child-Centred Education?**

No, two children are alike. Individuals differ in their physical characteristics, emotional characteristics, personality traits, achievement, interests, motivation etc. Mass procedures or class procedures, no matter how well intentioned, wall planned, well prepared and well executed do not adequately accomplish the objectives. Adequate attention to the learner is the most effective device to achieve the desired results.

Age, sex, aptitude, attitude, ability, achievement and socio-economic factors lead to individual differences.

It is observed that some children are physically weak and some physically strong. Some children are weak in observing things. Some are strong in this art. Some are fluent in the mother-tongue while others are strong in calculation. Now it is not a sound policy to treat all children in the same way.

The problems are as numerous as the children.

**Basic Tasks for Providing Child-Centred Education**

The task of providing child-centred Education is manifold. In addition to basic facilities, educational environment has to be made attractive, cheerful and pleasing. Buildings and classrooms should be kept clean, well lighted and airy. They need to be adorned with charts, coloured posters, suitable pictures and sometimes even with buntings.

Learning has to take place through play and activity. Effective learning comes from purposeful activities.

The following points deserve careful attention in this context:

1. The child is the agent of his own learning. Out of the three components of the teaching-learning situation, the child, the teacher and the environment, the child is the focal point. He must become the most important agent in his learning. This means that the curriculum, the content and the methods of teaching must be designed in terms of activities and experiences which appeal to the child.
2. It must always be remembered that most of the things a child gathers and learns itself until the age of three hold good to the last day of his life. Therefore, the parents, and the community should be made to recognise the significance of self-education of the child.
3. Children learn when they are active. Thus the medium of learning is the activities and experiences of children.
4. Child-centred approach is more psychological than logical. It emphasises the process rather than the product.
5. Child-centred approach gives freedom to the child under the care of the creative and sympathetic direction of the teacher.
6. The child's sense of astonishment and wonder and his natural curiosity lead to the effective learning process which should be encouraged.

**Role of the Teacher in Child-Centred Education**

1. The teacher must study the child thoroughly.
2. A child is likely to have misconceived ideas, forms and shapes of substances because of their similarities and dissimilarities. In this context, the teacher has to remain active to lead the child to develop right concepts and relationships.
3. A child is a unique being and has a unique role to play. The teacher's role is to help the child to conform to its unique role, both in spirit, choices, and consistent behaviour patterns.
4. The teacher must accept each child as he is.
5. He should motivate children to learn.
6. He should develop confidence and trust in children regarding their capacities to learn.
7. He should become an active member of the group.

8. He should possess enormous patience.
9. He should ensure the children that he is their best welfare and thereby win their confidence.
10. The teacher must provide a suitable environment.

**Important Methods of Making Child-Centred Education**

1. Assignment Method or Dalton Plan
2. Mastery Learning Method
3. Programmed Instruction
4. Computer-Assisted Learning
5. Internet Learning
6. Teaching Machines
7. Personalised System of Instruction
8. Gary System
9. Winnetka Plan
10. Basic System of Education
11. Montessori Method
12. Kindergarten Method
13. Discovery Method
14. Heuristic Method

**Limitations of Child-Centred Education**

Child-centred education has some important limitations which need to be taken note of.

Pragmatically speaking education cannot be totally child-centred. Child-centred education implies that each child may have a separate learning activity. All the actions involved in the activity must be carefully attended to and supervised by the teacher. It is common knowledge that there are so many children under the charge of a teacher in classes VI to VIII and onwards, that it is impossible to attend to the specific needs of children individually. For instance a Social Studies teacher has four to five sections to teach. Each section usually consists of forty students. This means that he has to guide nearly 200 students. To talk of paying individual attention or making learning child-centred will be a Utopian idea. The situation is so complex that sometimes a teacher fails to recognise his all students even in the class. Of course, at the nursery and primary stage, where there is one-teacher—one class system, child-centred education is possible to a considerable extent.

Perhaps no nation can afford to spend so much money, resources, time and energy on child-centred education.

*Summing up*: All possible efforts have to be made to find out the assets and limitations of each student. A comprehensive programme of guidance and counselling needs to be provided in every school. Specific needs of all categories of students i.e. slow learners, the talented, and the handicapped should be attended to and compensatory education should be arranged. Students belonging to deprived sections of the society should be provided special facilities. For some activities students may be divided in small groups. Effective guidance and supervision of the teacher will go a long way in meeting the specific needs of the students individually.

**Child-Centred Education and Teacher-Centred Education**

| *Dimensions* | *Child-Centred Education* | *Teacher-Centred Education* |
|---|---|---|
| 1. Goals | Goals set by the learner with assistance and guidance by the teacher to meet the diverse needs as they evolve. | Goals set by the teacher in advance to meet the needs that he has anticipated. |
| 2. Approach | Discovery and experience approach to learning. Situations and resources provided by the teacher for the learner to generate, experience and discover ideas for himself. | Information and ideas put over to the child a by the teacher. |
| 3. Homogeneity | Wide variety of activities at any one time. Various learners doing different activities suiting their needs at that point of time. | Same learning experiences for all students at any one time. All learners attend the same sessions and do the same things. |
| 4. Sequencing | Very flexible sequence. Sequence not determined in advance but according to the felt need of the learner. Similar items may be learned in different sequences by different learners. | Sequences or order fixed in advance. Sequences are determined according to the preferences of the teacher. |
| 5. Control | Decisions made by learners or jointly by the learners and the teacher. Hence joint control over the course. | Decisions made by the teacher and he maintains control over the course. |
| 6. Method | Wide variety of learning-teaching methods. Methods usually selected by the learners. | Relatively few teaching-learning methods. Methods selected by the teachers. |

| *Dimensions* | *Child-Centred Education* | *Teacher-Centred Education* |
|---|---|---|
| 7. Learner tutor relationship | Very close, open, personal relationship | Distant. Closed. Formal relationship. |
| 8. Group attitude | Trusting, Supportive. Close relationships | Not quite trusting. Not very supportive. Learners relatively distant from each other. |
| 9. Feelings | Full expression | Very restricted expression of feelings. |
| 10. Discipline | Free. Full of freedom. | Strict. Do's and Don'ts |

**Select Bibliography on Child-Centred Education**

*A Dictionary of Education*, P.J. Hills (Ed.), Routledge and Kegan Paul, London, 1982.

Aggarwal J.C., *Education Policy in India 1992: Retrospect and Prospect.* Shipra Publications, Delhi, 1992.

*The Concise Dictionary of Education*, Gene R. Howes and Lynne Salop Hawe (Eds.), Van Nostrend Reinhold Company, New York, 1982.

*Dictionary of Education*, Carter V. Good (Ed.), McGraw Hill Book Company, New York, 1973.

NCERT, *Readings in Child-Centred Education*, (Papers Presented at National Symposium on Child-Centred Education, Dec. 1988). Vol. I and II NCERT, New Delhi, 1988.

*Report of the Zakir Hussain Committee* and the *Detailed Syllabus*, Hindustani Talimi Sangh, Wardha, 1938.

*The Concept of Basic Education*, Ministry of Education, New Delhi, 1956.

*Report of the Education Commission* (1964-66), Ministry of Education, Government of India, 1966.

## 14.4 MORAL EDUCATION

**Meaning of Moral Education**

The Committee on Religious and Moral Instruction appointed by the Ministry of Education and headed by Sri Prakasa (1959) defined moral value as "Anything that helps us to behave properly towards others is of moral value". Moral education, therefore, is that which develops moral values.

Moral education particularly refers to the development of the conduct of man towards man in which human beings come together, in the home, the neighbourhood, the educational institutions and in all the social and economic fields.

### Why Moral Education?

Moral education is ingrained in the very tradition of Indian culture. Yet it is a matter of great regret that gradually we are losing our moral values with the result that we tend to become corrupt and hypocrite. This trend must be checked urgently if we are to restructure our society on solid foundations. Perhaps a major responsibility lies on our leaders in different walks of life and whom we usually emulate. Nevertheless educational institutions can also play a significant role in the promotion of moral values in our students.

It is the students of to-day who are to be in charge of various departments of life to-morrow. It they learn what morality is in their early years, they are likely to grow into individuals who are conscious keepers of the society. They will play their role effectively.

Without moral values, an individual will be no more than a *'Rakhshash'*.

Education is considered to be an important instrument of moulding the innate tendencies and instincts of the children according to moral standards accepted by the society. The content of the curriculum, the methods of teaching, the school activities and above all the teachers can play a prominent role in developing a 'moral person'.

In the Vedic period when a *'shishya'* (student) completed his education he, was exhorted by his *'guru'* (teacher) to follow certain moral values in his life.

(a) सत्यं वद् (Speak the truth)

(b) धर्मम् वद् (Do your duty)

The National Policy on Education has used the term value education which by and large implies moral education. It states, "The growing concern over the erosion of essential values and an increasing cynism in society has brought to focus the need for readjustments in the curriculum in order to make education a forceful tool for the cultivation of social and moral values."

### What Constitutes Moral Education?

The ultimate good of human society is the good of all. This idea has been very beautifully expressed in one of our ancient prayers.

सर्वे भवन्तु सुखिनः सर्वे सन्तु निरामयः।
सर्वे भद्राणि प यन्तु, मा कच्चिद् दुख भाग भवेत्।।

"Let all be happy and free from disease, let men see well of one another—let there be no unhappiness"

Swami Vivekananda has mentioned the following moral values:

1. Self sacrifice, 2. Service to others, 3. Sincere performance of our duties in whatever position, 4. Non-injury, 5. Purity, personal as well as social such as no yielding to corruption, 6. Fearlessness, 7. Cultivation of emotions, 8. Patriotism.

Gandhiji mention 11 vows or moral values 1. *'Ahimsa'* (Non-violence),

2. *'Satyam'* (truth), 3. *'Brahmacharya'* (celebacy), 4. *'Aparigarha'* (Non-acquisitiveness), 5. *'Asvada'* (Control of palate), 6. *'Sarvatra Bhayarjana'* (fearlessness), 7. *'Sarva Dharma Sambhava'* (Looking up all religions equally—toleration), 8. *Swadeshi* (Patriotism), 9. *'Sparsha Bhavana'* (Abolition of untouchability), 10. *'Sharivashram'* (Physical work), 11. *'Asatyam'* (Non-thieving).

The University Education Commission 1948-49 mentioned these moral values: courage, discipline, loyalty, self-sacrifice.

The Secondary Education Commission 1952-53 laid stress on the following moral values needed in the formation of character of the students: Co-operation. Discipline, Efficiency, Integrity, Good temper.

The Committee on Religious and Moral Instruction (1959) made special mention of:

Dignity of labour, Good manners. Love for humanity. Self-discipline.

The Committee on Emotional Integration (1961) referred to the following values.

Mutual appreciation of various religions. Unity of mankind. National unity. Spiritual values.

The Education Commission (1964-66) stressed the following moral values:—

Co-operation, Mutual regard, Honesty, Integrity, Discipline, Social responsibility.

*Value-Oriented School Education* (1972), a publication of the NCERT states the following: Cleanliness, Courage, Courtesy, Dignity of labour, Service, Universal love.

*Documents on Social Moral and Spiritual Values in Education*, (1979), published by NCERT lists 84 values in the alphabetical order. There is no categorisation of values in terms of social, moral and spiritual aspect.

The NPE uses the term 'Value Education' in Part VIII. Value education includes moral and social values. Values included are:

Universal and internal values oriented towards the unity and integration of our people. Such value education should eliminate obscurantism, religious toleration, violence, superstition and fatalism. Apart from the combative role, value education has a profound positive content, based on our heritage, national goals and universal perception. It should lay primary emphasis on this.

**Moral Education Programme: Documents on Moral Education**

At the outset it is observed that it is very difficult to draw a thin line between moral education, spiritual education, ethical education and religious education. Each is greatly influenced by the other. Some elements are common in all these types of education, while others differs. For instance performance of some religious rites does not come under the purview of moral education. Subjects like 'Unity with God', 'God realization', etc. are the main domains of spiritual education.

*I. Programme Suggested by the Secondary Education Commission (1952-53)*

*Three Essential Factors:*

1. Home can influence the moral behaviour of the child.
2. The conduct and behaviour of the teachers themselves and the life in the school community as a whole are the most important factors influencing the children.
3. The moral code of conduct of the public of the locality is another factor that influences the moral behaviour of the student.

The Commission recommended that such type of instruction through personal behaviour can be supplemented to a limited extent by properly organised instruction given in the school.

Moral instruction in the form of inspiring talks on the lives of great personalities of all times may be arranged in the morning assembly at the commencement of day's session.

*II. Programme Suggested by the Committee on Religious and Moral Instruction—1959*

The Committee defined moral instruction in terms of 'proper behaviour towards others'. The Committee laid stress on the importance of good manners. The Committee suggested the following programme:

*1. Elementary Stage*

(a) Holding of morning assembly for a few minutes for group singing.
(b) Simple and interesting stories about the lives and teachings of prophets, saints and religious leaders to be included in the syllabus for language teaching.
(c) Two periods a weak in the school programme to be set aside for moral instruction.
(d) Developing the attitude of 'service' and 'work is worship' in the students through school programme.
(e) Spirit of true sportsmanship to be developed in all schemes of physical education and all forms of play.

*2. Secondary Stage*

(i) Observance of silence for two minutes in the morning assembly.
(ii) Community singing in the morning assembly.
(iii) Moral instruction in the class for one hour a week.
(iv) Talks on moral and spiritual values.
(v) Organisation of social service programmes during holidays and outside class hours to be made an essential part of co-curricular activities. Emphasis to be laid on developing values like dignity of labour, love of humanity, patriotism and self-discipline.

(vi) Quality of character and behaviour of the students to form an essential part of overall assessment of a student's performance at school.

*III. Committee on Emotional Integration*

The Emotional Integration Committee appointed by the Government of India in 1961, made the following recommendations on moral education:

1. Fostering mutual appreciation of the various religions.
2. Introduction of ideals of the national unity and unity of mankind in the curriculum.

*IV. Education Commission 1964-66 on Moral Education: Recommendations*

1. There will be natural points of correlation between the moral values sought to be inculcated and the teachings of the great religions. All religions stress fundamental qualities of character, such as honesty and truthfulness, consideration of others, reverence of old age, kindness to animals, and compassion for the needy and the suffering.
2. Organised attempts should be made for inculcating the above mentioned values through direct and indirect methods with the help of ethical teachings of great religions.
3. The narration of stories by the teachers on moral education would be most effective, particularly in the lower classes.
4. Indirect influences of the school i.e. overall environment, the personality of the behaviour of the teachers, the facilities provided in the school, the co-curricular activities organised in the school have a great bearing on the development of the moral values in the students.

*V. National Curriculum Frame Work for School Education Published by NCERT (2000)*

It includes *'Value Education'* as an integral part of school curriculum. It observes, "Since India is the most enabling experiment in spiritual co-existence, education about social, moral and spiritual values and religions cannot be left entirely to home and the community." Further it observes, "This makes it imperative for the Indian School Curriculum to include inculcation of the basic values and an awareness of all the major religions of the country as one of the central components.

The publication makes the following recommendations:

(i) Value education and education about religions would not form a separate subject of study or examination at any stage.
(ii) These should be judiciously integrated with all subjects of study in the scholastic areas and all the activities and programmes in the co-scholastic areas—classrooms, school assembly place, playgrounds, cultural centres and such other places.

## Some Examples of Common Moral Values as Emphasised by Religions

### *Anger's Control*

*Buddhism* : One should not give way to anger, but should control it.
*Christianity* : The mark of a Christian is love, not hatred.
*Confucianism* : One should so conduct oneself as to avoid hatred or anger from others.
*Hinduism* : Anger breeds confusion.
*Islam* : The strong man is he who controls himself when he is angry.
*Jainism* : Anger is not for the wise or the religious.
*Judaism* : Anger causes strife and destruction.
*Sikhism* : Anger is the fire that burns as at cremation.
*Taoism* : Return anger with goodness.
*Zoroastrianism*: Never give way to the deadly emotion of anger.

### *Brotherhood*

*Buddhism* : One should make good men his closed friend.
*Christianity* : All men are brothers. Brotherly love should rule the world.
*Confucianism* : Friendship and brotherhood are the cardinal virtues.
*Hinduism* : The good man makes no distinction between friend and foe, brother and stranger.
*Islam* : All men are brothers and should live as such.
*Jainism* : Treat all men as brothers at all times.
*Judaism* : God has made all men brothers and they should be together as brothers all the times.
*Sikhism* : Get together my brothers. And remove all misunderstanding through regard for each other.

### *Duty*

*Buddhism* : One should be faithful to one's duty at all times.
*Christianity :* One has a duty to God and duties towards one's fellows.
*Confucianism* : The wise-man makes duty his aim at all times.
*Hinduism* : Never falter in doing your duty.
*Islam* : All men who do their duty will receive a fitting reward from God.
*Jainism* : It is the duty of all to be impartial.

### *Sincerity*

*Buddhism* : God loves the earnest, sincere man.
*Christianity* : At all times, a Christian is sincere.
*Confucianism* : Heaven will help the man who is sincere.
*Hinduism* : God does not favour those who are not sincere and honest.
*Islam* : God knows whether or not a man is earnest in his profession and will deal all men according to this knowledge.
*Jainism* : Clear thinking comes through sincere and earnest efforts.
*Judaism* : The Lord will help those who are earnest.
*Sikhism* : Earnestness is the only basis for true religious acts.

**Illustrative List of Activities Relating to Moral Education**

| *S. No.* | *Activity* | *Moral Value/Values to be Inculcated* |
|---|---|---|
| 1. | Celebration of National Days | Love for the country. National spirit |
| 2. | Community service | Dignity of labour. Spirit of social service. Love for the community. For courtesy. |
| 3. | Community singing, National Song, Bhajans etc. | Feeling of oneness. Patriotism |
| 4. | Cultural Programmes | Cooperation. Consideration for others. Sense of responsibility. Feeling of oneness. |
| 5. | Flag Hoisting | Discipline. Emotional Integration. Patriotism |
| 6. | Games and Sports | Cooperation. Consideration for others. Sense of responsibility.. Respect for rules. Team spirit. Sencerity. |
| 7. | Morning Assembly | Manners. Orderliness. Punctuality. Love and respect for great personalities. Peace of mind. |
| 8. | Scouting and Guiding. Red Cross etc. | Courage, Adventurous spirit. Sprit of Social Service. Compassion. Team spirit. Self Help Kindness. |
| 9. | Social Service Camps | Dignity of labour. Manners. Selfless service. Orderliness. Equality. Fellow feeling |
| 10. | School Co-operative Store | Honesty, Team Work. Co-operation Duty. Consciousness |
| 11. | Social Service in Fairs and on Other Occasions | Compassion. Dignity of labour. Spirit of service. Sincerity. Equality. |
| 12. | Student-self government | Appreciation of rights and responsibilities Team spirit. Mutual respect. Love for rules. Audience habits. |
| 13. | School Journeys | Team Work. Love for the Country Initiative. Friendship. Spirit of Equality. Resourcefulness. |

## Select Bibliography on Moral Education

Aggarwal, J.C., *Landmarks in the History of Modern Indian Education*, Vikas Publishing House Pvt. Ltd., New Delhi, 2000.

NCERT, *Documents on Social, Moral and Spiritual Values in Education*, NCERT, New Delhi, 1979.

NCERT, *National Curriculum Framework for School Education*, NCERT, New Delhi, 2000.

*Report of the University Education Commission* (1948-49), Vol. I. Manager of Publications, Delhi, 1949.

*Report of the Secondary Education Commission* (1952-53), Ministry of Education, New Delhi, 1953.

*Report of the Committee on Religious and Moral Education* (1959-60), Ministry of Education, Government of India, New Delhi, 1960.

*Report of the Committee on Emotional Integration* (1961), Ministry of Education, New Delhi, 1962.

*Report of the Education Commission* (1964-66), Ministry of Education, Government of India, New Delhi, 1966.

# PART II

# SOCIOLOGICAL PERSPECTIVES ON EDUCATION

# 15

# Meaning, Concept and Importance of Educational Sociology

## 15.1 MEANING AND CONCEPT OF EDUCATIONAL SOCIOLOGY

*E. George Payne* (USA) often called the 'Father of Educational Sociology' has given the meaning of educational sociology as "Educational Sociology is the science which describes and explains institutions, groups and social processes in relation to the educational system in its evolution and changing function." Ottoway explains the meaning of Educational Sociology as "Educational Sociology starts with the assumption that education is an activity which goes on in a society, and its aims and methods depend on the nature of the society, in which it takes place." According to Dan W. Dodson, "Educational Sociology is particularly interested in finding out how to manipulate the educational process to achieve better personality development." In the words of Brown, "Educational Sociology is the study of interaction of the individual and his cultural environment including other individuals, social groups and patterns of behaviour." In the words of Good, "Educational Sociology is the scientific study of how people live in social groups."

From above, it is clear that social interaction is the key problem of educational sociology.

Educational Sociology is the applied side of sociology which is the study of social relationships Social relationships are of various types and Educational Sociology covers educational relationships.

## 15.2 SCOPE OF EDUCATIONAL SOCIOLOGY AND ITS DEVELOPMENT

George Payne explained the various dimensions of educational sociology in his book '*The Principles of Educational Sociology*', published in 1928. In this book he explained the effects of learning on group life and that of the group life on learning. He further explained how education as a social process may eliminate social defects. He also described how education as a social process may strengthen desirable ideals and standards that a society aims to achieve.

John Dewey, a great American educational thinker did a lot of work to popularise the idea of Educational Sociology through his books "*Experience and Education*" (1938), "*Schools of Tomorrow*" (1942) and "*Education Today*" (1949). Dewey greatly emphasized the social function of education. He considered school as a social institution which 'purifies' and 'idealises' the existing social institutions.

The scope of educational sociology is very vast. It has constantly extended its domain. Its scope now includes as stated below :

1. It includes the relation of education to various social forces, particularly culture.
2. It includes how culture is handed over to coming generations through agencies like the school, the home, the religious organisations, the play-groups etc.
3. It includes how socialisation, especially of the child takes place as a result of social interaction.
4. It includes the role of these agencies in the educational process : (a) the school, (b) the press, (c) the radio, (d) the T.V., (e) the cinema.
5. It includes education as a mean of social change and social control.
6. It deals with the impact of sociological thinking on the meaning, aims and functions of education, the curricular including co-curricular activities, social organisation and methodology of teaching.

**Important Issues of Study in Educational Sociology.** These are :

1. Interrelation of education and sociology,
2. Education as an instrument of social progress.
3. Place of school in society.
4. Place of a teacher in society.
5. Mutual relations of students and teachers.
6. Social life in the school.
7. School and the community.
8. School and its relations with social institutions.
9. Promotion of social feeling in the students.
10. Social aspirations, needs and problems and educational system.
11. Curriculum and the needs of the society.
12. Promotion of critical and constructive approach.
13. Social advancements.
14. Equalisation of educational opportunities.
15. Role of the mass media in education and social progress
16. Use of group and co-operative methods of teaching.

**Aims of Studying Educational Sociology**

Harington has suggested the following aims of studying Educational Sociology.

1. To acquire knowledge about school work and the work of teachers

in relation to society and social progress.
2. To study the impact of social elements on the school.
3. To acquire knowledge of the effects of social elements on the individual.
4. To construct curriculum with comprehensive understanding of the economic and cultural tendencies of society.
5. To gain knowledge about the democratic ideals.
6. To employ research techniques for achieving the aims of Educational Sociology.

## 15.3 SOCIOLOGICAL PERSPECTIVE OF EDUCATION

Sociological perspective of education implies the following :
1. Education is essentially a social process.
2. Education takes place only in society.
3. Social millieu (environment) itself educates the child.
4. Education has an important social role to play.
5. Education is a life-long process.
6. School is just one but the most important of all the social institutions.

## 15.4 IMPORTANCE OF EDUCATIONAL SOCIOLOGY : CONTRIBUTION OF EDUCATIONAL SOCIOLOGY TO EDUCATION

Educational Sociology has a great bearing on education. As a matter of fact, there is no dimension of education which has remained unaffected by Educational Sociology. It is rightly stated by Zelong, "Educational Sociology today stands at the head of a great road of high promise, the road to practical technology that may contribute vitally to the development of a new kind of education – an education that actually develops citizens who know how to take part and delight in social participation and who have developed a truly sympathetic understanding of the emotional feeling of divergent groups, from those of the social community to those of the world".

Educational Sociology has influenced educational thought and practices in a number of ways. Some of the important influences are given below.
1. *Meaning of education.* In this regard, Brown's views have great significance. In his words, "Education is the consciously controlled process whereby changes in behaviour are produced in the person and through the person within the group."
2. *Aims of education.* The development of sociological tendency in education has put special emphasis as regards aims of education.
   (i) Development of social attitudes, feelings and qualities.
   (ii) Development of a socially efficient individual.
   (iii) Improvement in vocational efficiency.
   (iv) Effective use of leisure time and development of healthy recreational pursuits.

3. *Functions of education.* Monroe lays down the following main functions of education.
    a) Diffusion of more and more knowledge.
    b) Education as a means of social control.
    c) Education as a means of transmission of social heritage.
    d) Education as a means of social progress.
    e) Education as a means of developing constructive and creative outlook of the individuals.
4. *Educational Sociology and the Curriculum.* The primary concern of the curriculum is the development of "We feeling – a feeling that the student belongs to the society and has a spirit of social interaction."

    Following are the main educational considerations according to educational sociologists that should guide the construction of school curriculum :
    1. It should be based on the aspirations and the ideals of the society.
    2. It should be based on the needs and problems of the society.
    3. It should reflect the basic cultural values of the society.
    4. It should develop healthy human relations.
    5. It should enable the child to participate effectively in the civic life of the society.
    6. It should develop vocational efficiency in students.
    7. It should provide activities and programmes for wholesome participation in social life
    8. It should prepare students for world citizenship and international understanding.
    9. It should be flexible.
    10. It should be dynamic.
5. *Educational Sociology and Methods of Teaching.* Following are the chief characteristics of the methods of teaching :
    1. The methods of teaching should develop problem solving attitude among students.
    2. The methods of teaching should be based on group work and socialised techniques like project method.
    3. The methods of teaching should make use of social survey technique.
    4. The methods of teaching should enable the students acquire those skills in the classroom which are helpful to them in their adjustment to social situations.
6. *Educational Sociology and the Teacher.* The educational sociologists consider teacher as a 'social engineer' – an engineer who can play an important role in social reconstruction. The Education Commission (1964-66) observed that the "destiny of India is being shaped in its classroom." It is, therefore, the teacher

who is an important instrument in shaping the destiny through his influence on the children. A teacher is expected to :

1. possess right attitude of social behaviour.
2. remain above castism, regionism, etc.
3. give due regard to the dignity of the pupils.

## 15.5 CONCEPT OF EDUCATIONAL SOCIOLOGY AND ITS RELATIONS WITH OTHER DISCIPLINES

*Educational Sociology and Sociology of Education.* There is a lot of confusion over these terms. Some scholars have attempted to use these terms as if they are synonyms and have the same meaning. Others, however, seek to point out some difference. According to Prof. William Taylor of the Faculty of Education, University of Bristol, Educational Sociology is usually an activity of educators and sociology of education is an activity of sociologists.

Dr. S.P. Ruhela and Dr. Vyas point out that the Educational Sociology has been more or less concerned with the applied side of sociology and sociology of education with the theoretical side of sociology.

*Educational Sociology and Educational Psychology.* Both Educational Sociology and Educational Psychology deal with behaviour and personality of the child. Educational Psychology is concerned with the psychological side of the behaviour and personality of the child. Educational Sociology on the other hand studies those from a sociological angle—total environment. Educational Psychology is primarily concerned with the application of sociological factors to learning and teaching experience. It attempts to discuss the social conditions that are involved in the learning process.

*Sociology and Educational Sociology.* Educational Sociology is a branch of Sociology. While Sociology is the study of 'human relationships', Educational Sociology is concerned with human relations in educational setting.

# 16

# Sociological Bases of Education

## 16.1 MEANING OF SOCIOLOGY

Before discussing the sociological bases of education, it becomes necessary to understand the term sociology.

French mathematician and philosopher Auguste Comte (1798-1857) who coined the word sociology defined it as "the science of social phenomena." Comte observed that social phenomena were very complex.

Comte was followed by an English philosopher Herbert Spencer (1820 – 1903) who wrote his book "*Principles of Sociology*" in 1876. Spencer believed that the human individual was like the "*Cell*" and the society was like an "*organism*" composed of different cells.

Some of the important definitions of sociology are :

Duncan defined sociology as "the scientific study of the processes of interactions of persons."

In the words of E. Durkheim, "Sociology is the science of collective representation".

Gillin and Gillin state, "Sociology in its broadest sense may be said to be the study of interaction arising from the association of living beings.

Green states "Sociology is the synthesising and generalising science of man in all his social relationships."

Mac Iver and Page define sociology as "Sociology is about social relationships, the network of relationships we call society."

Thus sociology is the study of social relationships. It studies the human behaviour in groups. It studies the social structure and social phenomena. In the study of sociology different forms of human interrelations are involved.

Sociology is subdivided into different branches of specialization. Each branch has specialised methods of investigation and research. Important branches are:

1. Criminal Sociology.
2. Educational Sociology.
3. Industrial Sociology.
4. Medical Sociology.
5. Occupational Sociology.
6. Rural Sociology.

7. Social Stratification Sociology.
8. Urban Sociology.

## 16.2 SOCIETY AND EDUCATION

In the opinion of educational sociologists, the school is the focal point round which involves the life of the growing child. Man is a social being. He is a member of the society. The influence of society on education is imperative. Education involves several interrelations. Education must be a social activity. Education influences the society and is also influenced by the society. Educational reforms cannot be discussed in a vacuum. Social movements make charges in educational aims, contents, methods of teaching and its organisational set up. In fact the functions of education undergo radical changes. Clarke has very rightly observed, "No writer on education can wholly shake himself free from the influence of time and place." Dewey explains how the changing society affects education in his book "*The School and Society*" in these words, "Whenever we have in mind the discussion of a new movement in education, it is especially necessary to take the broader social view. Otherwise, changes in the social institutions and traditions will be looked at as the arbitrary invention of particular teachers. It is only by connecting education with the general march of events that the school can lose its isolated character."

## 16.3 SOCIOLOGICAL BASES OF EDUCATION

Of the several types of social factors that influence education, the most important are 'economic' and 'political' factors.

The study of the system of education during the British period illustrates how economic and political factors influenced education in numerous ways.

Communism leads to the development and promotion of communistic ideals and values among the students. The entire educational system is geared to serve the ends of the State. An individual child loses its individuality. There is no scope for sharing responsibility in educational administration. Curriculum becomes very rigid. Methods of teaching do not allow for question-answer techniques. The contents of the subject-matter is based on communistic ideals. Freedom of expression is denied. School discipline becomes military discipline.

In a country which follows a democratic system, the educational system becomes quite flexible. Democratic ideals and values pervade in the working of the educational system.

The economic system of a society greatly influences its educational system. The system of education of an agrarian society will be quite different from a industrial society.

The Industrial Revolution brought in its wake of changes in curriculum and methods of teaching. Stress was laid on the use of experimental and laboratory method in the teaching-learning process.

In a capitalist economy, schools are controlled by the capitalist class. There emerges a great cleavage in the outlook of the elite and the masses.

The need for the development of economy has increased the importance of vocational aim in education.

The economic standard of living also affects education.

Educational thinking underwent an important change with the end of the political domination of the British.

Sociology discharges five different types of functions as far education is concerned:

1. *Technical function.* The study of sociology helps to determine the functions of educational institutions and also suggests why they should be improved.
2. *Introductory function.* Sociology acquaints the people with the nature of the educational system and its processes and also indicates the directions which it should follow.
3. *Informative function.* A scientific study of sociology helps to get various functional information about the problems of society and provides guidelines to education for solving problems relating to it.
4. *Cultural function.* The study of sociology helps to develop a cosmopolitan outlook, universal brotherhood and tolerance towards other societies and outlines the role of education in this task.
5. *Democratic function.* The most important function discharged by sociology is the democratic function. This democratic function of sociology becomes the most dominant basis of education. Education is expected to provide great help in understanding the democratic structure and developing democratic skills and values in the students as well as the masses.

From above we conclude that the sociological bases of education are :

1. Education takes place in society.
2. Education is essentially a social process.
3. Social environment itself educates the child.
4. Education has a social role to play.
5. Education is a lifelong process.
6. Education is not schooling. It is more than that.
7. Education is formal, non-formal and informal.
8. School is not the only social institution of education. There are several other social institutions that impart education.
9. Economic and political factors of the society play a dominant role in educational reforms.
10. Education must be social in nature i.e. it must develop democratic skills and values in the students.

# 17

# Social Aims of Education

## 17.1 CONCEPTS AND TERMS ASSOCIATED WITH SOCIAL AIMS OF EDUCATION

The social aims in education find expression in the following concepts and terms :

—'Education for Citizenship'.
— 'Education for Emotional Integration'.
— 'Education for National Unity'.
— 'Education for Patriotism'.
— 'Education for Social Efficiency'.

## 17.2 NEED FOR SOCIAL AIMS OF EDUCATION

Education is a social activity. Education is an important instrument of social advancement. Good aims are related to real life of a society. An organised system must meet the real aspirations, goals, values and needs of the society. A child is not to be educated in a vacuum. He is a member of the society in which he lives and education must enable him to become a useful member of the society.

The individual is regarded as endowed with a social nature. He is social by nature. Without social relations an individual would not develop his innate powers. A new born baby would almost perish on the absence of social contacts.

As observed by Dewey, "Education is the process of reconstruction or reconstitution of experience, giving it a more socialised value through the medium of social efficiency".

The Education Commission (1964-66) has also observed, "Education cannot be considered in isolation or planned in a vacuum. It has to be used as a powerful instrument of social and political change."

## 17.3 DIFFERENT INTERPRETATIONS OF SOCIAL AIMS OF EDUCATION

Following are the different interpretations of social aims in education. By and large these are based on the nature of the State.

1. *Social Aim in a Totalitarian State*: In a totalitarian State, an individual

exists for the State and he has no individuality of his own. He is born for the State, lives for the State and dies for the State. In ancient times, in Sparta – a City State of ancient Greece (5th Century B.C.), an individual was educated to develop physical fitness and strict discipline so that he could become an excellent fighter. It may be stated that there was a great rivalry among some states for political supremacy.

The educational system of Germany under the Nazi Government led by Hitler was totally subservient. Social aim in education meant 'total surrender of individuality' to the State. Italy also followed this to a considerable extent under Mussolini (1922-1945). The erstwhile USSR also adopted an educational system in accordance with the tenets of Communism which meant unquestioned obedience to the State. The Japanese also had a strict control over the system of education during the first half of the 20th Century.

2. *Social Aim of Education According to Paternal Attitude:* The U.S.A., Great Britain and other democratic nations including India lay emphasis on these aims of education—'Education for Citizenship', Education for Social Service'. Values like sharing responsibility, co-operation etc. are cultivated through the educational system. Social aims of education also implies equlisation of educational opportunities so that an individual can develop his personality to the maximum.

3. *Social Aim of Education in Terms of Social Efficiency:* Prof. Dewey is the most ardent supporter of this aim of education. A socially efficient individual is one who is able to earn his livelihood and conforms to a certain standard of conduct known as the moral standard. A socially efficient individual is also a good citizen.

## 17.4 IMPORTANT SOCIAL AIMS OF EDUCATION ACCEPTED BY DEMOCRATIC STATES

Following are the important social aims usually accepted by democratic States :

1. *Development of Democratic Citizenship.* This implies :
   - (i) Clear thinking.
   - (ii) Receptivity to new ideas.
   - (iii) Clearness in speech and writing.
   - (iv) Passion for social justice.
   - (v) Development of an attitude of tolerance.
2. *Development of the Art of Living in a Community.* This means the development of the following qualities :
   - a) Appreciation of other's point of view.
   - b) Give and take attitude.
   - c) Sensitivity to the needs of the community.
3. *Development of True Patriotism.* This involves
   - (i) Sincere appreciation of cultural and social achievements of one's country.
   - (ii) Readiness to recognise weakness of one's country.

(iii) Strong will to work for removing weaknesses.
(iv) Resolve to serve one's country to the best of one's ability.
(v) Solid action to harmonise and subordinate individual interests to broader national interests.

4. *Improvement of Vocational Efficiency.* This implies
   (i) Creating a new attitude that means appreciation of dignity of labour.
   (ii) Making the students realize that vocational efficiency will lead to the maximum utilisation of the natural resources of the country.
   (iii) Developing good workmanship skills.
5. *Development of Qualities of Leadership and Followership.* This consists of initiative, deeper understanding of social issues, originality, love for duty and co-operation etc.

## 17.5 CHIEF SUPPORTERS OF THE SOCIAL AIMS OF EDUCATION

1. There are two elements in education. One should teach us how to make a living and the other how to live. *—Adams, John*
2. Education makes for effective participation in the social process of social interaction. *—Brown, Francis J.*
3. The teacher's aim is not to educate his pupils in the abstract, but for life in any existing society. *—Bruebacker, J.S.*
4. In our opinion, no reform is more important or more urgent than to transform education, to relate it to the life, needs and aspirations of the people. *—Education Commission 1964-66.*
5. Education is the development of all those capacities in the individual which will enable him to become a socially efficient individual. *—Dewey, John.*
6. An adequate educational programme will be concerned to help each individual child grow up into full participation in the richest available group life *—Kilpatric, William.*
7. I call a complete and generous education that fits a man to perform justly, skillfully and magnanimously all the offices, both private, and public of peace and war. *—Milton, John.*
8. I believe in a Socialist State and I would like to develop education towards that goal. *—Nehru, Jawaharlal*
9. The aim of secondary education is to train the youth of the country to be good citizens, who will be competent to play their part effectively in the social reconstruction and economic development of their country. *—Secondary Education Commission 1952-53*
10. Education is an attempt on the part of the adult members of the society to shape the development of the coming generation in accordance with its own ideals of life. *—Welton, James.*

## 17.6 WHY CLAIMS FOR SOCIAL AIMS OF EDUCATION

Following are the arguments of the supporters of the social aims in education :

1. *State or State alone is real.* As Ramount has said, "The isolated individual is a figment of the imagination."
2. *State is an idealised Superhuman Entity.* State is over and above the individual. The individuality is of no value, and personality a meaningless term apart from the social environment.
3. *Education is through Social Control.* The supporters of this view held that since education is provided through Government support in various ways, it therefore, should serve the ends of the State.

## 17.7 CRITICS OF SOCIAL AIMS OF EDUCATION

Social aims of education are criticised on account of the following reasons :

*Firstly*, social aim in its extreme form reduces the individual to a mere entity.

*Secondly*, the extreme concept of the all-powerful state or society ignores the legitimate desires and interests of the individual.

*Thirdly*, extreme nature of social aim kills all initiative and originality of the individual.

*Fourthly*, it attempts to make the individual only a tool of the Government or the State and demands an unquestioning loyalty and obedience form the individual.

*Fifthly*, it is against all concepts of education as individual development.

*Sixthly*, all out stress on social aim brought two World Wars in 1914-1919 and 1939-45.

## 17.8 SYNTHESIS BETWEEN SOCIAL AIMS OF EDUCATION AND INDIVIDUAL AIMS OF EDUCATION

Extreme postures are usually very harmful. Therefore, the extreme form of either of the two should be rejected.

It is wrong to think that in the ordinary course, they are opposed to each other. On the contrary, they are complementary to each other.

Individual and society are interdependent. Individuality cannot flourish without social medium and society cannot grow without the growth of the individuals.

We cannot think of a society without individuals.

The claims of the individual and the society are equally important.

We may sum up the discussion with the balanced and rational views of Ross, Huxley and Gandhiji. According to Ross : "There is always an interaction between the society and the individual. No individual can develop in a social vacuum. An individual can only develop in a progressive society and society can only make progress with developed individuals. The circle cannot be broken".

Aldous Huxley has also said, "A perfect education is one which trains up every human being to fit into place he or she is to occupy in the social hierachy, but without, in the process, destroying his or her individuality".

Mahatma Gandhi said, "I value individual freedom, but you must not forget that man is essentially a social being. He has risen to his present status by learning to adjust his individuality to the requirement of social progress."

# 18

# Contemporary Social System in India
## Its Structure (Caste and Class)

### 18.1 DIMENSIONS OF INDIAN SOCIETY

Broadly speaking, Indian society may be seen in terms of the following dimensions :

1. Cultural dimension of the society.
2. Economic dimension or economic system of the society.
3. Educational dimension or educational system of the society.
4. Political dimension or political system of the society.
5. Philosophical dimension or philosophical system of the society.
6. Religious dimension or religious system of the society.
7. Social dimension or social system of the society.
8. Spiritual dimension or spiritual system of the society.

While discussing any system, six points to be remembered are: (i) There are large regional variations from region to region. Nevertheless, there are several common characteristics also (ii) Each dimension is greatly affected by other dimensions. (iii) Each dimension or system of society is influenced by its past. (iv) Present system is greatly influenced by rapid, scientific and technological advances. (v) Present Indian system is greatly influenced by globalisation. (vi) Constitution of India is the most important source of change and reform of any system.

### 18.2 INDIAN SOCIAL STRUCTURE AND ITS MEANING

Modern sociology defines social system or social structure as a pattern developed and maintained by the 'institutions' of society.

The term 'institution' here means a device or a system of working that regulates the behaviour of members in certain typical or specific forms of relationships. The sociologists include family, marriage, religion, charity, education, economic system (like capitalism, communism and mixed economy etc.), political party, caste, social classes etc. as social institutions.

Some scholars make a distinction between cultural traditions and social traditions while others prefer not to make such distinction.

For our study, we will confine ourselves to caste and class structure of the Indian social system.

## 18.3 CASTE SYSTEM IN INDIA

*Meaning of a Caste.* Usually a caste is defined as a group of people having the following characteristics:

(i) A collection or group of families.

(ii) Common 'sur' name.

(iii) Common or related profession.

(iv) Common religion and rituals.

(v) Common code of conduct.

(vi) Common etiquettes and manners.

(vii)Common customs, ceremonies regarding marriages, birth and death, etc.

However, with the advancement of civilisation, all the features indicated above are not applicable. There has been a sea-change in the concept of a caste. Under the impact of the modernisation and, the efforts of social and political reformers, caste system has been gradually losing its old and traditional manners.

*Origin of Caste System.* It is very difficult to state when caste system originated in India. Scholars have given divergent views on this subject. However, it is admitted that the institution of caste is a blot on the Indian social structure. It has become a source of several evils.

*Classes based on Occupations.* During the Vedic period, there was no caste system in India. Society was divided on the basis of '*Varna*' which means 'choice of occupation'. Usually reference is made to the following hymn of the '*Rig Veda*'. "I am a poet composer of hymns, my father is a physician, my mother grinds corn. Being engaged in different professions, as cows seek food in different pastures, we worship Thee for bounties."

Such a division of functions on these sociological or occupational functions was considered very helpful in the harmonious functions of society.

Prof. Max Muller has observed that on the basis of available documents, we can emphatically say "No" to the prevalent of caste system in India in the Vedic period.

R.C. Dutt, a noted scholar also states, "We have not a single passage to show that the society was divided into hereditary classes".

Likewise Dr. V.S. Smith asserts, "I do not find any indication of the caste in the Rig Vedic times".

'*Yajur Veda*' – 16.15 reads as "The social organisation considered all human beings equal." All men are equal in brotherhood. There is no one small and no one big."

'*Rig Veda*' states, "May we divide our wealth equally among ourselves and reduce disparity, so that we may be welded into strong followship and unity." (R.V. 191.9).

### Growth of Caste System

During the course of its long history, several races from outside came to India and settle here. Gradually they mingled with the Indian people and also among themselves. This led to the multiplication of castes and sub-castes in India. With the passage of time, and inspite of the efforts of several religious and social reformers, caste system became very rigid. It also led to the attitude of 'big' and 'small' classes. Not only this, the caste system led to 'untouchability'. Touching to a Shudra by a person belonging to a higher caste, began to be considered as an act of 'pollution'.

No one really can give the exact number of all the castes and sub-castes in India. The general estimate is that the number exceeds 4000.

Not only the Hindus have castes, but also the Muslims, Buddhists, Jains and even Christians in India are divided into several castes of their own. Each caste is sub-divided into sub-castes.

### Important Merits claimed of the Caste System

1. Preservation of Hindu culture and religion.
2. Maintenance of purity of blood.
3. Economic prosperity on account of division of labour.
4. Opportunity of appreticeship training in different occupations on account of hereditary occupations.
5. Enforcement of morality and discipline by castes.

### Important Demerits of the Caste System

1. Social inequality.
2. Curse of untouchability.
3. Stumbling block to national and emotional integration.
4. Adverse effects of caste system on the working of democracy i.e. tendency to vote on the basis of caste.
5. Hatred among different classes.

## 18.4 CASTE AND EDUCATION IN INDIA

Following points deserve attention in this regard.

1. To what extent modern education has been successful in weaking caste system particularly the negative features of casteism, it is very difficult to state. There is no doubt that on account of the spread of education and the increased social status of some sections of the lower classes (because of economic advancement resulting from reservations in jobs etc.) educated classes have started more and more intercaste social interaction. Intercaste marriages and especially of I.A.S., I.P.S. and other officers belonging to lower castes with higher castes are on the increase.
2. Several caste organisations have started their own educational institutions. In matter of admission of students and appointments of

teachers, preference is usually given to the people belonging to the caste that manages the educational institution. This step has been very helpful in the promotion of education among these classes.

3. There are several constitutional provisions relating to the promotion of status and education of the 'Scheduled Castes', 'Scheduled Tribes' and 'Other Backward Classes'.
4. Several highly educated people in different walks of life consider it undesirable to provide special quotas in admissions and appointments to some classes. They view it as an onslaught on the concept of 'equality of opportunity'. They criticise such concessions as barriers to the recognition of merits.

## 18.5 CLASS STRUCTURE

*Meaning of a Social Class.* A class is generally a category of people having the following similar characteristics :

(i) Similar socio-economic system.
(ii) Similar types of occupations.
(iii) Similar types of aspirations.
(iv) Similar value system.
(v) Similar style of living.

It may be noted that there has been marked changes in recent years as regards the possession of similar characteristics of a social class. Social classes cannot be divided into watertight compartments.

## 18.6 SOCIAL CLASSES IN INDIA

There are several rough ways of dividing people into social classes in India. Among the important bases are :

1. Social classes according to income.
2. Social classes according to profession.
3. Social classes according to salary.
4. Social classes according to habitation i.e. urban or rural.
5. Social classes according to mobility : nomadic or otherwise.
6. Social classes according to the possession of land i.e. landlords and tenants etc.
7. Social classes according to type of accommodation allotted by the Government of India. There are nearly a dozen types of accommodation, ranging from one room to four or five rooms including bunglows.
8. Social classes according to the 34 scales of pay fixed by the Fifth Pay Commission.

## 18.7 CLASS STRUCTURE OR SOCIAL CLASSES IN INDIA ACCORDING TO GENERAL ACCEPTABILITY

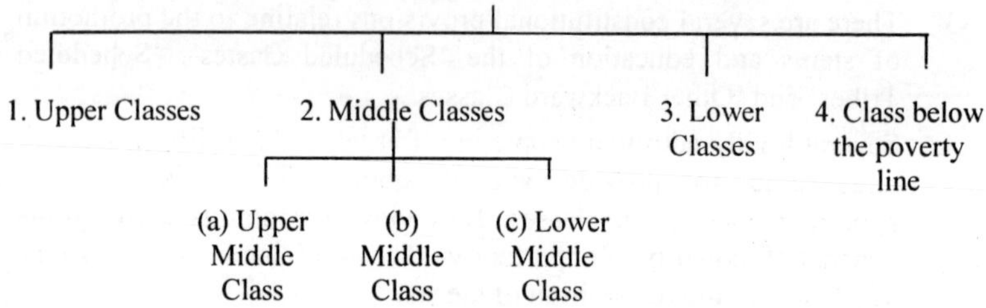


*Fig. 18.1: Social Stratification into Classes*

### Main Characteristics of Each Social Class

*The Upper Class*: This class includes very rich businessmen, industrialists, landlords, highly placed bureaucrats (very senior officers in government/ semi-government and autonomous organisations), politicians and professionals of a higher order. They enjoy very high economic as well as social status on account of their high positions and powers. This class enjoys several privileges. Nearly 5 per cent of India's population comes under this category.

*The Upper Middle Class:* People belonging to this class are usually doctors, engineers, lawyers, managers, professors and well-placed government officers. This class has lesser socio-economic status than the upper class. Their style of living approximates to that of the upper class.

*The Middle-Upper Middle Class:* People belonging to this class have limited resources but would like to enjoy standard of living as that of the two upper classes.

*The Lower Middle Class*: This class comprises clerks, school teachers, small shopkeepers, technicians and wage-earners, etc. Financial position of this class is quite low but people of this class like to dress, eat and live like the middle class people. The social status of this class is very low.

*The Lower Class:* This class is made of agricultural and industrial labourers, very low paid employees and daily wage earner etc. This class constitutes nearly 40 per cent of the total population of India. People of this class suffer from poverty, illiteracy etc.

*Class below the Poverty Line*: This forms about 30 per cent of the total population of India. People live from hand to mouth. They are very often homeless. They suffer from disease and hunger. They are totally illiterate.

## 18.8 SOCIAL STRUCTURE AND EDUCATION

Following are the main influences of the Indian social structure on education.

1. *Changing attitude towards girls education among lower classes:* The

traditional conservative attitude coupled with ignorance and poverty that have existed in the rural areas regarding indifference to the education of the girls have hindered the promotion of girls in the rural areas. However, in recent years, the lower middle class as well as the class below the poverty line has gradually recognised the importance of girls education. This has necessitated opening of more schools in rural areas.

2. *Changing attitude towards co-education:* The traditional conservative attitude regarding co-education has also radically changed. Co-educational institutions have been growing steadily.

3. *Changes in curriculum according to sex:* Earlier students belonging to lower middle class and middle-middle class were not interested in pursuing courses in engineering and accountancy etc. Now there is a growing demand from girls for these courses.

4. *Teaching profession:* At one time teaching especially at the school level was the monopoly of the middle-middle class. But now only females of this class join the teaching profession. Males of this class or above this class are very reluctant to become school teachers. This class considers it below its dignity to enter the teaching profession.

5. *Different level of schools:* Parallel to the social classes, have come into being educational institutions of different levels. Mention may be made of the following categories of schools :

1. Public schools like Doon, Modern and Delhi Public Schools etc.
2. Public schools of the second level.
3. Residential public schools.
4. Navodaya Schools.
5. Army and Airforce schools of a higher level.
6. Air, Army and Air Force schools of the second level
7. Central Schools.
8. Government schools (schools run by the State).
9. Aided schools (getting grant from the State).
10. Schools run by local bodies.

In general, it may be stated that there is a 'mad rush' from almost all classes except the lower middle and the lower class for public schools of varying standards.

6. *Craze for public schools:* The middle-middle class people, being conscious of the significance of education strive hard to send their children to public schools at great cost by making many sacrifices in their lives.

7. *Duality of education:* Dropping out of school, stagnation, and truancy among the students belonging to lower middle class and especially lower class are common. They receive poor quality education.

8. *Fee structure:* Education in government schools or schools run by local bodies is more or less free or very nominal. This has benefited the lower classes. Now they try to make use of educational facilities. Several incentives like free mid-day meals and books are also provided for the promotion of education among these classes.

# 19

# Guiding Principles of Indian Policy

## 19.1 CONSTITUTION AS THE GUIDING AND INSPIRATIONAL SOURCE OF INDIAN POLICY

The basic values that the Indian society upholds and that guide all individual as well as social life and group functioning are provided in the Indian Constitution. The Constitution of India and in fact of every country in the world determines its cultural, economic, educational, political, secular and social ideals and values. It also provides broad outlines for their fulfilment. While framing our Constitution, Constitution markers made a deep study of the Constitutions of various countries. At the same time they took note of our ancient ideals and values. The growing and changing needs of our country were also kept in view. Thereafter, the Constitution was framed. Suitable provisions, have been made to amend it according to needs and requirements of the times.

The Constitution of India was adopted by the Constituent Assembly on November 26, 1949 and it came into force on January 26, 1950.

The Constitution includes 395 Articles in XXII parts. Besides it has XII Schedules and III Appendices which provide details where required.

## 19.2 SALIENT IDEALS AND VALUES CONTAINED IN THE CONSTITUTION

The ideals and values provided for in the Constitution are in keeping with the cultural, philosophical, and social traditions of India. These ideals and values guided the freedom struggle also. Among the important ones are:

1. *Democratic Principles* such as freedom, equality, readiness to see the other person's point of view, tolerance, ability to adjust in and work with groups.
2. *Socialist Principles* such as respect for and commitment to equality in opportunity and status, maximising national production and wealth and equitable distribution of wealth.
3. *Secular Principles* such as freedom of worship, respect for all religions and readiness to manage civil affairs without reference to religion.

The Constitution of India which declares India to be a Sovereign Socialist secular Democratic Republic rests on the foundations of the above values.

The PREAMBLE of the constitution reads as WE, THE PEOPLE OF INDIA, having solemnly resolves to constitute India into a SOVEREIGN SOCIALIST SECULAR DEMOCRATIC REPUBLIC and to secure to all its citizens :

— *JUSTICE*, social economic and political;

— *LIBERTY* of thought, expression, belief, faith and worship,

— *EQUALITY* of status and of opportunity; and to promote among them all

— *FRATERNITY* assuring the dignity of the individual and the unity and integrity of the Nation;

— *IN OUR CONSTITUENT ASSENBLY* this twenty sixth day of November, 1949, do *HEREBY ADOPT, ENACT AND GIVE TO OURSELVES THIS CONSTITUTION*

(*Note*: Three new Terms SOCIALIST, SECULAR and INTERGRITY were added to the original text of the Preamble with the 42nd Amendment to the Constitution in 1976.

## 19.3 MAJOR POLICY PROVISIONS

1. *Appropriate Goals*. The goals of Socialism, Secularism and Democracy are set before the nation.
2. *Fundamental Rights*. PART III of the Constitution lays down the following fundamental rights which every citizen of India is entitled to in every walk of life including education.
    1. *Right to Equality*
        - (i) Equality before law (Article 14)
        - (ii) Prohibition of discrimination on grounds of religion race caste, sex or place of birth (Article 15)
        - (iii) Equality of opportunity in matters of public employment (Article 16)
        - (iv) Abolition of untouchability (Article 17)
    2. *Right to Freedom*. This includes freedom of speech etc.
    3. *Right against Exploitation*. This includes prohibition of forced labour and employment of children etc.
    4. *Right to Freedom of Religion*. This includes freedom of faith etc.
    5. *Cultural and Educational Rights*. It includes protection of minorities in various fields including education
3. *Fundamental Duties*. Chapter IVA includes ten fundamental duties of the citizens. This was incorporated with the $42^{nd}$ Amendment to the Constitution in 1976.
4. *Directive Principles of State Policy*. PART IV includes Articles 36 to 51 relating to providing guidance to the government that certain principles should be kept in view in formulating State policies. The

fulfilment of these principles is not binding on the government. Nevertheless government should make all efforts to the achievements of objectives as given in these principles. Article 45 regarding the provision for free and compulsory education for children forms a part of Directive Principles of State policy.

5. *Abolition of Untouchability.* Article 17 of the Constitution declares it an offence to practise untouchability against any citizen.
6. *Language of the Union.* Article 43 declares Hindi in the Devanagari script as the official language of the Union. English, however, has been allowed to be used as an alternate official language as long as it is felt desirable to do. Original a period of 15 years was fixed for this. Several articles relate to languages etc.

## 19.4 SPECIFIC ARTICLES IN THE CONSTITUTION RELATING TO EDUCATION POLICY

I. *Education in the Concurrent List.* Till 1976 education was a State subject, subject to certain provisions relating to higher education at the Central level. The Forty-Second Constitutional Amendment, 1976, affected the role of Central and State Governments in education.

Education was placed in the Concurrent List which implies that the Central Government as well as State Governments are responsible for the promotion of education. Entry 25 of the Concurrent List states, "Education including technical education, medical education and university education subject to the provisions of entries 63, 64, 65 and 66 of List I, vocational and technical training of labour".

Entries 63, 64, 65 and 66 of List I (Central List) pertain to Central Universities, Institutions of National Importance, coordination and determination of standards in institutions for higher education research and scientific and technical institutions.

In case of any dispute between the Central Government and State Government, legislation framed by the Central Government will have overriding authority.

II. *Free and Compulsory Education* (See next Chapter)

III. *Freedom to Attendance at Religious Instruction or Religious Worship in Certain Educational Institutions.* Article 28 reads as :

1. No religious instruction shall be provided in any educational institution wholly maintained out of State funds.
2. Nothing in Clause (1) shall apply to the educational institution which is administered by the State but has been established under any endownment or trust which requires that religious institution shall be imparted in such institution.
3. No person attending any educational institution recognised by the State or receiving aid out of State funds shall be required to take part in any religious worship that may be conducted in such institution or

to attend any religious worship that may be conducted in such institution or in any premises attached thereto unless such person or, if such person is a minor, his guardian has given his consent.

IV. *Protection of Interest of Minorities.* Article 29(1) states that any section of citizens residing in the territory of India or any part thereof having a distinct language, script or culture of its own shall have the right to conserve the same.

Article 29(2) reads that no citizen shall be denied admission into any educational institution maintained by the State or receiving aid out of State funds on grounds only of religion, race, caste, language or any of them.

V. *Right of Minorities to Establish and Administer Education Institutions.* Article 30(1) states that all minorities whether based on religion or language, shall have the right to establish and administer educational institutions of their choice.

Article 30(1A) reads that making any law providing for the compulsory acquisition of any property of any educational institution established and administered by a minority, referred to in Clause (1), the State shall ensure that the amount fixed by or determined under such law for the acquisition of such property is such as would not restrict or abrogate the right guaranteed under the Clause.

Article 32(2) states that the State shall, not in granting aid to educational institutions, discriminate against any educational institution on the ground that it is under the management of a minority, whether based on religion or language.

VI. *Promotion of Educational and Economic Interests of Scheduled Castes, Scheduled Tribes and other Weaker Sections.* Article 46 states that the State shall promote with special care the educational and economic interests of the weaker sections of the people, and in particular, of the Scheduled Castes and the Scheduled Tribes and shall protect them from social injustice and all forms of exploitations.

VII. *Facilities for Instruction in Mother-Tongue at Primary Stage.* Article 35-A states that it shall be the endeavour of every State and every local authority within the State to provide adequate facilities for instruction in the mother-tongue at the primary stage of education to children belonging to linguistic minority group; and the President may issue such directions to any State as he considers necessary or proper for securing the provision of such facilities.

## 19.5 SUMMARY OF POLICY DIRECTIONS

1. Policies in education should be guided by the principles contained in the Constitution.
2. Aims of education should be to promote ideals and values of socialism, secularism and democracy.
3. It is the responsibility of the Central Government and the State

Governments to promote education.

4. The language policy in the educational institutions should be as laid down in Article 43.
5. All possible efforts should be made to provide free and compulsory education to all children for eight years.
6. Religious education will not be compulsory in educational institutions.
7. Minorities can establish their own educational institutions.
8. Special measures will be taken to promote the education of the weaker sections.

# 20

# Secularism

## 20.1 INTRODUCTION

India has decided to build itself into a socialist, secular and democratic society in which different communities and groups belonging to all faiths can flourish side by side. All citizens, irrespective of any difference of caste, colour and religion etc. have the opportunities to make the best of their abilities for personal fulfilment and social progress. It is felt that only a secular framework is suitable for the growth of democracy in a multi-religious and multi-cultural society like India. Likewise secularism in India pre-supposes a democratic outlook.

While discussing the meaning of secularism, it must be stressed that Indian concept of secularism is quite different from the western concept of secularism. Thus secularism, like democracy has come to mean different things to different people.

It may also be noted that the word secularism did not occur in the Constitution when it was adopted in 1950. It was inserted in the Constitution in 1976 when it was feared that religious fundamentalism was on the increase and was posing a great threat to the national unity.

## 20.2 ORIGIN OF THE WORD SECULARISM

The word secularism was first used in the nineteenth century by George Jacob Holydake. Holydake based secularism as a social and ethical system, on the following principles :

1. Principle of material and cultural improvement of human beings.
2. Principle of respect and research of all truth, whatever be its source.
3. Principle of concern for 'this present age' or world and its improvement.
4. Principle of independent rational morality, which does not base itself on faith in divine order commandment.

The meaning attached to secularism tends to minimise the importance of the spirit and the DIVINE power. It also tends to ignore the spiritual side. Both the elements are considered basic to Indian thinkers. The definition lays stress on material improvement only. It also takes no notice of the religious element.

The word 'Secularism' is derived from the Latin word '*Saeculum*' meaning 'this present age'. Accordingly Holydake also emphasised the word 'this age'.

## 20.3 INDIAN CONCEPT OF SECULARISM AND A SECULAR STATE

The Indian concept of secularism is expressed in the following often quoted principles :

1. '*Sarva-dharma-samantva*' or '*Sarva-dharma-sambhava*'—equal regard for all faiths and creeds.
2. '*Ekam Brahma Vipra Bahuda Vadanti*'—God is one, wise men call Him by different names.

Although the word secularism was introduced only in 1976 in our Constitution, our secularism is historical. We have had great breadth of vision as expressed above.

Ashoka's secular outlook is one of the landmarks not only of Indian civilization but also of the human civilization. He made a passionate appeal for developing a spirit of reverence and tolerance for all faiths.

Dr. B.R. Ambedkar, the principal architect of our Constitution explains the concept of a Secular State in these words, "Secular does not mean that it shall not take into consideration the religious sentiments of the people. All that secular State means is that the Parliament shall not be competent to impose any particular religion upon the rest of the people."

Dr. Rajendra Prasad, the first President of India has very clearly explained the concept of secularism in the Indian context, "There are some who think that because we are a secular State, we do not believe in religion or spiritual values. Far from being so, it really means that in this country all are free to profess or preach the faith of their liking and that we wish well of all religions and want than to develop in their own way without any hindrance."

Jawaharlal Nehru, the first Prime Minister of India has explained the secular nature of Indian State as "It means while religion is completely free, the State including in its wide fold various religions and cultures, gives protection and opportunities to all and thus brings about an atmosphere of tolerance and co-operation."

Dr. S. Radhakrishnan has explained secularism as follows, "When India is said to be a secular State, it does not mean that we reject the reality of an unseen spirit or the relevance of religion to life. We hold that no one religion should be given preferential status or unique distinction."

## 20.4 SECULAR OUTLOOK OR CHARACTERISTICS OF A SECULAR-MINDED INDIVIDUAL

Following salient features of secularism emerge from the above stated views :

1. Secular outlook treats all religion on an equal footing.

2. Secular outlook accepts freedom of religion.
3. Secular outlook implies freedom of worship.
4. Secular outlook implies tolerance.
5. Secular outlook encourages rational thinking.
6. Secular outlook views all citizens with equal rights.
7. Secular outlook encourages moral and spiritual values.
8. Secular outlook believes in co-existence.
9. Secular outlook stresses free inquiry.
10. Secular outlook means freedom of mind from dogmatic ideas.
11. Secular outlook is not a negation of religion.

Accordingly the Secular State of India has the following main features :

1. Indian State treats all religions on equal footing.
2. Indian State neither interferes with nor promotes any religion.
3. It permits individual and collective freedom of religion to all citizens.
4. It views all individuals as citizens with equal rights and not as members of any particular religious group.
5. It is not against any religion.
6. It functions in a way independent of religion.
7. It allows religious education in some educational institutions run and managed by minorities subject to certain conditions.

## 20.5 CONSTITUTIONAL PROVISIONS AND SECULARISM

Often a question has been raised if India, being a secular State is not in essence hostile towards religion. The answer is an emphatic 'No'. This becomes very clear from the following provisions of the Constitution of India.

1. *Article 15. Prohibition of discrimination on grounds of religion, race, caste, sex or place of birth*: (i) The State shall not discriminate against any citizen on grounds only of religion, race, caste, sex, place of birth or any of them. (ii) No citizen on grounds only of religion, race, sex, place of birth shall be denied access to shops, wells, tanks etc.
2. *Article 25(1) Freedom of Conscience*: According to this Article, all citizens are equally entitled to freedom of conscience and the right to profess, practice and propagate religion. However, while the freedom of conscience is absolute i.e. without any restriction, the exercise of freedom of propagation of religion is subject to restrictions in the interest of harmony, public morality and order.
3. *Article 27. Exemption from the Payment of Taxes*: As per this Article, no person shall be compelled to pay any taxes, the proceeds of which are specifically appropriated in payment of expenses for the promotion or maintenance of any particular religion or religious denomination.

## 20.6 CONSTITUTIONAL PROVISIONS REGARDING IMPARTING OF RELIGIOUS AND SECULAR EDUCATION

1. Article 28 (1) states that no religious instruction shall be provided in any educational institution wholly maintained out of State funds.
2. Clause (1) shall not be applicable to any educational institution which is administered by the State but has been established by any trust which requires that religious instruction shall be imparted in such institution
3. No person attending any educational institution recognised by the State or receiving aid out of State funds shall be required to take part in any religious instruction without his consent. In the case of a minor, consent of his guardian is needed.

## 20.7 CONSTITUTIONAL PROVISIONS REGARDING ADMISSION AND ESTABLISHMENT OF EDUCATIONAL INSTITUTIONS BY RELIGIOUS MINORITIES

*Article 29(1)* states that no citizen shall be denied admission to any educational institution maintained by the State or receiving aid out of State funds on ground of religion only.

*Article 30(1)* provides for the establishment of educational institutions by minorities whether based on religion or language.

There shall be no discrimination in granting aid to any educational institution run by minorities whether based on religion or language.

## 20.8 REASONS FOR IMPARTING SECULAR EDUCATION

1. Secular education develops a moral outlook.
2. Secular education helps in the development of liberal attitudes and values.
3. Secular education develops wider-vision.
4. Secular education develops an attitude of appreciation and understanding of others' point of view.
5. Secular education develops democratic values.
6. Secular education develops scientific temper of mind.
7. Secular education develops humanistic outlook.
8. Secular education synthesises materialism and spiritualism.
9. Secular education serves as an antidote to religious fanaticism and hatred.

# 21

# Socialism

## 21.1 MEANING AND ORIGIN OF SOCIALISM

Socialism is a socio-economic-political doctrine which arose as a revolt against capitalism. Started in Europe in the19th century, it soon spread to almost all parts of the world. Karl Marx and Lenin in Russia and Mao in China were the chief architects of socialism.

Socialism aims at establishing a classless society based on the total supremacy of the State and total submission of the individual to the State.

During the course of time, several types of socialism have emerged. Each lays stress on different ways of achieving socialist goals. Following are the prominent types of socialism:

1. Christian Socialism.
2. Democratic Socialism.
3. Fabian Socialism.
4. Gandhian Socialism.
5. Guild Socialism.
6. Marxist-Leninist Socialism.
7. Scientific Socialism.

## 21.2 MAIN FEATURES OF SOCIALISM

1. Socialism aims at establishing a classless society.
2. Classless society is free from disparity, exploitation and oppression.
3. Socialism aims at social justice.
4. Socialism aims at equality.
5. Socialism believes in public ownership of the means of production, distribution and exchange.
6. Socialism aims at abolishing the capitalist system.
7. Socialism emphasizes mutual co-operation and fellowship.
8. Socialism aims at developing necessary skills and favourable attitudes towards work.
9. Socialism aims at the active participation of the individual in the productive process of society.
10. Socialism aims at the complete supremacy of the State.
11. Socialism aims at the complete subordination of the individual to the State.

12. Socialism has little faith in religious ideas and values.
13. Socialism ignores spiritual values.

## 21.3 METHODS OF ACHIEVING SOCIALIST GOALS

Socialism is usually associated with revolutionary methods. Cult of the 'bullet' rather than the cult of 'ballot' is the key note of socialism. Millions of people have lost their lives in civil wars in several countries on account of clash of socialist workers with their opponents. It is generally observed that without 'violence' socialist ideals could not spread.

## 21.4 DEMERITS OF SOCIALISM

1. Socialism sacrifices individual freedom.
2. Socialism gives undue importance to bureaucracy.
3. Responsibilities of the State under socialism increase, leading to overburden which results in corruption and inefficiency.
4. Under socialism production may decrease and lead to poverty.
5. Socialism failed in the origin of its country i.e. Russia. It remained in operation there for about ninety years.

## 21.5 INDIAN CONCEPT OF SOCIALISM

Gandhiji, Jawaharlal Nehru and Jai Prakash Narain are the great supporters of socialism. However, there is a marked difference between their approach and that of Marx.

Gandhiji saw socialism as a way of life. He called it '*Sarvodaya Samaj*' in which the '*greatest good of all*' is the end. He explained his socialism in an article in 1947 under the caption 'Who is a Socialist? Gandhiji wrote, "Under socialism all the members of society are equal—none low, none high. Under it the prince and the peasant, the wealthy and the poor, the employer and the employee are all on the same level." He further observed, "Socialism requires crystal – like (pure) means to achieve it. Only truthful, non-violent and pure-hearted socialists will be able to establish a socialist society in India and the world." Jawaharlal Nehru also held the similar views on socialism.

The distinguishing features of Indian socialism are :

1. It is based on equality between man and man.
2. Economic system must be based on human outlook.
3. Socialism does not sacrifice man for money.
4. It believes in building a classless and casteless society.
5. It stresses equality, freedom and social justice.
6. It believes in mixed economy i.e. public ownership as well as private ownership.
7. It aims at providing special facilities to the weaker sections of the society.

8. It believes in the growth of all types of industries—large scale, cottage and small scale.
9. It believes in free expression of views.
10. It is based on democratic ideals.
11. It believes in 'non-violent' means to achieve its goals.
12. It stresses decentralization in administration and planning.
13. Its goal is '*Sarvodaya Samaj*'.

## 21.6 EDUCATIONAL IMPLICATIONS OF SOCIALISM

*Socialism and Aims of Education*: Following are the aims of education for the establishment of the socialist, secular, democratic and modern Indian society.

1. Development of democratic outlook.
2. Development of socialist values.
3. Development of secular values.
4. Providing equality of opportunity to all for their all-round development and welfare.
5. Rapid expansion of educational facilities to all areas.
6. Developing values like '*Dharma*', dignity of labour, non-violence, unselfishness and selfless service etc.

### Socialism and Curricula (Curriculum)

1. Topics like democracy, duties of citizens, equality, freedom, rights, secularism, socialism, social reform movements, non-violence, etc. to be included in various subjects.
2. Group activities like debates, discussions, social service camps, social surveys, '*Shramdhan*' etc. to be organised.
3. Inclusion of Socially Useful Productive Work (SUPW) as an essential component of the school curriculum to be the key-note of the curriculum.
4. Emphasis to be laid on polytechnic education, vocational and professional courses.
5. Introduction of Information Technology and its effective use would enable to students to do well in the age of modernisation.

### Socialism and Methods of Teaching

1. Emphasis to be laid on group methods of teaching, seminars, projects, etc.
2. Self-discovery methods to be encouraged.

### Socialism and Control of Education

Education in India is a concurrent subject. The Central and State Government take several measures for the promotion of education. Local bodies are also responsible for education especially at the primary stage.

The Central Government has established several autonomous educational organisations and institutions to provide guidance in educational matters and also to run educational institutions.

The State Governments pass several Acts to regulate education.

**Socialism and Textbooks**

Several autonomous and semi-independent textbooks Bureaus and Boards have been established by States. These aim at providing books at reasonable prices. Textbooks at the primary and middle stages by large have been nationalised.

## 21.7 SOCIALISM AND EQUALISATION OF EDUCATIONAL OPPORTUNITIES

Following steps are being taken for providing equal opportunities.

(i) Tuition free education to economically and socially weaker sections of students.
(ii) Free textbooks and uniforms to weaker sections.
(iii) Award of scholarships.
(iv) Grant of loans.
(v) Admission facilities and special quotas for weaker sections, Scheduled Castes and Tribes
(vi) Hostel facilities.
(vii) Day-study centres.
(viii) 'Earn and Learn' facilities.
(ix) Special facilities for girls.
(x) Transport facilities.
(xi) Special stress on the education of the backward areas, hill areas, slum areas etc.
(xii) Running of government schools, local bodies schools.
(xiii) Common and neighbourhood school system at various places.

# 22

# Democracy

## 22.1 MEANING OF DEMOCRACY

*Democracy as way of life.* Etymologically the term democracy is derived from two Greek words namely, '*Demos*' and '*Krators*'. '*Demos*' means the 'the people' and '*Krators*' means 'power'. Thus democracy means 'power of the people'. Aristotle defined democracy as 'a government of many'. In the words of Abraham Lincoln, "Democracy is government of the people, by the people and for the people." Lord Bryce defines democracy as, "It is a government in which the will of the majority of qualified citizens rests." For Deway, "Democracy denotes a mode of government, a specified practice in selecting officials and regulating their conduct as officials." All these definitions are political in nature. These do not reflect the basic ideals and values for which democracy as a form of government functions.

A very appropriate definition of democracy is found in the observations of the University Education Commission. According to the Commission, "Democracy is the way of life and not a mere political arrangement. It is based on the principles of equal freedom and equal right for its members, regardless of race, religion, sex, occupation or economic stature." Thus 'equal freedom' and 'equal right' are the watchwords of democracy.

According to Henderson, "Democracy is based on the following assumptions :

1. Infinite value and worth of human personality.
2. Belief that are capable of managing their own affairs.
3. The affairs include promotion of the welfare of all.
4. For managing affairs, the people should have the freedom.

## 22.2 SIGNIFICANCE OF EACH LETTER OF THE WORD DEMOCRACY

The spirit of democracy as a way of life and a form of government may be explained by assigning ideals and values to each letter of democracy.

'D' stands for — Division of authority and power
— Dignity and worth of the individual.
— Duty–Consciousness.

'E' stands for — Equality.
— Ethical values.

| | |
|---|---|
| 'M' stands for | — Mutual understanding . |
| | — Mass education. |
| 'O' stands for | — Objective attitude. |
| | — Open mindness. |
| 'C' stands for | — Cooperation. |
| | — Classless society. |
| 'R' stands for | — Rational thinking. |
| | — Respect for others' ideas |
| | — Right relationship between rights and responsibilities. |
| 'A' stands for | — 'Appreciation of others' culture and belief. |
| | — Adult franchise. |
| | — Adult education. |
| 'C' stands for | — Caring and concern for others. |
| | — Constructive and creative attitude. |
| 'Y' stands for | — Yarning for living and walking together. |

## 22.2 DIMENSIONS OF DEMOCRACY

| 1 *Economic Dimension* | 2 *Educational Dimension* | 3 *Ethical Dimension* | 4 *Political Dimension* | 5 *Social Dimension* |
|---|---|---|---|---|
| This implies<br>1. Economic equality as far as possible.<br>2. Satisfaction of the basic needs of the people.<br>3. Equality of opportunity in undertaking economic activities.<br>4. Freedom from want | This implies<br>1. Equal opportunities in obtaining education<br>2. Maximum development of the individual<br>3. Sharing of responsibility in running the educational system | This implies faith that an individual is entitled to full respect for his individuality | This includes<br>1. Participation of the people in government.<br>2. Adult franchise.<br>3. Division of authority. | This implies equality of all irrespective of caste, class, colour, creed, sex and wealth. |

*Fig. 22.1 Illustrating various Dimensions of Democracy*

## 22.4 DEMOCRACY AND EDUCATION

The University Education Commission has explained the relationship of democracy and education in these words, "Democracy affirms that each individual is a unique adventure of life. The function of education is guidance of this adventure for the realisation of the potentialities of each individual."

Prof. Dewey in his book "*Democracy and Education*" has explained ve clearly the relationship between education and democracy in these words, "A society which makes provisions for participation in its good of all its members on equal terms and which secures flexible adjustment of its institutions through the interaction of the different forms of associated life is a democratic society. Such a society must have a type of education which gives individuals a personal interest in social changes without introducing disorder."

Prof. K.G. Saiyidain explains the functions of education and democracy in his book *Education, Culture and Social Order* in these words, "Education must be so oriented that it will develop the basic qualities of character which are necessary for the functioning of the democratic life." He lists the following qualities to be developed by education for the democratic life :

(i) Passion for social justice.
(ii) Quickening of social conscience.
(iii) Tolerance for cultural and intellectual differences in others.
(iv) Development of love for work.
(v) Deep and true love for the country.

## 22.5 IMPORTANCE OF EDUCATION IN DEMOCRACY

The following points may be mentioned regarding the importance of education in democracy :

1. Education enables the individual to understand his rights and duties.
2. Education develops the qualities of brotherhood, appreciation of other's point of view etc. – qualities essential for the successful functioning of democracy.
3. Education develops dignity of labour and a sense of personal worth.
4. Education broadens the mental horizon of the individual.
5. Education develops values of equality and fair-mindedness – important elements of democratic outlook.
6. Education helps to evaluate the policies and programmes of political parties.
7. Education helps to evaluate the merits and demerits of candidates contesting elections.
8. Education helps to prevent exploitation.
9. Education helps to develop qualities of followership and leadership.

## 22.6 SIGNIFICANT IMPLICATIONS OF DEMOCRACY IN EDUCATION

1. Education is essential to a citizen to function as a voter and a legislator.
2. Education is essential to a citizen to understand and discern intelligently the programmes of political parties.
3. Education is necessary to enable the citizens to prepare themselves for securing the means of livelihood without which a democracy is meaningless.

4. Education is essential to develop such attitudes, skills and knowledge which enable the citizens to participate intelligently in the social and other processes.
5. Education enables an individual to understand the laws of the land and their implications.
6. The right to education becomes a fundamental right in a genuine democracy.
7. The right to vote and the right to participate intelligently in shaping the policies of the State demands not merely the right to education but the right to education in the language of the people.
8. Education for all is a natural corollary of a democratic set-up.

## 22.7 VARIOUS DIMENSIONS OF EDUCATION AND DEMOCRACY

Democracy in Education

| 1 | 2 | 3 | 4 | 5 | 6 |
|---|---|---|---|---|---|
| Democracy and Aims of Education | Democracy and Curriculum | Democracy and Teaching-Learning Process | Democracy and Discipline | Democracy and the Teacher | Democracy and Educational Administration, Organisation and Supervision |

*Fig. 22.2: Illustrating Dimensions of Education Influenced by Democracy*

1. *Democracy and Aims of Education*: The *Educational Policies Commission of the U.S.A.* Laid down the four broad objectives of education in accordance with democracy.

a) The objective of self-realisation.
b) The objective of human relations.
c) The objective of economic efficiency.
d) The objective of civic responsibility.

*The Secondary Education Commission in India* included the development of democratic citizenship as one of the aims of education. Other aims are : improvement of vocational efficiency, development of personality and development of qualities for leadership.

Development of intellectual aim in a democracy implies the following aims :

(i) Education should aim at developing the skill of clear thinking in the students.
(ii) Education should aim at developing open-mindedness in the students.
(iii) Education should aim at enabling the student to express themselves clearly both in speech and writing.
(iv) Education should aim developing the ability to participate freely in discussion and exchange of ideas.

The moral aim of education for democracy implies tolerance, discipline and co-operation etc. and above all development of character.

The social aim of education in a democracy implies:

a) Art of living gracefully in a community.
b) Passion for social justice.
c) Development of true patriotism.
d) Development of internationalism.

2. *Democracy and Curriculum:* Curriculum in a democracy should be based on the following principles :

(i) Principles of relating content to the aspirations and needs of the people.
(ii) Principle of diversification i.e. providing courses according to the aptitudes and interest of the students.
(iii) Principle of vocational efficiency i.e. curriculum should prepare for a vocation so that children become socially useful productive individuals.
(iv) Principle of child-centred education i.e. maximum opportunities should be provided to the child to remain active and participate effectively in the teaching-learning process.

3. *Democracy and Methods of Teaching-Learning:* Methods of teaching-learning should be activity-centred, child-centred and life-centred.

Following are the important methods of teaching-learning visualised in a democracy.

(i) Group work.
(ii) Project method.
(iii) Socialised recitation.
(iv) Survey method.
(v) Enquiry methods and techniques.

4. *Democracy and Discipline:* Discipline in a democratic educational set up implies self-discipline and social discipline. Attempts are made to provide social situations which encourage and direct the impulses of the pupils in common purposes and co-operative activities.

Students are provided opportunities to conduct some of their own affairs. Student council, class committees etc. are formed.

Provision for participation in a number of co-curricular activities – cultural, civic, social etc. is made so that students learn to work in groups and appreciate the values of co-operation, tolerance etc.

5. *Democracy and the Teacher:* A teacher can play an important role in developing democratic attitudes, ideals and values in the students. He, therefore, himself should posses a democratic outlook. He should give due regard to the individuality of the students. He should appreciate the individual differences of the students and accordingly arrange his teaching-learning.

6. *Democracy and School Administration:* There should be a proper

division of powers and responsibilities at various levels. 'Decentralisation' and 'human relationships' should be the watchwords of educational administration.

7. *Democracy and the School:* Thomas H. Briggs has observed that "School is truly the guardian of democracy."

William Kilpatru assigns the following functions to school in democracy.

1. To give its pupils an intelligent understanding of the issues of democracy.
2. To make its pupils well disposed towards democracy as a way of life.
3. To make its pupils skilful in the co-operative activities through which democracy must function.

(*Details regarding the functions of the school are given in a separate Chapter*).

## 22.8 MEASURES FOR EDUCATING AND TRAINING THE STUDENTS FOR DEMOCRACY

1. Introduction of self-government in school.
2. Organisations of group activities for providing opportunities to develop democratic values.
3. Use of democratic methods of instruction for allowing them simple scope for free expression.
4. Provision for manual work for developing dignity of labour.
5. Giving equal treatment to all students, irrespective of any consideration.
6. Recognising the individuality of each student.
7. Providing opportunities for social service.
8. Organisation of camps.
9. Organising programmes of community kitchen where possible.
10. Arranging hostel facilities where feasible.
11. Making equal opportunities for admission.
12. Encouraging different hobbies.
13. Organising visits to legislatures.

# 23

# National Integration and the Role of the Teacher

## 23.1 MEANING OF NATIONAL INTEGRATION

National integration touches almost all points of national life. It is a 'feeling of oneness' or 'we feeling' and a feeling of solidarity which transcends all cultural or group differences and synthesises the different castes; linguistic, regional and religious communities emotionally into a compact whole. It binds the citizens in a unity. It checks narrow tendencies which are a great hindrance to national unity and national progress National integration is the 'unity of heart and mind'.

National integration implies :

1. A feeling of brotherhood in the minds of the citizens of a country.
2. A feeling of cohesion.
3. A feeling of harmony.
4. A feeling of loyalty to the country.
5. A feeling of patriotism.
6. A feeling of oneness.
7. A feeling of solidarity.
8. A feeling of tolerance, especially tolerance of others' beliefs etc.
9. A feeling of unity of the country.
10. We feeling and not 'I feeling'.

## 23.2 WHY NATIONAL INTEGRATION

We frequently notice incidents of disputes, disturbances and even bloodshed in various parts of the country in the name of caste, language, region or religion etc. Demonstrations and strikes in the interest of one particular group take place which paralyse economic and industrial activities. There is great economic loss. Educational institutions on very narrow considerations are closed for a number of days. Even the work of State Assemblies and Parliament comes to a standstill.

The narrow considerations pose a threat to national unity also.

History teaches us that all types of development in art and culture, philosophy and literature etc. is possible only when there is peace in the country.

Internal disputes and rivalries in the past failed to check the foreign powers. It was the lack of national unity that was responsible for the conquest of India by the British. The Jats, the Marathas, the Nizams, the Rajputs, the Rohilas and the Sikhs etc. failed to unite against the foreign aggression.

Lack of national unity is likely to create hindrances in achieving our ideals and values of democracy, secularism and socialism enshrined in our Constitution.

## 23.3 HINDRANCES AND OBSTACLES IN NATIONAL INTEGRATION

Following are the main factors responsible for separatist tendencies. These create hindrances in national integration.

1. Casteism
2. Classism
3. Communalism
4. Economic disparities
5. Educational disparities
6. Illiteracy
7. Ignorance
8. Linguism
9. Localism
10. Narrow political loyalties
11. Over ambitiousness of some leaders
12. Favourtism
13. Poverty
14. Provincialism
15. Regionalism
16. Religious fanaticism
17. Reservations and quotas
18. Sectorianism
19. Selfishness
20. Unemployment
21. Untouchability

It may be stressed that these factors singly or jointly create unfavourable situations to the promotion of national integration.

The Education Commission1964-66 pointed out that old values which held society together have been disappearing. Their place has not taken by a new sense of social responsibility.

## 23.4 ROLE OF EDUCATION IN NATIONAL INTEGRATION

The Emotional Integration Committee, appointed in 1961 by the Ministry of Education, Government of India considered various aspects of national integration and gave valuable suggestions. The Committee is also known as Sampurnand Committee after the name of its Chairman.

Regarding the role of education in national integration, the Committee stated, "Education can play a vital role in strengthening emotional integration. Education should not only aim at imparting knowledge but should also develop all aspects of a student's personality. It should broader his outlook, foster a feeling of oneness and nationalism and a spirit of sacrifice and tolerance so that the narrow group interests are submerged in the larger interest of the country."

Dr. Radhakrishnan explained the role of education in emotional integration as, "If India is to remain free, united and democratic, education should train people for unity and not localism, for democracy and not dictatorship."

## 23.5 WAYS AND MEANS OF PROMOTING NATIONAL INTEGRATION THROUGH EDUCATIONAL PROGRAMMES

The Sampurnanand Committee made the following suggestions for strengthening emotional and national integration.

1. *Reorganisation of Curriculum* (i) Stress should be laid on the inclusion of material that promotes values of secularism, socialism and democracy.

(ii) Achievements of different leaders belonging to all sections of the society should be highlighted.

(iii) A core curriculum including the freedom movement should be included.

(iv) *Co-curricular Activities.* Co-curricular activities like scouts and guides, student camps, student tours, community service should be organised.

(v) *Teaching of Social Studies.* In every lesson, as far as possible, emphasis should be laid on the interdependence of each region in various fields like agriculture, commerce and industry.

(vi) *Textbooks.* Textbooks should be prepared in such a way that they do not include any material which in any form is likely to offend any section of the society. They should not create any kind of prejudice in the minds of the students.

(vi) *Language and Script.* It is necessary that in implementing a language policy, the rights of the minority languages should be kept in view.

(viii) *Uniform for School Children.* A common uniform for the students in the entire country may be prescribed.

(ix) *Singing of national anthem.* Children should be taught to show due respect to the national anthem. It should be ensured that while singing the anthem, students behave in a disciplined manner. Its meaning and significance should be properly explained.

(x) *Reverence for the National Flag.* Students should be told the significance and history of the national flag. An attitude of reverence for it should be inculcated in the students.

(xi) *Celebration of National Days*. The students, the teachers and the other staff should participate in the celebration of National Days i.e. January 26, August 15 and October 2.

(xii) *Special Talks on the Unity of the Country*. Topics dealing with the unity of the country should be taken up in the morning assembly from time to time.

(xiii) *Admission Policy*. Domicile restrictions on admission in educational institutions should be removed.

(xiv) *Recognition of Institutions*. Only those institutions should be recognised that work for national unity.

(xv) *Common School System*. A common school system should be adopted. This is likely to remove class distinctions.

(xvi) *Community Development Programmes*. Students should be provided opportunities to participate in community service programmes

## 23.6 ROLE OF THE TEACHERS IN PROMOTING NATIONAL INTEGRATION

Teachers can play an important role in developing values of national integration among the students. Following are the important measures which can prove very helpful in this regard:

1. Teachers should set ideal examples of national integration through their behaviour, ways of thinking and doing things.
2. Teachers should present historical facts in an impartial and objective manner.
3. They should not discriminate students on the basis of caste, colour, language, region or religion.
4. They should lay balanced stress on the achievements of great leaders belonging to different communities and regions etc.
5. In Geography and Indian Economics, the importance of interdependence of different regions and States should be highlighted.
6. All possible efforts should be made to inculcate an attitude of rational thinking in the students.
7. Community dinner, camps, educational excursions and tours may be organised so that students get opportunities to appreciate the concept of unity and diversity.
8. Deeds of patriotism of great persons belonging to all communities should be suitably explained.

## 23.7 PLEDGE FOR NATIONAL INTEGRATION

The Emotional Integration Committee recommend that the following pledge should be taken by the school community from time to time.

"*India is my country, all Indians are my brothers and sisters. I love my country, and I am proud of its rich and varied heritage. I shall always strive to be worthy of it.*

*I shall give my parents, teachers and all elders respect and treat everyone with courtesy. I shall be kind to animals.*

*To my country and my people, I pledge my devotion. In their well-being and prosperity alone lies my happiness."*

*Concluding Observations.* National integration is a challenge. It is true that educational institutions can play an important role in inculcating ideals and values of national integration among the students. Nevertheless, it is more important that leaders, especially political and religious, who are trend setters in national life, must rise above petty considerations and set high examples of national integration through their daily actions. India has already paid a heavy price in the division of the country on account of lack of national integration. History should not be allowed to repeat itself.

# 24

# Socialisation and Education

## 24.1 MEANING OF SOCIALISATION

Socialisation means the development of social behaviour. This social behaviour is developed through the process of social interaction among individuals. Social interaction must take place in a suitable social environment and this environment for the child is provided basically by the school.

Following definitions of prominent thinkers help us to understand the various dimensions of socialisation.

Drever thinks that "Socialisation is a process by which the individual is adopted to his social environment and becomes a recognised, co-operating and efficient member of it."

Bogardus defines socialisation as the "process whereby persons learn to behave dependently together for human welfare."

Gandhiji observe, "I value individual freedom but you must not forget than man is essentially a social being and socialisation is the process of making a social being."

According to Guskin and Guskin , "Socialisation is the process by which an individual learns the behaviour, the values and the expectation of others that enable him to take on particular roles in society."

Havighurst and Newgarton are of the view that "Socialisation is the process by which children learn the ways of their society and make those ways part of their personality".

Mac Iver writes, "Socialisation and Individualisation are the two sides of a single process."

Ross observes, "Socialisation is the development of we-feeling in associates and the growth in their capacity and will to act together."

According to Dewey, socialisation is a process by which the individual becomes a 'socially efficient individual'.

Cook regards socialisation as a process as a result of which individuals take on themselves the various social learnings, social roles and developmental tasks.

Moore and Cole point out that it is through group relations that an individual is socialised and he becomes aware of what it means to work with a purpose and he identifies himself with the group.

Margaret Mead and several other scholars regard socialisation 'as a process of acculturation'. Acculturation implies acquiring the culture of the society. Culture refers to the total way of life of people. Thus culture includes attitudes, beliefs, customs, folkways, habits, morals, traditions, knowledge, arts, law etc. of a group or a society.

In simple words, it may be stated that socialisation is a process in which an individual identifies himself with the society. An individual learns social attitudes, social skills and social knowledge which lead to his social maturity and social adjustment.

## 24.2 IMPORTANCE AND OBJECTIVE OF SOCIALISATION

Man becomes a human being only as a member of society. By nature, he cannot live alone or in isolation. He is compelled by his biological and social requirements to live in a group or society. Even a '*Sanayasi*' living in a cave or a very isolated place needs some company at least for some time to survive. Each of us is a social product. Therefore, the main objective of socialisation is to enable the individual to conform to the norms of the group or the society to which he belongs.

## 24.3 MAIN CHARACTERISTICS OF THE PROCESS OF SOCIALISATION

1. Socialisation is a continuous process.
2. Socialisation is a visible as well as non-visible process.
3. Socialisation is a deliberate and also an unconscious process.
4. A democratic approach to socialisation is the appropriate approach. Autocratic approach leads to regimentation.
5. The process of socialisation aims at enabling the individual to become a self-realised socially useful member of the society.
6. Socialisation improves the individual as well as the society.
7. There are several agencies and groups which are engaged in the process of socialisation of the individual—the family, the peer group, the club, the media and the school. But the school is the most important agency of socialisation.

## 24.4 EDUCATION AND SOCIALISATION

A noted French educational socialogist Emile Durkheim has explained the role of education in the socialisation of the child in these words, "Education is the influence exercised by adult generation on those that are not yet ready for social life. Its object is to arouse and to develop in the child a certain number of physical, intellectual and moral traits that are demanded of him by the society. More briefly, education is a socialisation of the young generation". He further explains that education is the means by which every society prepares, within children, the essential conditions of its very existence. The schools, colleges and other educational institutions have the responsibility of socialising the child by inculcating in him appropriate behaviour patterns, knowledge, attitudes and skills so that he adapts himself to a democratic, secular, socialist and modern society.

## 24.5 DIFFICULT TASK OF SOCIALISATION OF THE CHILD

Earlier the society was very simple. There were only a few well-established roles for the individual. He did not face much stress and strain. Family was an important agency that enabled the individual to play his role. School was expected to teach knowledge of 3 R's i.e. reading, writing and arithmetic and this was considered adequate for adapting an individual to his environment.

Now the society has become very complex. An individual is expected to acquire various types of knowledge, skills and attitudes to enable him to adjust himself to the environment.

## 24.6 ROLE OF THE SCHOOL IN THE SOCIALISATION OF THE CHILD: IMPORTANT PROGRAMMES OF SOCIALISATION

The school is one of the most important social institutions of the society. It has its disposal several means of socialising the child. In fact each aspect of school programme has some potential influencing the child. Through the contents of the curriculum of various subjects, co-curricular programmes, group life in the form of class and the interaction of students with teachers, the school socialises the child.

Following are the important measures of socialising the child :

1. The adoption of the common school system is the most effective way of socialising the child.
2. School curriculum should at every stage lay stress upon the unity of the different sections of the society.
3. Interdependence of States/regions should be brought out clearly so that the students evaluate the values of co-operation.
4. The school programme should be enriched with numerous curricular and co-curricular programmes in which children participate interact, co-operate and learn to live work together.
5. Children may be taken from time to time to places of cultural, economic, geographical, historical etc. to enable them to understand the contribution of various places to emotional unity and oneness of the country.
6. Exhibitions on 'know your country' may be organised.
7. Children should be acquainted with the work of great men of all regions.
8. Children should be provided opportunities to participate in social events like celebration of birthdays of leaders.
9. Children should be told about the socially accepted institutions and

norms of the society.

10. The introduction of common school dress, common lunch etc. in the schools will save children of the lower middle family from suffering the agony due to the inflated ego of the children of the well-to-do families.
11. Communities activities like common meals, camps, social service, etc. should be frequently organised.
12. The mechanism of praise and blame, reward and punishment should be carefully used to socialise the child.
13. The teachers should demonstrate social and democratic outlook.
14. School should become the centre of the community for various purposes.
15. Group singing on national themes should be popularised.
16. Special lectures on socialisation should be arranged.

## 24.7 ROLE OF THE TEACHER IN THE SOCIALISATION OF THE CHILD

The teachers can exist a great influence on the child in inculcating attitudes and values of socialisation in various ways. The first step is that they should give due respect to the personality of the child. They should encourage the children to mix up in inter-caste rather than intra-caste and inter-regional rather than the intra-regional groups. They should not show any favour to the students belonging to upper class. They should try to understand the limitations of the students of the backwards classes. Any impression of discrimination should not be allowed to develop in the minds of the students. They should always impress upon the students that there are no high or low castes. They should encourage the students to develop friendship without any class bias. They should refrain from projecting their class images on the students. The must make all possible efforts to provide a healthy social environment in which students imbibe desirable values of equality, freedom, patriotism etc.

*Summing up.* Essential conditions for making the process of socialisation most effective in the school are :

1. A democratic social climate in the school.
2. Effective inter-personal relationships.
3. Motivating teaching-learning situations.
4. Harmonious school-community inter-relationships.
5. Student involvement and participation in school management.
6. Rich programme of co-curricular and group activities.

# 25

# Social Change, Nature, Process, Causes and Effects

## 25.1 MEANING OF SOCIAL CHANGE

In simple words, social change implies change in the social structure and functions of the various units which form society. Social structure includes social institutions like the family, the marriage system, caste system, educational institutions, customs, manners, literacy forms, language, dress and food habits etc.

Kingslay Davis defines social change as "only alternations as occur in social organisation, i.e. in the structure and functions of society."

B.B. Mathur explains social change as, "Social change refers to the modifications in the organisation and behaviour of the group as expressed in its laws, customs, modes and beliefs."

According to B. Kuppasmwami, "When we speak of social change we might assert that there is some change in social behaviour and in the social structure."

Henry Johnson would like to include five kinds of charges in social change. These are as under :

1. Change in social values.
2. Institutional changes.
3. Change in distribution of possessions and rewards.
4. Change in personnel.
5. Change in abilities and attitudes of personnel.

According to Mac Iver and Page, "Social change is a process responsive to many types of changes—changes in the man-made conditions of living, changes in the attitude of man and changes that go beyond human control to the biological and physical nature."

Delbert C. Miller observes, "Social change refers to a pattern of social relationship in a given setting."

## 25.2 NATURE AND CHARACTERISTICS OF SOCIAL CHANGE

Social change is inevitable. Society is dynamic. It is in a constant flux. Whether we want a change, whether we like it or not, times are moving fast. Change is the law of nature.

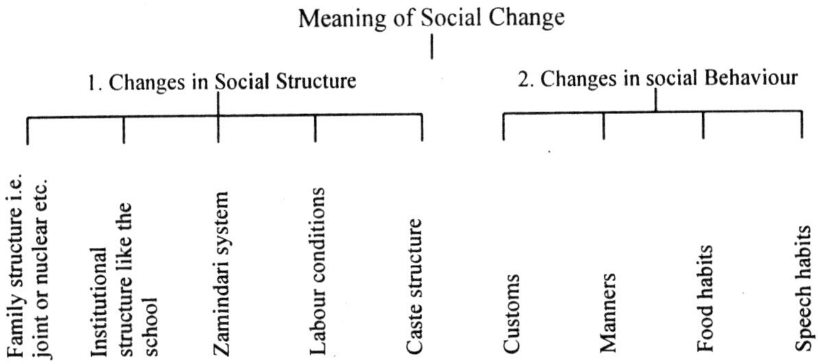


*Fig. 25.1: Illustrative Areas of Changes in Social Structure*

(*Note* : The list is not exhaustive. Only some examples of various areas of social life are mentioned)

Following characteristics of the change reflect the nature of social change:

1. Social change may be sudden, slow or rapid.
2. All aspects or elements of the social structure may not change.
3. Each aspect of social change may not change with same intensity.
4. Social change may mean discarding some old things or elements.
5. Social change may mean addition of new things or elements.
6. Social change may be brought through non-violent or violent means.
7. Social change may be outcome of only one factor or number of factors.
8. Social change may be for the good of the society or otherwise.

## 25.3 PROCESS OF SOCIAL CHANGE

Process of social change may be classified in a number of ways.

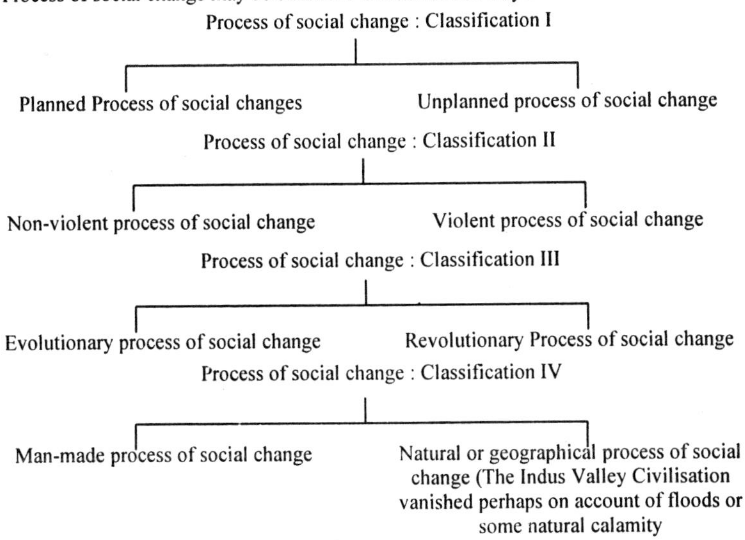


*Fig. 25.2: Illustration of the Process of Social Change*

S.P. Ruhela mentions the most significant processes of social change as under :

1. Westernization.
2. Industrialization.
3. Urbanization.
4. Sanskritization.
5. Secularization.
6. Social Mobility.
7. Politicization.
8. Hinduization.
9. Indianization.
10. Modernization.

A brief analysis of each process of social change is given here.

*Westernization.* This is the process of social change in India which has influenced culture, living styles, values etc. of the Indian people as a result of western impact, especially during the British rule.

*Industrialization.* Industrialization is the process of social change which has given rise to crimes, drinking, trade union activities, growth of slums, educational institutions, banks, roads etc.

*Urbanization.* This is the process of social change which has led to continuous migration from rural areas to towns. This results in the same social problems as industrialization.

*Sanskritization.* In this process, low caste Hindu or tribe or other group attempts to change its customs, ideologies, rituals and ways of life in the direction of a high caste.

*Secularization.* Movements like Arya Samaj and Brahmo Samaj have promoted the process of secularisation. It is a process of change which views events, things and ideals from a rational point of view.

*Social Mobility.* Social mobility is the process of change in status.

*Politicalization.* It is the process of social change through the spread of knowledge about political ideologies, parties and leaders. In this process of social change, people become aware of their rights and responsibilities.

*Hinduization.* This process of social changes consists of the attempts of many tribal communities in India to enter the broad field of Hindu social structure. Also attempts are made to popularise Hindu beliefs and customs etc.

*Indianization.* This is the process of social change in which several people belonging to difficult faiths, tend to identify themselves with Indian culture. In several catholic churches in South India and elsewhere, it is observed that many nuns wear Indian dresses—Sarees and blouses. Worship is also done in Indian style. Lamps, candles, incense, '*prasad*' etc. are used in the Indian style. Instead of English, regional languages are used in religious songs and prayers.

*Modernization.* Modernization is a process of social change which emphasises rational, secular and scientific approach in one's life.

A persual of above would indicate that processes of social changes cannot be divided into water tight compartments. They are inter-related.

Sometimes it becomes very difficult to make a clear-cut distinction between process, cause and effect of social change. All are inter-related.

## 25.4 CAUSES/FACTORS OF SOCIAL CHANGE

There are a large number of causes or factors that bring about social changes. Sometimes even one cause may become responsible for social change. At other times, some factors or causes jointly act in such a way that social change becomes inevitable. Again it is stressed that the processes, causes and effects of social change work simultaneously.

Ideas and ideologies of great leaders have played an important role in social change. The influence of prominent personalities like Marx and Lenin in Russia, Mao Tse Tung in China and Gandhiji in India are some of the well-known examples of modern history.

Ideas like 'Liberty', 'Equality' and 'Fraternity' proved great forces in giving birth to French Revolution which in turn immensely changed the French society.

Industrial Revolution resulted in marked social changes.

The American War of Independence was the outcome of the social and economic causes. This brought about revolutionary changes in the social life of the people of America.

**Causes of Social Change**

| 1 | 2 | 3 | 4 | 5 | 6 | 7 | 8 | 9 | 10 | 11 | 12 | 13 |
|---|---|---|---|---|---|---|---|---|---|---|---|---|
| Climatic and weather causes of social change | Demographic causes of social change | Economic causes of social change | Educational causes of social change | Industrialisation causes of social changes | Legislation as a cause of social change | Natural causes of social change | Philosophical causes of social change | Political causes of social change | Religious causes of social change | Urbanisation causes of social change | Westernisation causes of social change | Scientific and Technological causes of social change |

*Fig. 25.3: Illustration of Causes of Social Change (See also 26.1)*

## 25.5 EFFECTS OF SOCIAL CHANGES

Following are some of the examples of marked social changes.

1. Climatic factors led to the disappearance of the Indus Valley. The entire civilisation collapsed and new civilisation came up.
2. The British rulers introduced a new system of education which changed the etiquettes, habits and manners etc. of the several sections of Indian society. New dresses emerged.
3. Lack of occupational opportunities in the villages led to migration of people to towns. Several slums in the towns changed the life style of the people.
4. Natural factors like earth-quakes, droughts and floods etc. may people render homeless and force the people to change their life style.
5. Political factors like the rise of Communism, Fascism, Nazism entirely changed the social structure of several societies.
6. Religious and social reformers become responsible for changes in rites, customs, modes of worship etc.
7. Scientific and technological causes exert far-reaching influence on social changes.
8. Political change like the end of foreign rule in India altogether changed the social outlook of the people. New aspirations, ideals and values like democracy, secularism and socialism became the cornerstones of social life.
9. Religious reformers like Gautama Buddha and Vardhamana Mahavir greatly influenced the social life of the people.
10. Religious and social reformers like Swami Dayanand and Swami Vivekananda of the 19th century made the people of India conscious of their social responsibility.
11. Mahatma Gandhi's work touched almost all dimensions of life including social.

# 26

# Education as a Means and Product of Social Change

## 26.1 EDUCATION AS A MEANS OF SOCIAL CHANGE

It is not without reason that education has received great attention at the hands of leaders, religious and social reformers. They have strongly advocated the use of education as the most important agent/means or instrument of bringing about changes in the society. Education is not for the sake of learning or knowledge only.

The British rulers in India introduced a system of education in India which would enable the Indians to imbibe British culture, and manners. Lord Macaulay, the architect of the British System of education in India, in a letter to his father in 1836 wrote, "Hindus are much influenced with education. There is no Hindu who may keep faith in his religion after studying English." Earlier in 1835 in his Minute on Education which was accepted by Lord William Bentinck as the basis of the system of education in India, Lord Macaulay had written, "We must at present do our best to form a class of persons, Indian in blood and colour, but English in taste, in opinions, in morals and intellect." This indicates the importance of education as an agent or means of social change. Religious and social reformers Raja Rammohan Roy, Swami Dayananda and Vivekananda considered education as the potent weapon of social reform. Freedom fighters, political leaders and statesmen like Gandhiji laid great stress on education for improving the economic and social conditions of the people.

Gandhiji wanted his scheme of Basic Education to be the main instrument of social change. In his words, "The Basic School should be the searhead of a non-violent social revolution."

The well-known American philosopher and educationist, John Dewey observes, "Education is the fundamental method of social progress and reform. This it does in two ways : by guiding children towards new values and by assisting the development of intelligence in individual children and increasing society' potential for its own transformation".

J.S. Brubacher has explained the role of education in the process of social change in these words." If the lamp of reason is not lit or if the light is blown out, it but remains to struggle. When rational processes are put aside, it is only too likely that clubs and machine guns will become the social arbiters. Bullet will replace ballots."

The report of the Education Commission 1964-66 begins with these words, "The destiny of India is being shaped in her classrooms. This we believe is no mere rhetoric." The Commission further observed that if social change is to be achieved on a grand scale, there is one instrument and one instrument only that can be used is 'Education'.

## 26.2 BROAD AREAS OF SOCIAL CHANGE AND TRANSFORMATION THROUGH EDUCATION

*Developing Awareness.* Education is considered as an important means of making people aware of their weakness and enabling them to gain necessary knowledge for bringing about social changes in a non-violent, rational and scientific manner.

*Developing Appropriate Values.* Education is expected to change the attitudes and values of the people to create in them necessary motivation for social change.

*Realisation of Important Goals.* Education is considered to be of immense help in realising the national goals of social change like democracy, secularism and socialism.

*Providing Necessary Skills.* It is generally accepted that education will provide necessary training in skills and occupations so as to produce competent personnel needed for manning the different jobs in agricultural, business, commerce, educational, industrial and research establishments etc. in accordance with the requirements of social change.

## 26.3 FUNCTIONS OF EDUCATION IN SOCIAL CHANGE

According to H.C. Dent, a national system of education has two functions to perform: a traditional preservation function and a growth facilitating function. In a time of social flux both these functions become overwhelmingly important.

Some scholars are of the view that education has to perform the following three functions :

1. Conservation of traditional heritage.
2. Adjustment and growth of the present society.
3. Creation of a suitable base for new order and new ideas which should become an instrument of social change in the future.

For performing the above mentioned social functions, education has to establish the following linkages :

1. Education should link the past with existing realities of the present national identity and the emerging future goals and aspirations of the society.
2. For achieving meaningful national integration, education should establish proper linkage of the urban elite and the rural people. This

task can be performed through providing equal opportunities for education. Programmes of formal and non-formal education through various types of institutions should be organised extensively in the rural areas.

3. There is a need for closer involvement of the students and the community in educational programmes for a developing a 'sense of belonging' and creating necessary enthusiasm for social change.
4. Science and spirituality should be linked together.
5. Formal education should be linked to the world of work and the world of culture to serve the needs of the social change.

## 26.4 EQUALITY OF OPPORTUNITY IN EDUCATION AND SOCIAL CHANGE

Equality of opportunity in education is very helpful in promoting social change. The National Policy of Education 1986 has observed, "The New Policy will lay special emphasis on the removal of disparities and to equalise educational opportunity by attending to the specific needs of those who have been denied equality so far."

## 26.5 AGENCIES OF EDUCATION AND SOCIAL CHANGE

There are a large number of agencies of education – formal, informal and non-formal agencies that can be used effectively for bringing about social change in the society. (The details of these agencies are provided in a separate Chapter).

## 26.6 LIMITATIONS OF EDUCATION IN BRINGING ABOUT CHANGES

1. *Limited Resources*. Adequate funds are needed for providing educational facilities on a large scale. Besides funds are needed for qualitative improvement of education. Ill-equipped individuals cannot bring about social changes in the society.
2. *Attitude of 'No Change'*. People in general and even educated people are reluctant to follow new paths.
3. *Poverty and Ignorance of the Masses*. Percentage of literacy remained very low in India for a number of years. It is only recently that considerable improvement has become visible. Likewise a substantial percentage of people are still below the poverty line. In such a situation, social reforms cannot take place.
4. *Lack of 'Political Will'*. Revolutionary constructive educational reforms could not be carried out on account of the non-availability of necessary political support. Thus education remained ineffective to a considerable extent in playing its role in social change.

## 26.7 TEACHER AS AN AGENT OF SOCIAL CHANGE

Prof. Ottaway is convinced that teachers in the schools can exercise a powerful influence on the community if they choose to do so.

Edmund W. Gordon, an American educationist has explained the role of the teacher in social change in these words, "It is the task of the teacher to educate – to educate for change – to educate through change – to educate for orderly planned revolution".

The McNair Report on the Training of Teachers in England states, "It is a truism to say that every teacher, in however humble a capacity he or she may be serving, is directly involved in the moulding the shape of things to come."

Prof. W.O. Smith of the University of London observed that those who aspire to teach should think about the problems of society and work accordingly.

The role of the teachers in social change in the context of situation in India is questioned by S.P. Ruhela and K.C. Vyas. They advance three important reasons for this (i) Occupation of school teachers has so far not emerged as a profession in the strict sense of the term. (ii) Several teacher's training institutions continue to be disgusting educational slums. (iii) School teacher's professional organisations are not duly committed.

## 26.8 EDUCATION AS A PRODUCT OF SOCIAL CHANGE

Social reformers advocated several reforms for bringing about social change in the society. They called for the removal of superstition and ignorance. They encouraged the people to develop a sense of equality and self-improvement to improve their lot rather than depending upon destiny. They encouraged them to read scriptures and other books to gain knowledge and insight. They promoted rational and scientific thinking.

Swami Dayananda made the Vedas as the basis of social reforms. He asked people to read them thoroughly. For spreading his message, his followers opened a chain of educational institutions in various parts of India.

Raja Rammohan and Swami Vivekananda urged the people to study western science and literature also so that they could acquaint themselves with the progress made by foreign countries.

Thus on account of the emphasis on various aspects of social reforms, people began to realise that it was not possible to develop self-confidence, self-respect and status without obtaining education. The social reformers themselves started educational institutions at various places to create necessary awareness among the people. Therefore, we say that education is the product of social change.

Under the British rule, the social life of the people and especially of higher sections of society was geared to meet the requirements of the colonial power. Accordingly education system became subservient to social change. This necessitated far reaching changes in all dimensions of education—aims of education, contents of education, methods of instruction and discipline etc.

## 26.9 INTERDEPENDENT ROLE OF EDUCATION AND SOCIAL CHANGE

Education is a means as well as a product of social change. This implies that educational changes and social changes are complementary. An educational change leads over time to a social change and social change in turn intensifies and strengthens the social change.

The process of change may be in the reverse order. A social change may lead to an educational change. The educational change in turn may intensify and strengthen social change.

Let us explain the mutual relationship of educational change and social change by taking an example. The spread of education among the Scheduled Castes helped to improve their socio-economic conditions and this brought about some social changes. They became more aware of the importance of education. They began to avail benefits themselves of the opportunities provided in the formal and non-formal system of education.

The constant emphasis on equality by the political and social reformers developed a desire of social change among the Scheduled Castes. They, therefore, saw in education as the promoter of their status. They began to avail themselves of educational opportunities in a great measure. In this way through education the process of social change was intensified and strengthened.

The spread of education among females led to a new awareness among them. Their social status underwent changes. With the improvement in the social status of women they become more conscious of education and this strengthened the process of educational change among them.

# 27

# Role of Education in the Preservation of Cultural Heritage of India

## 27.1 RICH CULTURAL HERITAGE OF INDIA

Sir James, an English thinker has paid the following glowing tribute to the cultural heritage of India :

"At a time when our ancestors were thinking of killing animals or one another, India, perhaps had philosophy which was very nature, also in art, poetry, literature and in fact everything."

About the richness of ancient Indian education (a vital element of culture), Dr. F.W. Thomas, one of the most distinguished indologists has written, "Education is no exotic in India. There is no country where the love of learning had so early an origin or has exercised so lasting and powerful an influence."

Regarding India's cultural contribution to world culture, Swami Vivekananda has remarked, "Even as the gentle dew of the morning blossoms forth the fairest of flowers, the Indian culture has contributed to the thought and culture of the world."

## 27.2 MEANING OF CULTURAL HERITAGE

With a view to understand the meaning of cultural heritage, we may first consider the meaning of the term culture. Culture has been seen and defined differently by scholars. Here only some important definitions of culture are given.

According to Brown, culture cannot be defined. It is better to describe it. He describes culture as :

(i) Culture is a way of life of people.
(ii) Culture is the things they value.
(iii) Culture is their habits.
(iv) Culture is their works of art.
(v) Culture is their music.
(vi) Culture is their history.

In brief Brown regards culture as "What they are, what they do and what they like". This definition is very comprehensive but at the same time very vague.

In the words of Brown, "Culture is composed of integrated customs, traditions and current behaviour patterns of human groups."

Ellwood describes culture as, "Culture includes all man's material civilisation, tools, weapons, clothing, shelter, machines and even systems of industry." This is a very narrow view of culture. It excludes non-material elements of culture.

Mac Iver states, "Culture is the expression of our nature in modes of living and thinking in everyday intercourse in arts, in literature, in religion and enjoyment."

Mathew Arnold views culture as "the best that man has thought and known."

Taylor defines culture as, "The complex whole which includes knowledge, belief, art, morals, law, customs and any other capabilities and habits, acquired by man as a member of society."

According to T.S. Eliot, "The term culture includes all the characteristic activities and interests of the people."

Swami Dayananda considers culture as "acceptance of truth and abandonment of untruth."

Jawaharlal Nehru points out that "Culture is the widening of the mind and of the spirit."

Gandhiji has described culture in these words, "Culture is the foundation, the primary thing. It should show itself in the smallest details of your conduct and personality behaviour, how you sit, how you walk, how you dress etc. Inner culture must be reflected in your speech, the way in which you treat visitors and guests, and behave towards one another and towards your teacher and elders."

The University Education Commission 1948–49 defines culture as "an attitude of mind, an inclination of the spirit."

In simple words, culture is a system or a way of live consisting of ideals and values of the people of a country. It also consists of material things.

Heritage implies something acquired, inherited, and possessed from the predecessor or prodecessors.

Thus Indian cultural heritage means our ideals and values as expressed in our way of life, art and architecture, history and philosophy.

Indian cultural heritage consists of primarily four elements :

1. Common outlook on life – spiritual element.
2. Intellectual influences of various movements – humanism, liberalism, tolerance, universalism.
3. Cultural objects – achievements in arts and sciences.
4. Common ways of living with minor deviations.

## 27.3 CHIEF CHARACTERISTICS OF INDIAN CULTURAL HERITAGE

Indian culture is the outcome of thousands years of interaction. It is the result of mutual give and take. It has assimilated the richness and variety of several cultures. Following are its chief characteristics:

1. Indian culture is very old.
2. Indian culture is very rich.
3. Indian culture is composite.
4. Indian culture denotes unity in diversity.

## 27.4 COMPOSITE CULTURAL HERITAGE OF INDIA

Some people compare Indian culture with a 'banyan tree' which has a number of aerial roots to support it. The different aerial roots are sub-cultural patterns which give strength to the cultural stems of the Indian culture.

Indian culture has been compared by some people with a 'bouquet of flowers' in which we find that flowers of different colours and fragrance are tied together and they present a unique and colourful appearance. Such is the background of our culture.

1. The composite culture of India is the product of interaction and intermingling among the Aryans, the Dravidians, the Sakas, the Kushans, the Huns, the Afghans, the Pathans, and the Mughals. The Britishes also influenced it.
2. It is the product of the contribution of the Hinduism, Buddhism, Jainism and Sikhism. Islam and Christianity also contributed to it.
3. Composite culture of India includes the influences of
   a) The Vedic vision.
   b) Philosophy of Bhagvad Gita.
   c) Bhakti Marg Saints.
   d) Muslim Sufi Saints.
   e) Indian Nationalist Movement.
   f) Gandhian thought.
4. The most illustrious representatives of the composite culture of India of the medieval period and modern period are : Amir Khushan, Sant Kabir, Guru Nanak (13th, 14th and 15–16th century), Prince Dara Shkuh (17th century), Raja Rammohan Roy (19th century) and Mahatma Gandhi (20th century).

Essence of Indian cultural heritage may be expressed as under.

1. '*Sarva-dharma-Sambhave*' – Equal regard for all religions.
2. *Ekam Bhahma Vipra Bahuda Vadanti* – God is one, wise man call Him by different names.
   This is reflected in :
   (i) Composite nature of culture of India.
   (ii) Unity in Diversity.
   (iii) Tolerance.
   (iv) Equality.
   (v) Humanism.
   (vi) Universalism.
   (vii) Spiritualism.

## 27.5 CULTURAL HERITAGE AND EDUCATION

1. *Interrelatedness of Education and Culture:* Education and culture are inter-related. Education is conceived as a systematic effort to maintain a culture. Education is regarded as an effective instrument of social change. Education can impart knowledge, training and skill as well as inculcate new ideas, attitudes and values among the young. It can also preserve past culture and enrich it.

On the other hand, it is the culture in which education germinates and flowers. It is the culture, also upon which education exerts a nourishing influence.

2. *Functions of Education Relating to Cultural Heritage:* The National Policy on Education 1986 and as amended in 1992 has observed that education can and must bring about the fine synthesis between change oriented technologies and country's continuity of cultural heritage. It further observed that de-culturalisation and dehumanisation must be avoided at all costs.

Society is very keen that its education should perform the following functions in relation to its cultural heritage.

1. Education should transmit cultural heritage.
2. Education should improve cultural heritage where needed.
   In short, the students should be taught to get due aspiration from the lofty past heritage, to live amicably in the dynamic and complex present and to face boldly and effectively the challenging of the uncertain future.
3. *Measures through which Education Performs Its Functions Relating to Cultural Heritage.*

The entire process of education must be enriched by cultural content in as many dimensions as possible. Following are the important means in this regard.

1. Contents of school curriculum.
2. Methods of teaching.
3. Co-curricular activities.
4. Textbooks and cultural values.
5. Synthesis of moral and spiritual values with scientific values.
6. Cultural tours.
7. Personality of the teacher.
8. Value education.

*Summing up.* As observed in the National Policy on Education, "In our culturally plural society education should foster universal and external values, oriented towards the unity and integration of our people."

# 28

# Informal, Formal and Non-Formal Agencies

## 28.1 NEED FOR DIFFERENT TYPES OF AGENCIES OF EDUCATION

It is rightly observed by Counts that "The school is but one among many educational agencies." The common belief that education is confined to schools and colleges is not entirely true. No doubt schools and colleges do occupy the most predominant place in the society as educational institutions. But when we use the word 'education' to denote the idea of the all-round development of the personality of the individual, we must recognise the role of other agencies of the society besides the schools and the colleges. Schools function for a short time daily. They function for nearly seven months only during the year. The rest of the time of the students is spent outside the school premises – in the family, in the neighbourhood and with the peer groups. They are influenced by mass communication media and other agencies like class, social education centres, libraries etc.

According to some educators, of all the education we receive, we learn one-fourth from our teachers, one-fourth from books, one-fourth from our colleagues and one-fourth from the overall environment. This indicates the type of education and the multitude of agencies of education.

Education in a wider sense takes place from the womb to the tomb i.e. from the conception to cremation. Education is a life-long process. Education goes on whether we are aware of it or unaware of it. Thus there are several types of social institutions that impart education. There are active as well as passive agencies of education. Likewise there are formal, non-formal and informal agencies of education. They are agencies of education run and managed by the Government. Private agencies are also involved in running different types of educational institutions.

Education imparted in formal agencies is called formal education. Education given in non-formal agencies is called non-formal education. Education received in informal ways is called informal education.

While discussing different types of agencies, it may be borne in mind that teachers are not the only educators. As observed by T. Ramount, "Let us agree to recognise explicitly that in a real sense teachers are not the only educators. In other words it is life that educates, the school provides a part of life's experience".

## 28.2 BROAD CLASSIFICATIONS OF AGENCIES OF EDUCATION

Broad Classification of Agencies of Education : No. 1

| 1. *Formal Agencies of Education* (Active Agencies of Education) | 2. *Informal Agencies of Education* (Passive Agencies of Education) | 3. *Non-formal Agencies of Education* (Active-Passive Agencies of Education) |
|---|---|---|
| 1. School | 1. Art Gallery | 1. Adult and Social Education Centres |
| 2. College | 2. Cinema | 2. Play ground (when regular physical education is organised) |
| 3. Home or Family (in the Past) | 3. Home/Family | 3. Radio (Educational Programmes) |
| 4. Church (in the past) | 4. Library | 4. T.V. (Educational Programmes) |
| 5. Adult school (on regular basis) | 5. Museum | 5. Professional Organisations like Teachers' Associations when they organise seminars, workshops etc. |
| 6. Open school (when contact classes are also arranged) | 6. Peer group | 6. Clubs when educational talks etc. are organised. |
| 7. T.V. (When used as an integral part of the curriculum and pre-telecast and post-telecast teaching is organised) | 7. Play-ground (when not supervised by the teacher) | 7. Cinema (When educational pictures are organised) |
| 8. Radio (When used as an integral part of the curriculum and pre-broadcast and post-broadcast lessons are organised) | 8. Press | 8. Internet (When some educational course is organised) |
| | 9. Reading Room | 9. Correspondence Institutions |
| | 10. Radio (Normal Programme) | 10. Open Learning Institutions |
| | 11. Television (Normal Programme) | 11. Distance Learning Institutions |
| | 12. Voluntary Organisations like Bharat Sewak Samaj, Boy Scouts etc. | |
| | 13. Internet | |

Agencies of Education : Classification No. II

| *Active Agencies of Education* | *Passive Agencies of Education* |
|---|---|
| 1. The Family | 1. Cinema |
| 2. The School | 2. Radio |
| 3. The Community | 3. T.V. |
| 4. The Religion | 4. Internet |
| 5. The State | 5. Library |
| 6. Social Clubs | 6. Magazines |
| 7. Peers | 7. Newspapers |
| 8. Neighbourhood | 8. Market places |

**Formal Agencies of Education and Formal Education**

Formal agencies of education like schools and colleges impart formal education. These agencies are consciously and deliberately planned to bring about specific influences on the educand. They have regular working hours. They prepare students for taking public examinations on regular basis. Usually they employ full time staff. They follow prescribed curriculum and textbooks. They have to conform to rigid departmental rules and regulations.

**Informal Agencies of Education and Informal Education**

The informal agencies do not follow any set pattern of instruction or education. In fact they impart education incidentally. Education is not organised deliberately in these institutions. These are informal groups. Education is indirect. One may learn without being conscious of it. Nevertheless influence of informal agencies of education is quite significant.

**Non-Formal Agencies of Education**

'Flexibility' is the key-word in the case of non-formal agencies of education. The system is an 'open one' with regard to : (1) Admission (2) Curricular work (3) Place of instruction (4) Mode of instruction (5) Time and duration of instruction (6) Regular/temporary/part time staff. Open School, Open University, Open Learning Institutions and agencies imparting correspondence education come under non-formal agencies of education. Adult education agencies are usually placed under this category.

## 28.3 NO WATERTIGHT DIVISION OF AGENCIES OF EDUCATION

There is no clear-cut dividing time in classifying educational agencies into formal, non-formal and informal agencies. Even a school can take the form of a non-formal agency of education when it organises adult education classes and programmes. Students in the school acquire a good deal of education through informal contacts with the peers and the teachers. The press, the radio and the T.V. are normally termed as informal agencies of education. However, when they take up occasional programmes of formal education, they assume the form of non-formal agencies of education. Regular school broadcasts and T.V. lessons based on the school curriculum may be considered as programmes of formal education and radio and T.V. as agencies of formal education.

The entire programme of correspondence/distance education/open education may be classified both formal as well as non-formal, depending upon the type and mode of educational activity.

An adult school which follows a regular programme of education comes under the category of formal agency of education. However, when it is used for educational work, for sometime it is placed under the category of non-formal agency of education. Recreational programme of an adult school may be placed under the category of informal education. Now this comes under the category of an informal agency of education.

## 28.4 BROAD COMPARISON BETWEEN FORMAL AND NON-FORMAL AGENCIES OF EDUCATION

| *Item* | *Formal Agency of Education* | *Non-Formal Agency of Education* |
|---|---|---|
| 1. *Learners* | It caters to learners who can attend full time courses | It caters to those learners who cannot attend full time courses or have dropped from school. It also includes learners who want to improve their qualifications |
| 2. *Aims* | To get a certificate, diploma or degree needed for a job or self-employment | (i) To increase knowledge<br>(ii) To better skills<br>(iii) To improve qualifications |
| 3. *Place* | An educational institution with more or less permanent location. School or College | No specific place, can be home, factory, farm library, open space etc. |
| 4. *Age* | Usually prescribed age | Usually no age limit |
| 5. *Grade/Class* | Students are grouped into classes | Usually flexible groups |
| 6. *Curriculum* | Almost fixed and rigid | Almost flexible |
| 7. *Text books* | Prescribed text books as well as recommended text books | Usually general books on the subjects |
| 8. *Teachers* | Normally almost all teachers on full time basis | Very few full time teachers. Mostly part time teachers or on contract basis |
| 9. *Examinations* | Examinations at regular intervals<br>Tests of different kinds | Normally no examinations or very few examinations, assignments |
| 10. *Methods of Teaching* | Face to face teaching | Contact programmes, correspondence lessons<br>Radio, T.V. |
| 11. *Status* | Normally high status | Usually not considered at par with regular full time courses. |
| 12. *Degrees/ Diplomas* | Degrees/Diplomas awarded to successful candidates | 1. Normally certificates awarded<br>2. Degrees and diplomas are awarded for courses planned in accordance with the prescribed syllabi – B.Ed., M. Ed., M.A. etc. |

With the increasing use of new educational technology and science, it has become very difficult to divide educational agencies into water-tight compartments.

## 28.5 MASS MEDIA AS AGENCIES OF EDUCATION

*Meaning of Mass Media.* Mass media are means or instruments of communication that reach large number of people or pupils. The media may be printed like newspapers or may take the form of cinema, radio and T.V. Now new media like Internet and e-mail etc. are also increasingly being used. As observed by Erickson and others, "In recent years technology has swept through society from research laboratories into manufacturing communications, the space age and finally now, into education".

Prof. Marrshall MC Luhan (1911-1980) who has written extensively on 'Understanding Media' observes, "Education will no longer depend entirely on obtaining knowledge through the print media. The visual approach to learning is fast changing to total sensory involvement (visual auditory, mots etc.) in the process of acquiring knowledge". His slogan was 'Medium is the message'.

Earlier the teacher was the only medium of communication for children. Now we see new media like radio and T.V. making their inroads into education. A close look at the use of new media of education indicates that they are supplementary to teacher's work. They do not and cannot replace the teacher.

**Importance of Mass Media in Education**

1. Mass media is very helpful in spreading literacy.
2. Mass media is very useful in social education.
3. Mass media provides very useful information on almost all matters of significance in life.
4. It can bring the entire world in the classroom.
5. It sends information to remote places and helps in distant learning.
6. It helps in providing a simplified and vivid description even of complicated skills like performing of operations, experiments etc.
7. It helps in the modification of attitudes and values of individuals.
8. It provides information very speedily.
9. It is useful in reinforcing group dynamics.
10. It appeals to various senses and this is helpful in developing motivation.

## 28.6 RADIO AS AGENCY OF EDUCATION

In the words of R.G. Reynolds, "Radio is the most significant medium of education in its broadest sense. As a supplement to classroom teaching its possibilities are almost unlimited". Frederic Wittis has observed, "I like to think of education by radio as a timely, vital and dramatic thing".

**Merits of School Broadcasts**

1. They enrich the school programmes.
2. They provide latest information on a variety of topics of interests to students.
3. They bring the school into contact with the world around.
4. They develop leisure time interests among students.
5. They provide opportunities for student participation.
6. They impart vocational skills.
7. They develop scientific temper of mind.
8. They promote emotional and national integration.
9. They provide useful information on population education, energy conservation, preservation of wild life etc.
10. They serve as instruments of teacher training.
11. They reach the masses, conquering the barriers of space and time.
12. They are very helpful in adult education programmes.
13. Various radio programmes like 'Children's programme', 'University Broadcast', 'Youth Programme', etc. reach varied sections of society and provide informal but effective and meaningful education.

**Deficiencies and Limitations of Radio Broadcasts**

1. Broadcast exposition leaves some gaps.
2. Broadcast time may not be suitable.
3. Radio sets may develop defects and need immediate repairs.

**Suggestions for the Improvement of School Broadcast Programmes**

(i) The broadcasts should have a wider horizon of application in day-to-day life.

(ii) The school broadcasts should also be designed according to the needs of the syllabus.

(iii) Teachers should be actively involved in various dimensions of broadcasts meant for the students.

(iv) The radio programmes should be intended to give supplementary information on the various topics in the curriculum.

(v) Teachers should occasionally meet, discuss and plan the type of assistance required in producing effective broadcast programmes.

(vi) Students should be asked to give suitable suggestions to make further improvement in broadcasts.

(vii) Every school should have one teacher trained in the electronic media.

(viii) Proper follow-up may be taken up on school broadcasts.

(ix) Suitable listing facilities should be provided to the students in the school.

(x) Broadcasts should be made in a pleasing style.

(xi) Language used in school broadcasts should be easy, simple but forceful.

**History of School Broadcasts**

Since 1920 when the British Broadcasting Corporation (BBC) started the programme of school broadcasts, it has made rapid strides in making sound contribution to formal education.

In the U.S.A., broadcast programmes in accounts were planned from New York in 1923, programmes in arithmetic and literature from Oakland in 1924, music appreciation lessons in 1925 from Cleveland. By 1952, 20 States in the U.S.A. had made provision for educational broadcasting.

Around 1952, nearly 98 per cent of the schools in U.K. were equipped with radio and there were regular daily programmes.

January 1929 was the beginning of radio programmes of interest to students from the Bombay radio station. From April 30, the Corporation of Madras had regular school broadcasts for half an hour on all working days. Similar programmes were introduced by Calcutta Station in 1932.

At present, following types of programmes are produced by Akashvani Stations :

a) Programmes for children of primary classes.
b) Programmes for children of secondary and higher secondary classes.
c) Review lessons for secondary and higher secondary classes on the eve of annual examinations.
d) Programmes for teachers
e) General enrichment programmes for children

## 28.7 TELEVISION AS AN EDUCATIONAL MEDIUM

*Importance of Television.* For a country like India which has vast and inaccessible areas, T.V. can serve as one of the important media of educating the masses. It can be used as formal, non-formal and informal agency of education. It attracts attention which is essential for learning. Following are the important merits of T.V.:

1. T.V. comes to the assistance of those persons who are unable to acquire education through the traditional system.
2. It promotes the goal of equalisation of educational opportunity by reaching the remote areas.
3. It provides technical advantages which normally are not readily available in normal classroom for demonstration or illustration.
4. It makes possible close-up magnification of small objects, components, intricate mechanisms, diagrams, etc. by providing students a 'front-row-seat automatically.
5. It makes quick and lasting visual and aural impressions.
6. It makes possible to bring large, scarce or new equipment into the classroom electronically.

7. It saves time, effort and cost of setting up classroom projection equipment.
8. It brings into the classroom demonstration, videotape or film presentations at the instant or immediately after they occur.
9. It allows relationship between two illustrations or time lapse between two stages of a process by dissolving one picture into another.
10. It directs the attention of the student to the exact details of an object.
11. It permits inclusion of up-to-the-moment information, modifications, new equipment or techniques into classroom instruction.
12. It permits the use of the services of the best available teachers to teach a subject to a large member of viewer students.
13. It permits to preserve the expert teaching skills on video tape or film for later use.
14. It provides a uniform experience to all students when they see the basic ideas or techniques on television.
15. It provides classroom teachers the opportunity to observe the teaching process of the best teachers and to increase their skills of teaching.
16. It incorporates useful film sequences, slides, graphic art and makes teaching aids available within the T.V. presentation, tailored to meet the needs of a particular topic.
17. Educational telecasts can re-create the past through dramatisation, films or lectures.
18. Educational telecasts can explain several scientific phenomena which are to small, too slow, too fast or too dangerous to be observed first hand, by sound films.
19. Educational T.V. has both amusement and instruction value.
20. Education T.V. reduces dependence on the classroom teachers.
21. It bridges the gap between the private school and public school to some extent by making the best teachers available to all students.
22. Educational T.V. helps in the in-service training of teachers.
23. In case of distance learning, television reduces cost of instruction.
24. On account of the combination of audio and video components, T.V. has great appeal than radio and print media.

**Limitations of T.V. Instruction**

1. There is one-way communication from teacher to students.
2. It does not provide opportunity for question-answer, discussion and interaction of the viewers with the T.V. teacher at the time of telecast.
3. Educational T.V. expects thousands of students who view telecasts to be of the same educational standard.
4. T.V. teachers cannot cater to the individual differences of the students.

5. Teaching through T.V. is a costly affair. It is not within the reach of every school.
6. All schools do not have the proper viewing facilities.
7. T.V. lessons to large number of students in the hall may create disciplinary problems.

**Suggestion for Making T.V. Instruction More Effective**

1. Effective arrangement for pre-telecast and post-telecast should be made.
2. There should be interaction among the students, subject teachers and the teachers who telecast, irrespective of the fact whether teachers who telecast are practising teachers or not.
3. There should be proper seating arrangements so that all the students have a proper view of the lesson.
4. Provision for T.V. repairs should be made suitably.

**History of T.V. Instruction**

Regular T.V. programmes began by B.B.C. in1936. By 1958 more than 98 per cent population in the U.S.A. and U.K. was covered by television transmission. By 1962, American engineers succeeded in bouncing T.V. waves across the Atlantic on Satellite Telestor. In 1967, the first regular service of colour T.V. began on BBC-2 in Europe.

On October 2, 1961, the Delhi School T.V. Project was launched by the 'All India Radio (AIR), in collaboration with the Directorate of Education, Delhi and the Ford Foundation. The project was taken up in 140 schools with 300 T.V. sets. It covered nearly 29,000 students.

## 28.8 PEER GROUP AND EDUCATION

*Meaning of a Peer Group.* Broadly speaking a peer group may be thought of as a social group with limited number of members who have same common objects of loyalty. Social relations are fundamental to peer group.

*Chief Characteristics of a Peer Group.* Some of the salient characteristics of a peer group are as under.

1. The group has a feeling of oneness and unity.
2. The members of the group posses 'we feeling'.
3. There is a similarity of behaviour among the peers.
4. The members have common interests.
5. The members are expected to obey the social norms.
6. The members have mutual obligations.
7. The members have common interests.
8. The members have common values.
9. The members have high expectations.
10. The members of a peer group are interrelated in various respects.

*Peer Group as an Informal Agency of Education.* The peer group primarily operates in the area of recreational, social and vocational activities. Members of the peer group become sources of sex education. A peer group attempts to assist its member i.e. the teenager in the process of self identification and individualisation. It also helps in socialisation. It develops a co-operative spirit. Members learn to appreciate difference of opinion. Qualities of followership and leadership are strengthened.

A peer group serves as an important social agency of education during adolescence.

# 29

# Role of the Family, School, Community (NGOs) and State in Education

## 29.1 ROLE OF THE FAMILY IN EDUCATION

**Views of Great Philosophers and Thinkers on the Role of the Family**

Home/family is the first social institution where a child learns his first lessons of living together, working together, helping each other and learning lessons of mutual help and adjustment. Originally the family was the all inclusive social institution. It is only recently that the role of the school has expanded.

Following views of great thinkers reflect the role of the family/home on the education of the child :

*Forebel* – Mothers are the ideal teachers and informal education given in home is the most affective and natural.

*Mazzini* – Child leans the first lesson of citizenship between the kiss of mother and care of father.

*Pestalozzi* – Home – a centre of love and affection, is the best place and the first school of the child.

*Raymont* – The home is the soil in which spring up those virtues of which 'sympathy' is the common characteristic. It is here that the warmest and most intimate affection flourishes. It is here that the child learns the difference between generosity and meanness, considerateness and selfishness, justice and injustice, truth and falsehood, industry and idleness.

*Rousseau* – Education begins at birth and proper nurse is the mother.

*Frank states* – It is the only institution which is an essential agency for child rearing, socialisation, and for introducing the child to the culture of the society thereby shaping his basic character – structure and personality.

*Henderson* remarks – A child's education begins in his home.

*Swami Dayanand* – Blessed is the family, fortunate is the child whose parents be godly and learned.

*Saiyidain* – The education of man depends on the environments that he enjoins. If the environments are based on good customs and traditions of the family, they will spread beneficial influence on his ideas and development and his education will be useful not only to him but to the whole community.

**Important Educational Functions of the Family**

1. Providing environment and necessary facilities for proper physical development of the child.
2. Providing suitable moral environment for the moral development of the child.
3. Exploring and developing aesthetic and intellectual interests in the child.
4. Providing opportunities to the child for participation in routine household responsibilities.
5. Understanding the nature of the child and acting accordingly.
6. Understanding the importance of the individual differences of their children and treating accordingly.
7. Providing opportunities for self-expression.
8. Following a proper code of discipline.
9. Providing learning equipment at the proper time.
10. Realising the limitations of the school.

**Effects of Industrialisation on the Role of the Family**

1. Very few opportunities for vocational guidance.
2. Less opportunities for social contacts.
3. Less time available for looking after the child.

*Summing up.* In spite of the limitations of the role of the family, it can still play a prominent role in providing proper care, guidance and learning experiences to the child. There is no doubt that home can do a lot in 'making the man'. As the popular saying goes, "A wise father is more than a hundred school masters. The mother's face is the child's first lesson-book."

The great scientist J.C. Bose got an insight into his scientific in-genuity from his mother's conservation during childhood.

## 29.2 SCHOOL AS AN AGENCY OF EDUCATION

**Importance of School as a Social Institution and a Formal Agency of Education : Select views**

A school is one of the most important formal agencies of education. It plays a very significant role in discovering, and moulding the innate capacities, attitudes, habits and ideas of the children with a view to producing well balanced personalities : aesthetically rich, culturally refined, emotionally stable, mentally alert, morally sound, physically strong, socially efficient and spiritually enlightened.

Following quotations of the eminent thinkers illustrate suitably the importance of the school :

1. In the words of Kandel, "The school exists to accelerate the impact of the essential aspects of culture which prevails in the society".

2. J.S. Ross observes, "Schools ought to stress the duties and responsibilities of individual citizen. They ought to train their pupils on the spirit of cheerful willing and effective service".
3. H.G. Wells has remarked, "A world whose schools are unreformed is an unreformed world."
4. According to Dewey, "The school is primarily a social institution – an effective agency in bringing the child to share in the inherited resources of the race, and to use his own powers for social ends."
5. Nunn has stated, "A nation's school are an organ of its life, whose special function is to consolidate its spiritual strength, to maintain its historic continuity, to secure its past achievements, and to guarantee its future."
6. In the opinion of the Secondary Education Commission (1952 – 53), "The school must be transformed into an activity school – whose main concern is training its pupils in the gracious art of living".
7. The Education Commission 1964-66 remarked, "The destiny of India is being shaped in her classrooms".
8. Harold Rugg thinks of school as an "enterprise in living, both social and personal."

**Functions and Roles of the School in the Society**

The school is expected to perform the following functions and roles :

1. School as the transmitter of cultural heritage of the society.
2. School as the conserver of cultural heritage of the society.
3. School as the promoter of cultural heritage of the society.
4. School as the connecting link between home and the community.
5. School as the provider of special environment for the all round development of the child.
6. School as the provider of a planned scheme of things for the child.
7. School as the promoter of cultural pluralism i.e. tolerance of all cultures.
8. School as the promoter of ideals of the State.
9. School as the promoter of social development of the child.
10. School as the promoter of democratic values in the child.
11. School as the promoter of secular values in the child.
12. School as the promoter of ethical, moral and spiritual values of the child.
13. School as the promoter of scientific values in the child.
14. School as the promoter of professional and vocational skills and values in the child.
15. School as a promoter of egalitarian values in the child.
16. School as a promoter of innate abilities of the child.
17. School as a promoter of values of international understanding and peace.

18. School as a centre of community.
19. School as a trainer in the art of living together.

*Summing up*. In the words of S. Balakrishna Joshi, "In a word, a well-conducted school is a happy home, a sacred shrine, a social centre, a State in miniature and bewitching Brindavan – all beautifully blended into a synthetic structure."

**Measures to be Taken by the School to Perform Its Functions**

1. *Balanced and simplified environment.* The school discharges this function through curriculum. The school becomes a 'miniature community'.
2. *Art of living together.* The school provides a number of group activities through which students get a lot of training in the art of living together.
3. *Training in democratic living.* School incorporates activities like student self-government.
4. *Opportunities for Vocational Training.* School includes several programmes and activities like work experience and vocational subjects.
5. *Development of Child's entire personality.* The school makes all possible efforts to provide a pleasant and stimulating intellectual, physical and spiritual environment which will evoke the manifold interests of the students and develop them creatively and constructively. It formulates a programme of hobbies, occupations and projects that cater to the varying aptitudes and temperaments of the students.

   The school library, laboratory and workshop become the humble of stimulating activities.
6. *Spirit of co-operation.* The head of school should develop an environment of co-operation and harmony among staff members so that the students also imbibe this attitude.
7. *Co-operation with Several Agencies of Education.* School enlists the co-operation of the various formal, non-formal and informal agencies wherever considered necessary.
8. *School as a Centre of Community Service.* School can organise adult education classes. It can take up community service programmes.

## 29.3 FUNCTIONS OF THE SCHOOL IN BEHAVIOURAL TERMS : HISTORICAL LETTER OF ABRAHAM LINCOLN (1809-1865), 16TH PRESIDENT OF THE U.S. (1861-1863), TO THE HEADMASTER OF THE SCHOOL IN WHICH HIS SON WAS STUDYING

The word of wisdom stated more than one hundred years ago are still valid to-day. (extracts)

He will have to learn, I know that all men are not just, all men are not true. But teach him also that for every scoundrel, there is hero, that for every selfish politician, there is a dedicated leader.

It will take time, I know; but teach him, if you can that a dollar earned is of more than five thousand ...

Teach him to learn to lose and also to enjoy winning.

Steer him away from envy if you can.

Teach him to learn that the bullies are the easiest to lick.

Teach him if you can, the wonder of books but also give him quite time to ponder over the eternal mystery of birds in the sky, bees in the sun and flowers on a green hillside.

Teach him it is far more honourable to fail than to cheat.

Teach him to have faith in his own ideas, even if anybody tells him they are wrong.

Teach him to be gentle with gentle people and tough with the tough.

Try to give my son the strength not to follow the crowd when everyone is getting on the band-wagon.

Teach him to listen to all men. Teach him also to filter all he hears on a screen of truth and take on the good that comes through.

Teach him, if you can how to laugh when he is sad.

Teach him there is no shame tears

Teach him to scoof at cynics and to be beware of too much sweetness.

Teach him to sell his brawn and brain to the highest bidders, but never to put a price tog on his heart and soul.

Teach him to close his ears to a howling mob.

Teach him to stand and fight if he thinks he's right.

Teach him gently but do not cuddle him because only the tests of fire make fine steel.

Let him have the courage to be impatient. Let him have the patience to be brave.

Teach him always to have sublime faith in himself because then he will always have sublime faith in mankind.

## 29.4 COMMUNITY AS AN AGENCY OF EDUCATION

*Meaning of a Community.* In simple words, a community may be defined as a cluster of people living within a small area and sharing a common way of life to a considerable extent. Some of the important definitions of a community are :

According to Mac Iver and Page, "Community is an area of social living marked by some degree of social coherence. The bases of community are locality and common sentiment."

Alvin Goods defines a community as, "A community is a primary group resulting from social contacts, largely direct of those residing in a small area."

Ottaway states, "A community is everybody – adults and children, social and non-social persons living in a certain territory where all share a mode of life"

In the words of Brownell, "Community is meant a small diversified group of people, male and females with different skills and abilities living together as kin-neighbours."

From above, we note the following characteristics of a community :

(i) Community has a population.
(ii) Community lives in a territory.
(iii) Community has a historical heritage.
(iv) Community shares a common mode of life.
(v) Community provides different kinds of services to its members through its various institutions.
(vi) The members of the community work in co-operation and help each other in times of need.

**Role of the Community in Education**

Community is an important agency of education. It is child's laboratory which provides him first hand learning experiences of different kinds. The community with its various resources can enrich and supplement learning. Community socialises the child through its various institutions. It provides 'concrete', 'seeable' and 'tangible' resources which are dynamic, interesting and meaningful for the learners (children).

A community performs some specific functions as an agency of education. These are as :

1. It provides educational facilities in the locality/territory in the form of schools.
2. It co-ordinates the efforts of various agencies working in the field of education.
3. It undertakes several school improvement projects.
4. It establishes, libraries and social education centres.
5. It takes steps for promoting democratic attitudes among the people through organising conferences.
6. It conducts fairs, festivals and exhibitions which are of great cultural, educational and recreational values.
7. It sometimes encourages experimentation in the curricula and methods of teaching.
8. It co-operates with the school in providing better and effective teaching-learning experiences.

## 29.5 INTERACTION BETWEEN THE COMMUNITY AND THE SCHOOL

| *Community* | *School* |
|---|---|
| 1. The community opens and maintains schools. | 1. The school fulfills the educational needs of the community. |
| 2. The community has a certain philosophy or objective of life. | 2. The school translates the philosophy of the community into practice by educating the children accordingly. |
| 3. Community requires various categories of works, doctors, engineers, | 3. The school prepares the children for taking up various jobs and services |

| Community | School |
|---|---|
| lawyers, scientists, etc. | needed by the community. |
| 4. Community provides the traditioı culture. | 4. The school balances, purifies and simplifies the complex activities of the traditional community. It also enriches its traditional culture. |

There is a great need of co-operation between the home/family, the community and the school. The home/family and the school are an integral part of the community.

## 29.6 NON-GOVERNMENTAL ORGANISATIONS (NGOS) AND EDUCATION

**Significant Role of NGOs**

From time immemorial, non-voluntary effort has played an important role in the promotion of education. In earlier times, private enterprise in education was by and large unorganised.

Since the 19th century several non-governmental organisations have been playing a major role in the field of education in India. The beginning of British system of education in India may be traced to the efforts of several Christian missionaries who worked singly or under the auspices of some voluntary organisation.

Philanthrophists, religious and social organisations, social workers, etc. have set up a number of voluntary organisations which work in different dimensions of education i.e. primary, middle, secondary, higher secondary and college level education. They also work in the field of adult and social education. There is a net-work of D.A.V. educational institutions under the D.A.V. Management. Ramakrishna Mission, Sanatam Dharam Sabhas, Shromani Gurudwara Prabandank Committee, Christian Association, Muslim Associations, Parsee Associations etc. are running several types of educational institutions. There are also several educational institutions run by Delhi Public School Society, Modern School Society etc.

Recently some Non-Governmental Organisation have came up for the promotion of environmental education, family planning population education etc.

The area of operation of voluntary organisation is as broad as the life itself.

The Ministry of Human Resource Development, Department of Education, Government of India is providing grants and other assistance to hundreds of non-governmental organisations for the following purposes :

1. Promotion of adult education.
2. Promotion of literacy among women.
3. Promotion of vocational education.

4. Environmental orientation to school education.
5. Improvement of science education in schools.
6. Strengthening culture and values in education.
7. Strengthening of boarding/hostel facilities for girl students.
8. Integrated education for disabled children.
9. Promotion of yoga.
10. Languages development.
11. Non-formal education.

Several other Ministries of the Government of India also are encouraging non-governmental organisations to work in the educational and social field.

Likewise State Governments are also seeking the co-operation of several non-governmental organisations in undertaking programmes for community development.

### Classification of Non-Governmental Organisations

Following are the important ways of classifying non-governmental organisations.

**Classification of NGO-I**

- Work limited to one community
- Work extended to several communities

*Fig. 29.1: Classification of NGO according to territory of operation*

**Classification of NGO-II**

- Religion based NGO
- Secular NGO

*Fig. 29.2: Classification of NGO : Religious or Secular*

**Classification of NGO-III**

- Formal Education
- Non-formal Education
- Informal Education

*Fig. 29.3: Classification of NGO according to type of education*

**Classification of NGO-IV**

- Government recognised
- Not recognised by the government

*Fig. 29.4: Classification according to recognition*

**Classification of NGO-V**

- Government aided
- Non-government aided

*Fig. 29.5: Classification of NGO according to grant*

*Fig. 29.6: Classification of NGO according to purpose*

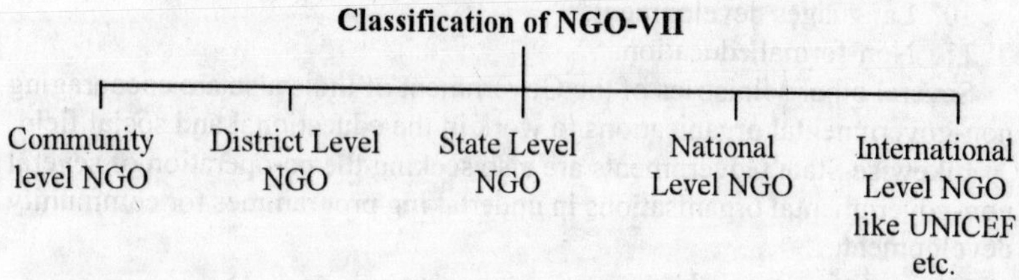


*Fig. 29.7: NGO according to level*

## 29.7 POLICY STATEMENTS ON THE ROLE OF NGOs

### Education Commission (1964-66) on the Role of NGOs

The Education Commission (1964-66) recognised the role of the non-governmental organisations (private enterprises) in the development of education in India. It, therefore, recommended that all possible use of their assistance must be made by the Government/State. It felt that the growing educational needs of a modern society cannot be met by government efforts alone. Nevertheless, it should be ensured that the non-governmental organisations, do not include in malpractices.

*National Policy on Education (NPE) (1986 and as amended in 1992) on the Role of NGO*

In Part X the NPE has laid down that

"Non-government and voluntary effort including social activist groups will be encouraged and financial assistance provided. Of course, their work and management would be supervised."

## 29.8 ROLE OF THE STATE IN EDUCATION

### Form of State and Educational Enterprise

In a totalitarian State, the entire responsibility of education is of the State. It establishes and manages all educational institutions. It determines the aims, contents, methods of teaching and discipline etc. in the field of education. There is no scope for private enterprise in education.

In a Laissez-faire State, there is an attitude like 'as you please' i.e. the State does not interfere in education and in fact in almost all area of national life.

## Education a Joint Enterprise in India

It is universally accepted that a democratic State should not claim monopoly in running and managing educational institutions. It should encourage private enterprise in education also.

The National Policy on Education (1986 and as amended in 1992) has laid down the following directions in the management of education :

1. Decentralisation and the creation of a spirit of autonomy for educational institutions.
2. Giving pre-eminence to people's involvement, including association of non-government agencies and voluntary effort.

## Merits of State Control of Education

1. State having large funds at its disposal, can make huge investment in education.
2. State control can ensure universal, compulsory and free education to all children of a certain age group.
3. State can ensure a uniform system of education.
4. State can prescribe a common curriculum.
5. State can introduce an egalitarian element in the provision of educational opportunities.
6. State can ensure suitable standard of education.
7. State can ensure suitable service conditions for teachers.
8. State can ensure secular education.
9. State can ensure quality in teacher training and also availability of the required number of teachers.

## Demerits of State Control of Education

1. Education will be politicalised.
2. Indoctrination, brain washing and brain storming would become the order of the day.
3. Teachers committed to a particular ideology will be recruited.
4. Individuality of the students is likely to be made subservient and not allowed to develop harmoniously and naturally.
5. Individual differences of children are likely to be ignored.
6. Qualities like initiative and enterprise would tend to receive set-back.
7. There will be regimentation. Democratic ideals would recede to the background.
8. Work ethics may wither away.
9. The family will be deprived of its fundamental right to look after its children.
10. A narrow view of education will predominate.

**Educational Functions of a Modern Democratic State**

A democratic State like India is expected to perform the following functions:

1. Provision of adequate educational facilities in institutions.
2. Raising the quality of education.
3. Making primary education compulsory, universal and free.
4. Assisting private enterprise in education.
5. Providing adult education to all illiterate adults.
6. Exercising general control and guidance.
7. Training young men and women in citizenship.
8. Providing competent educators.
9. Evolving a national system of education.
10. Ensuring availability of adequate teaching-learning material to students.
11. Encouraging research in education.
12. Awarding sufficient number of scholarship to the talented.
13. Preparing and implementing educational plans.
14. Preparing suitable manpower for various technical, vocational, professional and other fields.
15. Appointing education committees and commissions for suggesting suitable changes in the light of new developments in economy industry, science and technology etc.
16. Instituting cadres of Indian Education Service (IES) and State Education Service (SES) to manage the educational enterprise.
17. Constituting working groups and advisory bodies of cross–section experts to link education with various disciplines and fields.
18. Organising boards and committees relating to framing of curriculum, preparation of teaching material, recognition of educational institutions and conduct of examinations.

# 30

# Constitutional Provisions Regarding Elementary Education Concept and Importance

## 30.1 CONCEPT OF ELEMENTARY EDUCATION

*Historical Review.* There is a good deal of confusion and variation in the use of terms like primary education, lower primary education higher, primary education, middle education and elementary education. These terms have been variously defined in the educational literature and by educationists.

As per the Indian Constitution, the country is committed to providing free and compulsory education to all children up to the age of 14. The constitution has not used any term for this.

The Zakir Hussain Committee (1938) which prepared a detailed scheme of Basic Education/Wardha Scheme, considered Basic Education, covering a period of several years. It did not use any term like primary etc.

Gandhiji (1937) explained the concept of primary education as, "Primary education extending over a period of seven years or longer and covering all the subjects upto the matriculation standard except English, plus a vocation used as the vehicle for drawing out the best in the mind of boys and girls in all departments of knowledge, should take place what passes to-day under the name of primary, middle and high school education."

The Sargent Report (1944) stated, "Basic Education, while preserving the essential unity, will consist of two stages – the junior (or primary) stage, covering a period of five years and the senior (or middle) stage, covering three years."

Article 45 of the Constitution (1949) uses neither the term primary education nor elementary education. It simply reads, "Compulsory education for all children until they complete the age of fourteen years."

The Secondary Education Committee (1952-53) has recommended, "four or five years of primary or Junior Basic Education, Middle or Junior Secondary or Senior Basic Stage which should cover a period of 3 years."

The Education Commission (1964-66) used the terms 'primary' and 'lower secondary' as under :

a) Lower Primary : Classes I to IV or I to V
b) Higher Primary : Classes V to VII or VI to VIII
c) Lower Secondary Classes : Classes VIII to X or IX to X

The National Policy on Education (1968) referred to the Directive Principles under Article 45 of the Constitution seeking to provide free and compulsory education for all children up to the age of 14.

An NCERT publication '*The Curriculum for the Ten-year School: A Framework*' (1975) used primary stage and middle stage Primary stage of education covers roughly, the children of age 6+ to 11+ studying in classes I to V. In some parts the age may be 5+ to 10+. Classes VI to VIII cover the middle stage when the normal age groups should be 11+ to 14+."

According to Ishwarbhai Patel Committee (1977), Primary Education includes classes I to VII/VIII divided into two parts : Classes I to IV/V and classes V/VI to VII/VIII. It also used the terms lower primary stage and upper primary stage.

The National Policy on Education (1986) and as amended in 1992 uses the term "Elementary Education", "Universal retention of children up to 14 years of age.

NCERT's *(National Curriculum for Elementary and Secondary Education: A Framework* (1988), treats elementary education of 8 years duration. It includes : Primary Stage (5 years) and Upper Primary Stage (3 years).

*The Fifth All India Education Survey: Selected Statistics* (1989) published by NCERT has used the terms primary stage for classes I to V and upper primary stage for classes VI to VIII.

Ramamurti Review Committee for Review of NPE in its report entitled '*Towards an Enlightened and Human Society : NPE 1986 : A Review*' (1990) uses the term elementary education which includes primary level (classes I to V) and Upper Primary (classes VI to VIII). It also uses middle school level and upper primary (VI to VIII) interchangeably.

A publication '*Selected Educational Statistics 1998-99*' (2000) of the Government of India, Ministry of Human Resources Development, Department of Secondary Education and Higher Education, (2000) uses the terms primary (classes I – V), upper primary middle (classes VI to VIII) and elementary classes I to VIII.

*National Curriculum Framework for School Education* (2000) published by NCERT mentions 'Elementary Education (8 years) : Primary stage (5 years) – Class I to V and Upper primary stage (3 years) – Classes VI to VIII.

*Present Position of Elementary Education* (2000). In 19 States and Union Territories primary education includes five classes (I to V) and in 13 States and Union Territories, it includes six classes (I to VI). Eighteen States and Union Territories have been VI to VIII at the Upper Primary/Middle Stage, I State classes VI and VII, II states V to VII and 2

States V to VIII. Thirteen States and Union Territories have classes VIII to X at the Secondary stage.

*Summing up.* Elementary education generally extends over classes/standards/grades I to VIII. It ordinarily covers the age group 6 to 14 years. It comprises two distinct stages referred to as the primary stage (classes I to V) and the upper primary or middle stage (classes VI to VIII). Generally, the class teacher system is followed at the primary stage. Class teacher system requires a teacher to teach almost all the academic subjects to one class. Special interest, proficiency and qualifications of the teachers are taken into consideration at the upper primary stage.

## 30.2 IMPORTANCE OF ELEMENTARY EDUCATION

The importance of elementary education has been very aptly described by J.P. Naik, an eminent educationist, and an expert educational planner in these words, "The progress of primary education is one important index of the general, social and economic development of the country as a whole."

Studies have clearly established that countries which have made adequate provision for elementary education are far ahead of those with inadequate provision. In this context it must be remembered that in developed countries, almost 99 per cent of the population have access to elementary education (See Table 30.1).

A well-planned and properly implemented system of elementary education plays a very significant role in laying down the proper foundation of child's cultural, emotional, ethical, intellectual, moral physical, social and spiritual development.

Elementary education contributes a lot to foster values of emotional and national integration.

Elementary education is very helpful in developing scientific temper among the students.

Elementary education is an instrument of accelerating the spread of adult education in the country.

India is wedded to a democratic system not only in political life but also in other areas. Elementary education provides necessary knowledge of the rights and responsibilities of an enlightened citizen.

Elementary education assumes all the more importance in a country where a majority of the children do not go for further education. In other words it prepares children to enter life. This means that the knowledges, skills and values developed in the would-be-citizens would be such as they can face the challenges amicably, boldly and effectively.

Elementary education is important on account of its contribution to the development of the following knowledges, skills and virtues :

1. It enables the child to learn and practise the basic principles of healthy living in individual and social respects.
2. It develops in the child qualities of mind which will help him to lead a mentally healthy life.
3. it develops desire for knowledge and mastery over its processes so

that the child develops critical thinking, rational outlook and creativity.

4. It develops in the child the skill to appreciate his home, to recognise his duties and responsibilities and try to help members of his family in all sorts of work done for the happiness of the family.
5. It enables the child to get opportunities to take active interest in the community and to appreciate the value of cooperative and democratic living.
6. It enables the child to develop a rational and scientific outlook.
7. It enables the child to develop national outlook through the study of various subjects and practice experiences.
8. It enables the child to develop the art of communication of his feelings and thoughts orally and in writing or through some other medium.
9. It enables the child to develop his aesthetic sense – an important element in all round development.
10. It enables the child to understand the place of moral values and encourage him to behave accordingly in social life of the community.
11. It enables the child to develop understanding of the democratic social structure.
12. It enables the child to develop knowledge, skills and attitudes required for the progressive economic development of the individual and the society.
13. It enables the child to develop the skills of application of systematic, scientific and technological advancement.
14. It enables the child to develop understandings, skills and attitudes required for buying and selling commodities.
15. It enables the child to develop international understanding.
16. It enables to child to develop secular outlook.

## 30.3 COMPARATIVE DATA ON PRIMARY EDUCATION AND ALLIED INDICATORS OF DEVELOPMENT OF SELECT COUNTRIES

**Table 30.1**

| *Countries and territories* | *Total population (thousands)* | *GNI per capita (US$)* | *Life expectancy at birth (years)* | *Total adult literacy rate* | *Primary school net enrolment/ attendance (%)* |
|---|---|---|---|---|---|
| | *2006* | *2006* | *2006* | *2000-2005* | *2000-2006* |
| Afghanistan | 26088 | 250 | 43 | 28 | 53 |
| Australia | 20530 | 35990 | 81 | - | 97 |
| Austria | 8327 | 39590 | 80 | - | 97 |
| Bangladesh | 155991 | 480 | 63 | 48 | 81 |
| Bhutan | 649 | 1410 | 65 | - | 70 |
| Brazil | 189323 | 4730 | 72 | 89 | 95 |

| *Countries and territories* | *Total population (thousands)* | *GNI per capita (US$)* | *Life expectancy at birth (years)* | *Total adult literacy rate* | *Primary school net enrolment/ attendance (%)* |
|---|---|---|---|---|---|
| | *2006* | *2006* | *2006* | *2000-2005* | *2000-2006* |
| Canada | 32577 | 36170 | 80 | – | 100 |
| China | 1320864 | 2010 | 73 | 91 | 99 |
| Denmark | 5430 | 51700 | 78 | – | 95 |
| Egypt | 74166 | 1350 | 71 | 71 | 94 |
| Finland | 5261 | 40650 | 79 | – | 98 |
| France | 61330 | 36550 | 80 | – | 99 |
| Germany | 82641 | 36620 | 79 | – | 96 |
| **India** | **1151751** | **820** | **64** | **61** | **84** |
| Indonesia | 228864 | 1420 | 70 | 90 | 96 |
| Iran (Islamic Republic of) | 70270 | 3000 | 71 | 82 | 95 |
| Iraq | 28506 | 2170 | 58 | 74 | 88 |
| Japan | 127953 | 38410 | 82 | – | 100 |
| Korea, Democratic People's Republic | 23708 | a | 67 | – | – |
| Korea Republic of | 48050 | 17690 | 78 | – | 100 |
| Mexico | 105342 | 7870 | 76 | 92 | 98 |
| Myanmar | 48379 | 220 | 61 | 90 | 84 |
| Nepal | 27641 | 290 | 63 | 49 | 87 |
| Nigeria | 144720 | 640 | 47 | 69 | 68 |
| Pakistan | 160943 | 770 | 65 | 50 | 68 |
| Russian Federation | 143221 | 5780 | 65 | 99 | 92 |
| Sri Lanka | 19207 | 1300 | 72 | 91 | 97 |
| Switzerland | 7455 | 57230 | 81 | – | 93 |
| United Kingdom | 60512 | 40180 | 79 | – | 99 |
| United States | 302841 | 44970 | 78 | – | 92 |
| Zimbabve | 13228 | 340 | 42 | 89 | 82 |
| **SUMMARY INDICATORS** | | | | | |
| Industrialized countries | 969949 | 37217 | 79 | – | 96 |
| Developing countries | 5358223 | 1967 | 66 | 76 | 84 |
| Least developed countries | 785444 | 438 | 55 | 55 | 65 |
| World | 6577236 | 7406 | 68 | 78 | 86 |

| Notes : | | |
|---|---|---|
| (1) | Reference year | Around 2006 AD |
| (2) | Source | The State of the World's Children 2008 |
| (3) | Observations | In general it is observed that countries with higher percentage of children completing primary age have higher per capita income |

## 30.4 IMPLICATIONS OF CONSTITUTIONAL PROVISIONS ON ELEMENTARY EDUCATION

Following are the important implications of the constitutional provisions on elementary education :

1. Universal provision at the elementary stage.
2. Universal enrolment at the elementary stage.

3. Universal retention at the elementary stage.
4. Universal free education at the elementary stage.

**Universal Provision on Universalisation of Education at the Elementary Stage.**

This implies that school facilities should be provided to all the children between the age group 6 to 14 years in the country. The schools should be within the walking distance of a child. In this respect we have fairly succeeded. At the primary stage, nearly 95 per cent of the country's rural population now has schools within a distance of one kilometre. At the upper primary stage, nearly 85 per cent of the rural population have schools within a distance of three kilometres.

*Universal enrolment at the elementary stage.* The Gross Enrolment Ratio (GER) at the primary stage, in the country as a whole, and in most States exceeds 100 per cent. In some States like Uttar Pradesh, Bihar, Rajasthan, Haryana, Jammu & Kashmir and Meghalaya, the ratio is considerable lower. At the upper primary stage, in addition to the above mentioned States, Andhra Pradesh, Orissa and Sikkim have GER lower than the national average. In most of these States, the literacy rates are lower than the national average.

*Universal retention at the elementary stage.* Situation in this respect is very discouraging. Nearly 60 per cent children enrolled, complete primary education. In other words nearly 40 per cent students leave school after completing the primary stage. At the upper primary stage, retention rate is nearly 34 per cent. This means that 56 per cent children leave school without completing elementary education. Nearly 68 per cent students drop before completing class X. This clearly shows that there is lot of wastage and stagnation in education at the school stage.

**Universal Free Education at the Elementary Stage**

In advanced countries universal elementary education implies free education – tuition fee as well as free textbooks and some other learning material. Some countries make provision for free mid-day meals or subsidised meals and free transport. But in several developing countries like India, it has not been possible to do so. Of course, education at this stage is tuition free in Government schools, Government aided schools and local bodies schools. Other facilities on a selective basis are provided.

## 30.4 PROBLEMS, ISSUES, REMEDIES AND CONSTITUTIONAL PROVISIONS

(*See Chapter 14.2, 31, 32, 33, 34 and 35*)

# 31

# Girl's Education

## 31.1 IMPORTANCE OF GIRL'S AND WOMEN'S EDUCATION

There is no doubt that the families play an important role in the cultural, economic, political, religious and social life of a country. The people of ancient India fully recognised this fact. They accordingly accorded a reasonable status to women. Their education was duly encouraged. More than 400 verses in the Vedas are ascribed to 24 women sers. It was only in the middle ages that their education and status began to decline.

Here we give a few quotes from the Vedas and other ancient literature to highlight the factual position of the status and education of women in earlier times in this country.

"Just as boys acquire sound knowledge and education by the practice of Brahmacharya", so should girls." (*Athava Veda*', XI. 16.3.18)

"O learned lady! All life is dependent upon you because you impart education to all." (R.V. 2,49.17)

"Women have the opportunity to attain knowledge of the Vedas from all the four corners" (R.V. 14.9.64).

"In the battle field, in the absence of the king the queen should take command of the forces and inspire then." (A. V. XI. 16.3.18).

"From the point of view of reverence due, a teacher is ten-fold superior to a lecturer, a father hundred-fold to teacher, and a mother a thousand-fold to father." ('*Vashishta Dharmsutra*' – 13.480)

What can the fire not burn.
What cannot merge into the ocean.
What can the weaker section (women) not achieve.
And what can escape death. (*Ayodhyakand, Ramcharitmanas*)

"Where women are respected, there the gods delight, And where they are not, there works and efforts come to naught. There is no hope of rise for that family or country where they live in sadness." *Manusmriti"*

Prominent makers of history and thinkers have also laid strees on the status and education of the girls and women.

Swami Vivekananda said, "If you do not raise the women who are living embodiment of the divine mother, don't think that you have any other way to rise."

Gandhiji observed, "I am strongly of the opinion that women should have the same facilities as men and even special facilities where necessary."

In the words of Jawaharlal Nehru, "Education of the boy is the education of one person but education of a girl is the education of the entire family."

## 31.2 CONSTITUTIONAL PROVISIONS REGARDING GIRLS EDUCATION: EXPANSION IN EDUCATIONAL FACILITIES

There has been a spectacular progress in the expansion of educational facilities for girls in India after independence. The increase in girls' enrolment at the primary level (class I to V) was 12 times during the period 1950-51 to 2009-10. From 5.4 million it rose to 64.70 million. At the upper primary stage (class VI to VIII), the girls' enrolment increased nearly by 52 times i.e. from 0.5 million to 26.20 million. The female literacy rate is 65.46 as per census 2011 against 74.04 all India and 82.14 of male.

**Table 31.1 Enrolment of Girls Since 1950-51 (in Million)**

| *Year* | *Primary (Classes I to V)* | *Upper Primary (Classes VI to VIII)* | *Elementary (Classes I to VIII)* |
|---|---|---|---|
| 1950-51 | 5.4 | 0.5 | 5.9 |
| 1960-61 | 11.4 | 1.6 | 13.0 |
| 1970-71 | 21.3 | 3.9 | 25.2 |
| 1980-81 | 28.5 | 6.8 | 35.3 |
| 1990-91 | 40.4 | 12.5 | 52.9 |
| 1995-96 | 47.4 | 16.0 | 63.4 |
| 2003-04 | 59.9 | 21.5 | 81.4 |
| 2009-10 | 64.1 | 26.2 | 90.9 |

**Table 31.2 Girls' Gross Enrolment Ratio Since 1950-51**

| *Year* | *Primary (Classes I to V)* | *Upper Primary (Classes VI to VIII)* | *Elementary (Classes I to VIII)* |
|---|---|---|---|
| 1950-51 | 24.8% | 4.6% | 17.7% |
| 1960-61 | 41.4% | 11.3% | 30.9% |
| 1970-71 | 60.5% | 20.5% | 44.4% |
| 1980-81 | 64.1% | 28.6% | 52.1% |
| 1990-91 | 85.5% | 47.0% | 70.8% |
| 1995-96 | 93.3% | 55.0% | 79.3% |
| 2004-05 | 107.8% | 69.3% | 93.5% |
| 2009-10 | 115.4% | 78.3% | 101.1% |

*Note* : Gross Enrolment Ratio (GER) is defined as the percentage of the enrolment in classes I-V and VI-VIII and/or I-VIII to the estimated child population in the age groups 6-11 years and 11-14 and or 6-14 years respectively.

## 31.3 GENDER DISPARITY

The rate of growth as stated above in the case of girls has been higher than boys. But disparities still persist. Girls account for only 48.46 per cent of enrolment at the primary stage and 48.12 per cent at primary stage (Table 31.3).

**Table 31.3 Percentage of Girls' Enrolment to Total Enrolment at the Elementary Level Since 1950-51**

| *Year* | *Primary (Classes I to V)* | *Upper Primary/Middle (Classes VI to VIII)* |
|---|---|---|
| 1950-51 | 28.1% | 16.1% |
| 1960-61 | 32.6% | 23.9% |
| 1970-71 | 37.4% | 29.3% |
| 1980-81 | 38.6% | 32.9% |
| 1990-91 | 41.5% | 36.7% |
| 1995-96 | 43.2% | 39.0% |
| 2004-05 | 46.7% | 44.0% |
| 2009-10 | 48.5% | 48.1% |

**Table 31.4 Drop-out Rates at Primary and Middle Stages Since 1960-61**

| *Year/ Classes* | *1970-71* | *1980-81* | *1990-91* | *1998-99* | *2004-05* | *2009-10* |
|---|---|---|---|---|---|---|
| *Class I – V* | | | | | | |
| Boys | 64.5 | 56.2 | 40.1 | 40.6 | 31.08 | 30.25 |
| Girls | 70.9 | 62.5 | 46.0 | 44.7 | 25.04 | 27.25 |
| Total | 67.0 | 58.7 | 42.6 | 42.4 | 29.00 | 28.86 |
| *Classes I – VIII* | | | | | | |
| Boys | 74.6 | 68.0 | 59.1 | 54.4 | 50.50 | 40.59 |
| Girls | 83.4 | 79.4 | 65.1 | 60.0 | 51.30 | 44.39 |
| Total | 77.9 | 72.7 | 60.9 | 56.8 | 50.80 | 42.39 |

## 31.4 VARIATIONS IN GIRLS ENROLMENT RATE IN STATES

There is a great variation among states as regards girls enrolment ratio in classes I-V and VI-VIII. A few examples are given below. The most distinguishing aspect is that the populous states like Bihar and UP have very low enrolment ratios.

**Table 31.5 Showing Variation Among States as Enrolment Rate of Girls (2009-10)**

| *Sl. No.* | *State* | *Classes I-V (6-10 years)* | *Classes VI-VIII (11-14 years)* |
|---|---|---|---|
| 1. | Andhra Pradesh | 98.29 | 77.37 |
| 2. | Arunachal Pradesh | 163.42 | 96.21 |
| 3. | Bihar | 109.20 | 49.70 |
| 4. | Maharashtra | 102.30 | 86.93 |
| 5. | Mizoram | 162.20 | 94.98 |
| 6. | Rajasthan | 115.05 | 72.75 |
| 7. | Sikkim | 152.75 | 86.59 |
| 8. | Uttar Pradesh | 114.70 | 65.88 |
| 9. | West Bengal | 126.42 | 87.00 |
| 10. | Delhi | 122.54 | 106.95 |

## 31.5 CAUSES OF SLOW PROGRESS OF GIRLS' EDUCATION

Usually following causes of slow progress of girls are mentioned :

(i) Lack of proper social attitudes in the rural and backward areas for the education of girls.
(ii) Lack of educational facilities in rural areas.
(iii) Economic backwardness of the rural community.
(iv) Conservative nature and co-educational aspects.
(v) Lack of suitable curriculum.
(vi) Lack of proper incentives to parents and children.
(vii) Lack of women teachers.
(viii) Lack of proper supervision and guidance due to inadequate women personnel in the Inspectorate.
(ix) Uneducated adult women and lack of social education.
(x) Girls as helping hand to parents in various ways including earning.
(xi) Inadequate systematic publicity.
(xii) Indifference of Panchayats.

## 31.6 MEASURES FOR THE PROMOTION OF GIRLS' AND WOMEN'S EDUCATION

Following measures are suggested :

I. *Creating Proper Social Attitude and Environment in the Rural and Backward Areas for the Education of Girls* : Following measures may be taken :

1. To study the problems relating to women's education and to get detailed scientific data, a thorough research should be taken up by the Institutes of Education and allied institutions in different States and co-ordinated at the national level.
2. Separate schools for girls at the middle and high school stages should be established where needed.

3. School Mothers in co-education primary schools should be appointed.
4. Creches and nursery classes wherever possible should be opened.
5. Public opinion in favour of girls' education should be created.

II. *Providing Adequate Educational Facilities in Backward and Rural Areas* : The target should be to have at least one primary school within a radius of one kilometer from every home which is within the walking distance of a child. Following steps are needed :

1. Hostel for girls at the middle and high school stages.
2. maintenance stipends to girls residing in hostels for meeting their board and lodging expenses, at least in part.
3. Subsidised transport facilities, wherever necessary and possible.
4. All priority to be given to the construction of suitable buildings for girl's schools.
5. Free education for girls.

III. *Removing Economic Backwardness of the Rural and Backward Areas :* The girls are very useful at home for carrying out domestic duties and so mothers are reluctant to send them to school. A large number of children in the rural areas are under-nourished. They hardly have a square meal a day. Unless the parents are given some kind of economic relief, it will be impossible to achieve the targets. Following measures should prove very useful :

1. Free uniforms and free books to the needy and deserving children should be provided.
2. Attendance scholarships which serve as a compensation to the parents should be given. This will also ensure reduction of wastage and stagnation.
3. Mid-day meals should be made available free of charge.

IV. *Conservative Nature of Parents and Co-education* : Parents in rural areas and backward communities tend not to send the girls to co-educational schools. Their apprehensions have to be removed with a thought-out plan of education them in this regard.

V. *Provision of Suitable Curriculum* : Curriculum, by and large, has not met the requirements of women. Following suggestions made by Smt. Hansa Mehta Committee (1962) deserve careful consideration:

1. No differentiation should be made in the curricula for boys and girls at the primary and middle stages of education.
2. Steps should be taken to improve the instruction of home economics.
3. Steps should be taken to improve the teaching of music and fine arts and liberal financial assistance should also be made available to girls' schools for the introduction of these courses.

4. Universities should review periodically the provision they have made for the courses designed to meet the special needs of girls and take necessary action to remove the deficiencies discovered.

VI. *Proper Incentives to Parents and Girls* : The following measures have been suggested :

1. The number of attendance scholarships be doubled in the Tenth Plan.
2. The allowance of the School Mothers should be enhanced so that qualified women may be attracted to take up the work.
3. The number of maintenance stipends should be doubled and the rate of such stipends should be adequately increased in view of the rising prices all over the country.
4. The number of sanitary blocks in co-educational primary schools be adequately increased.
5. Larger allocation of funds should be made in the budget for construction of hostels for girls.

VII. *Provision for Providing Adequate Number of Women Teachers* : Following steps are suggested :

1. A large number of training institutions have to be provided for women, especially in the backward States. These institutions should generally be located in rural areas and they should generally recruit their trainees from that area.
2. Condensed course centres should be started in these backward areas to open up avenues to adult unqualified women for employment as teachers. Wherever possible such centres should be attached to the training institutions.
3. A large number of quarters for women teachers should be provided, particularly in rural areas. Our target should be to provide at least 50 per cent of the women teachers with quarters in primary schools.
4. All women teachers employed in rural areas should be given adequate rural allowance.
5. Special stipends should be given to girls in high and higher secondary schools with aptitude for teaching.
6. Whenever possible husbands and wives should be posted in the same place even if they work in different departments of the Government.
7. Free training should be imparted with stipends to all candidates of training institutions.
8. In-service education training should be given to untrained women teachers who have put in at least two years of service. The period of training of education should be treated as on duty.

VIII. *Proper Supervision and Guidance* : For providing proper guidance and supervision, following steps should be taken :

a) Increase in the number of women inspecting officers, particularly in the backward States, at different levels including State level and Directorate level.

b) Provision of adequate transport for all district women inspecting officers.

c) Adequate office staff and equipments.

d) Residential facilities to all women officers at the levels.

e) Adequate funds at the disposal of the State Council for closer contact with rural areas.

IX. *Facilities for Education of Adult Women* : Girls education and education of adult women suffers on account of lack of social education. This problem can be tackled in the following ways :

1. By opening adult literacy classes in large number.
2. By teaching simple skills like sewing, knitting, handicrafts etc., and knowledge of basic principles of health and food habits.
3. By developing proper attitudes towards community living, family planning, superstitions, caste, etc.

X. *Eradicating Social Ills* : The Purdah system (in some States such as in Orissa, Uttar Pradesh, Bihar and Rajasthan) and certain other harmful social customs in these States and in others stand in the way of the development of girls' education. In some places caste barriers also contribute to this. Social reformers and other voluntary organisations may be motivated to take up this work.

XI. *Wide Systematic Publicity* : For educating the parents to take interest in the education of girls, press and electronic media may be used extensively.

XII. *Awards to Panchayats* : Panchayats should be given some motivation to take up work in this area.

*Concluding Remarks* : The role of women outside the home has become an important feature of the social and economic life of the country and in the years to come this will become still more significant. From this point of view greater attention will have to be paid to the problems of training and development of women. The education of girls, therefore, should be emphasised not only on grounds of social justice, but also because it accelerates economic and social transformation. SSA has consistently worked on improving girl's access to elementary education.

# 32

# Problems, Issues and Remedies Regarding Child Labour Education and Welfare

## 32.1 CONSTITUTIONAL PROVISIONS REGARDING CHILD LABOUR

Independence ushered in a new era in the field of child development and welfare. Concerted efforts in this regard are being made by the Central Government and the State Governments. Among the several problems relating to the advancement of the child, the problem of child labour has also received attention. The Constitution of India includes the following provisions in this regard :

*Article 24. Prohibition of Employment of Children in Factories, etc.* According to this Article, no child below the age of fourteen years can be employed to work in any factory or mine or engaged in any other hazardous employment.

*Article 39(e). Prohibition of Abuse of Children.* This provision states that it will be secured that the health and strength of workers, men and women, and the tender age of the children are not abused. It will also be ensured that the children are not forced by economic necessity to enter vocations not suited to their age.

*Article 39(f). Opportunities and Facilities to Develop.* This Article mentions that children will be given opportunities and facilities to develop in a healthy manner and in a condition of freedom and dignity. It also ensure protection of childhood and youth against exploitation.

## 32.2 WHO IS A CHILD

According to the U.N. Convention on the Rights of the Child, "A child means every human being below the age of eighteen years unless, under the law applicable to the child, majority is attained earlier."

The legal position of a child varies in countries depending upon the purpose.

According to the Indian Constitution, no child below the age of 14 years shall be employed to work in any factory or mine or engaged in any other hazardous employment (Article 23).

A publication of the Ministry of Human Reason Development entitled 'Selected *Educational Statistics* (2000) considers a child upto the age of 18 years. According to Labour laws in India and the Apprentices Act 1951, and the Child Labour (Prohibition and Regulation) Act 1986, "Child means a person who has not completed his fourteenth years of age".

## 32.3 POVERTY AND CHILD LABOUR

Child labour perpetuates poverty as children become part of the vicious circle of poverty from generation to generation.

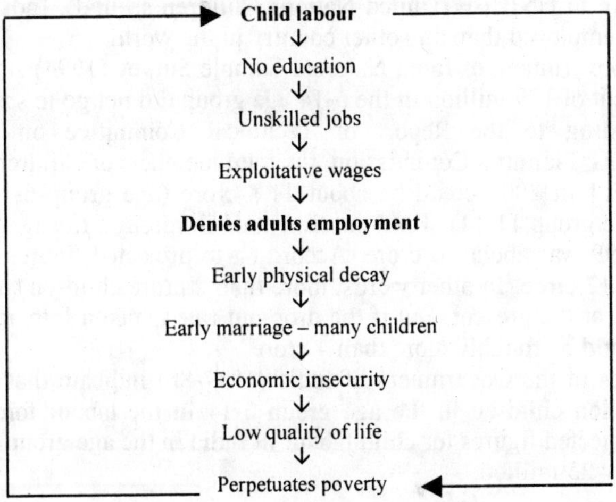


*Fig. 32.1: Poverty and Child Labour*

## 32.4 THE PREFERRED PICTURE OF CHILD LABOUR AND WELFARE

If child labour were to be abolished and all children were to go to school, it is likely that the problems of over-population would decrease and India's prosperity would increase.

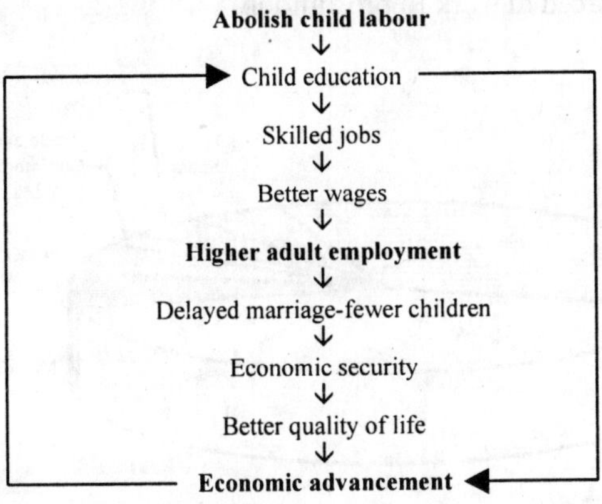


*Fig. 32.2: The preferred picture of child labour*

## 32.5 WHAT IS CHILD LABOUR

According to UNICEF, children whose main occupation is work, rarely if ever go to school and are sometimes the family breadwinners working in difficult conditions upto 14 hours a day are child labourers."

## 32.6 CHILD LABOUR IN INDIA

According to UNICEF (United Nations Children's Fund), India has more children employed than any other country in the world.

The Government of India National Sample Survey (1994) states that 90 million out of 179 million in the 6-14 age group did not go to school.

According to the Report of Technical Committee on Population Projections, Planning Commission, the total members of children in the age group 6-14 in 2001 could be about 11.8 crore (age group 6-11) and 7.5 crore (age group 11-14). Total enrolment of children in the age group 6-14 in 1998-99 was about 16 crore. According to projected figures in 2001, it could be 17 crore. In other words, more than 2 crore children would be out of school at the present. But if the drop-out rate is taken into account, this figure could be roughly more than 4 crore.

Figures of the Government of India (1987-88) indicate that there were 17.5 million children in the age group 5-14 in the labour force. On this basis, projected figures for child labour in India in the age group may be put at roughly 25 million.

## 32.7 TYPES OF CHILD LABOUR : WHERE DO CHILDREN WORK

Children are found at work in all parts of the economy. According to the Registrar General of India, official figures show that a huge 42.2% of child labourers are employed as agricultural workers, which includes tea plantations. They work in leather goods factories, hosiery units, the carpet, glass, textile and plastics industries and private homes as domestic servants. They are also forced to work in prostitution.

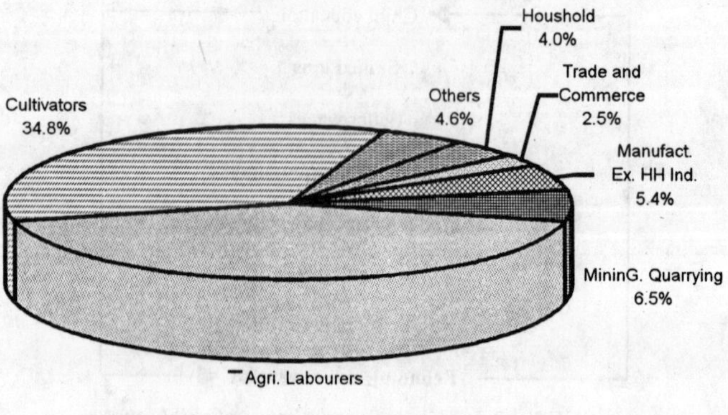


*Fig. 32.3: Percentage of child labour in India working in different occupations*

## 32.8 MEASURES TAKEN IN INDIA FOR ELIMINATING AND CHECKING EXPLOITATION OF CHILD LABOUR

1. *Laws Framed to Check Exploitation of the Children*

(i) *Factories Act, 1948*: No child who has not completed his fourteenth years of age shall be required or allowed to work in any factory.

(ii) *Labour Laws: Apprentice's Act, 1951*: A person shall not be qualified to be engaged as an apprentice unless he is not less than fourteen years of age.

(iii) *Mines (Amendment Act), 1983*: No person below eighteen years of age shall be allowed to work in any mine or in any factory.

(iv) *Child Labour (Prohibition and Regulation) Act, 1986:* It prohibits children to work unless they have completed fourteenth years of age.

(v) *Ban on Child Labour, 2006:* It bans the employment of children as domestic and *dhaba* servant.

2. *National Policy on Child Labour (1987):* Important features of the policy are :

(i) Enforcement of legal provisions to protect the interest of children.

(ii) Preparing development programmes for the benefit of child labour.

(iii) Formulating and implementing National Child Labour Projects (NCLP).

(iv) Establishment of special schools to provide non-formal education and vocational training to children withdrawn from work.

(v) Participation in the international programme on Elimination of Child Labour (IPEC), launched by the ILO (International Labour Organisation) in 1991.

3. *The National Policy for Children (1974):* The National Policy for Children formulated by the Government of India reaffirmed the Constitutional provisions and declared that "it shall be the policy of the State to provide adequate services to children, both before and after birth and through the period of growth, to ensure their full physical, mental and social development. The State shall progressively increase the scope of such services so that, within a reasonable time, all children in the country enjoy optimum conditions for their balanced growth."

4. *Ratification of the U.N. Convention on the Rights of the Child*: The Government of India, ratified the Convention on the Rights of the Child (CRC) on December 2, 1992. It may be recalled that the Convention on the Rights of the Child was adopted by the United Nations General Assembly in its Special Session in 1989 (November 20, 1989). Thereafter the World Summit for Children was held in 1990. By ratifying the Convention the India has made itself subject to International Laws. There are 54 Articles relating to children's rights. Article 32 of the Convention specifically

outlaws child labour.

5. *Recent Supreme Court Judgments on Child Labour*: Following are the recent Supreme Court judgments relating to improvement in the condition of child labour :

1. 1993 Supreme Court Judgment – *Unni Krishnan J.P. and Others us. State of Andhra Pradesh.*
2. 1996 Supreme Court Judgment – *M.C. Mehta us. State of Tamil Nadu and Others.*

The Supreme Court in 1996 *inter alia* reiterated its earlier judgment of 1993 regarding right to free and compulsory education for children up to the age of 14 years. It also directed that the concerned employer who employs a child in contravention of the provisions of Child Labour Act 1986, shall pay as compensation a sum of Rs. 20,000 per child.

6. *Goals Set for the year 2000 by the National Plan of Action: A Commitment to the Child – Government of India* (1992): Among other measures, it envisages an accelerated programme for the elimination of child labour.

## 32.9 SUGGESTIVE MEASURES FOR IMPROVING THE CONDITION OF CHILD LABOUR AND ELIMINATING CHILD LABOUR IN INDIA

Following measures are suggested :

1. Making right to education as fundamental right for children between the age group 6-14 as per the Supreme Court Judgment 1996.
2. Increasing investment in education. South Korea invests $ 130 per person every year on education, Malaysia $ 128 and India just $ 9 (nine), of which 90 per cent goes on teachers' salaries.
3. Enforcing all child labour laws strictly. It must be ensured that no child under the age of 14 is employed. The proper place for a child is at school and not working at home or in factories or plantation.
4. No purchases to be made from suppliers who employ child labour. Some times back, reports of extreme types of exploitation of child labour in crackers' factories at Shivakashi and in various factories at Moradabad appeared in the press which startled the entire nation.
5. Making adequate provision as directed in NPE, 1986 in the form of non-formal education for drop-outs and other types of children who are unable to attend full time school.
6. Ensuring decent ways.

# 33

# Problems, Issues and Remedies Regarding Children with Special Needs

## 33.1 MEANING OF CHILDREN WITH SPECIAL NEEDS

There is a good deal of confusion regarding the use of terms 'Children with special needs', 'Exceptional children', 'Handicapped children', 'Disabled children' and 'Special education'. Several authors use these terms simultaneously.

By children with special needs we mean those children whose needs cannot be met within the ordinary classroom environment. Such children need special types of teaching content, teaching material, teaching staff and even special schools. Children are considered special when they have characteristics that deviate from the normal or average child.

A working definition of a child with special needs may be given as. "A child with special needs is one who deviates from an average or normal child, emotionally, intellectually, physically and socially to such an extent that he cannot be benefited from a regular classroom programme and needs special treatment in order to develop to his optimum capacity."

## 33.2 MAIN CHARACTERISTICS OF CHILDREN WITH SPECIAL NEEDS

1. They are markedly different from the normal children.
2. Their differences may be emotional, intellectual, physical or social.
3. They need a special environment.
4. The special environment may be provided in the normal system of schooling or in special schools, meeting with special types of needs.
5. They need more care than normal children.
6. Their education is more expensive.

## 33.3 CLASSIFICATION OF CHILDREN WITH SPECIAL NEEDS

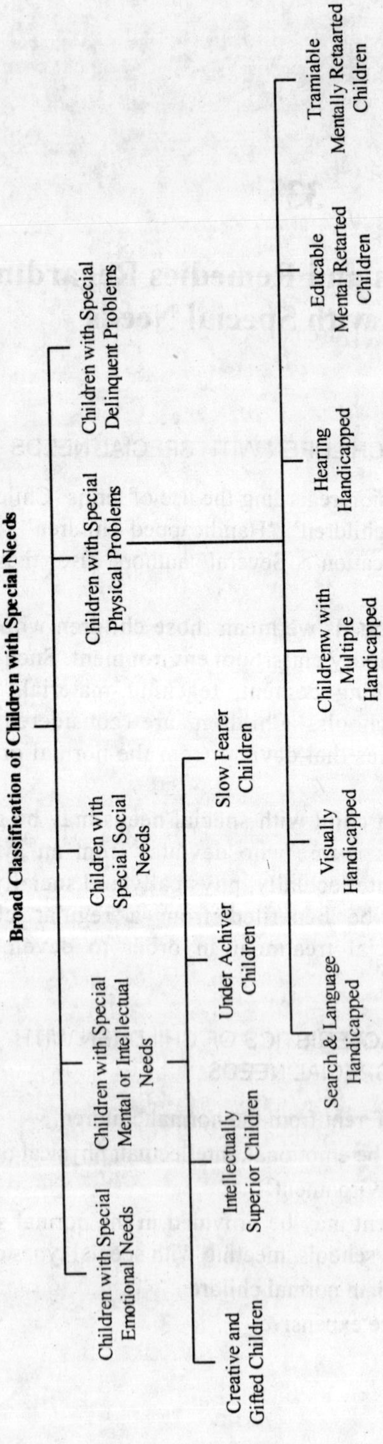

### 33.4 WHY EDUCATION AND TRAINING OF CHILDREN WITH SPECIAL NEEDS

Following are the major considerations for making provisions for the children with special needs :

1. The aim of equalisation of educational opportunities in a democratic set up highlights the fact that children with special needs should have proper opportunities to develop their potentials to the optimum level.
2. Proper opportunities will enable them to make them economically self-sufficient.
3. Regular classroom environment does not meet their needs.
4. Under normal classroom environment, they may develop behavioural problems and acquire anti-social tendencies.
5. Special categories of children like the blind, the deaf and the dumb etc. need special schools.

### 33.5 CONSTITUTIONAL PROVISIONS REGARDING EDUCATION AND TRAINING OF CHILDREN WITH SPECIAL NEEDS

No specific provision for the education and training of children with special needs exists in the Constitution. They are covered under Article 45 of the Constitution.

Article 46 makes specific provision for the promotion of educational and economic interests of Scheduled Castes, Scheduled Tribes and weaker sections of the society.

The National Policy on Education States, "In our national perception education is essentially for all." (Part 3.1) This includes the children with special needs also.

The NPE will lay special emphasis on the removal of disparities and to equalise educational opportunity by attending to the specific needs of those who have denied equality so far." (Part 4.1).

In Part 4.9, the NPE provides for the education of the handicapped with the objective of integrating them with the general community as equal partners, to prepare them for normal growth and to enable them to face life with courage and confidence.

### 33.6 PATTERNS/SYSTEMS OF EDUCATION FOR CHILDREN WITH SPECIAL NEEDS

Following are the usual patterns of education for children with special needs:

1. Integration
2. Partial Integration
3. Total Segregation

*Integration.* Integration implies that the education of children with special needs should be so organised that they mix up with normal children. The NPE states, "Wherever it is feasible, the education of children with major handicaps and other mild handicaps will be common with that of others."

*Partial Integration.* Children with special needs join with regular groups for carefully selected experiences, games and play.

*Total Segaregation.* Under this system, children with special needs are totally segregated from children studying in schools. They are taught in special schools.

## 33.7 INTEGRATED EDUCATION FOR THE DISABLED CHILDREN (IEDC) — INTEGRATED EDUCATION OF CHILDREN WITH SPECIAL NEEDS

Considerable concern has been shown in recent years on the need to equalise educational opportunity among special groups of children. To provide equal educational opportunities, specific strategies need to be evolved. Integrated education for disabled children has been considered to be a viable approach.

Integration implies the existence of the following elements in the regular system of education.

1. Sharing the same classroom, resources and opportunities by the children having special needs as well as the regular students.
2. Providing special services needed for the children with specific needs in the regular schools.
3. Having children with special needs to follow the same schedule as normal students.
4. Involving children with special needs in several academic courses and co-curricular activities including art, field trips, music and exercises etc.
5. Enabling the children with special needs to use library, play-ground, other facilities at the same time as normal students use.
6. Advising all students to understand the limitations of the children with special needs.
7. Encouraging friendly relations among normal children and children with special needs.
8. Providing an appropriate individualised programme to children with special needs.

**Role of the Regular Teacher when Integrated System is Followed**

1. He should make a thorough study of the problems of children with special needs.
2. He should understand the common characteristics of children with special needs.
3. **He should fully appreciate the common difficulties that the children**

with special needs face.

4. He should acquaint himself with the special materials the children with special needs use, e.g. pushing a wheel chair up or downstairs etc.
5. He should seek the willing cooperation of normal children to improve the psychological climate and environment of the class so that children with special needs feel at home and put in their best.
6. He should occasionally discuss the problems of children with special needs with the special education teacher.

**Role of the Special Education Teacher**

1. He should identify the academic or physical adaptations needed in the classroom for children with special needs.
2. He should develop programmes to prepare children with special needs for entry into regular classes.
3. He should design a variety of activities that will involve the entire class in grouping patterns that are flexible.
4. He should devise a variety of alternative techniques.
5. He should prepare a flexible time schedule for learning as well as physical and social needs of each student.
6. He should extend full co-operation to the regular teacher.
7. He should involve parents also.
8. He should procure special material and equipment needed for meeting the specific requirements of children with special needs.

**Merits of the Integrated System**

1. It reduces cost of education.
2. It promotes mutual understanding between normal children and children with special needs.
3. It is in conformity with democratic ideals

**Demerits of the Integrated System**

1. Normal children do not get adequate opportunities to display their talents.
2. Children with special needs find it psychologically disturbing to be placed in the normal school.

(*See also Chapter 35.2*)

# 34

# Problems, Issues and Remedies Regarding Disadvantaged Sections (Economically, Socially and Culturally)

## 34.1 MEANING OF DISADVANTAGED SECTIONS

Disadvantaged sections can be classified in a number of ways, for instance those suffering from economic deprivation (poverty), suffering from social deprivation (social low status) and cultural deprivation (outmoded ways of life). The traditional method of classification is in terms of Scheduled Castes, Scheduled Tribes and Other Backward classes.

People belonging to remote hilly areas, forest areas, desert areas and slum areas etc. are also included in the category of the deprived sections. Here the basis is economic deprivation in general.

The entire tribal population comes under the category of deprived sections.

Sometimes women are also included in the category of deprived sections.

The handicapped children may also be included in this category.

The Education Commission (1964-66), has not used the term 'deprived sections'. In Chapter VI '*Towards Equalisation of Educational Opportunity*', it uses the terms like 'backward', 'underpriviliged', 'Scheduled Castes' and 'Scheduled Tribes'.

The *National Policy on Education* (1986) in Part IV entitled 'Education for Equality' under the caption 'Disparities' includes the following categories :

1. Education for women's equality.
2. Education of Scheduled Castes.
3. Education of Scheduled Tribes.
4. Other Educationally Backward Sections and Areas.
5. The Handicapped.

'*National Curriculum Framework for School Education*' (2000) published by the NCERT uses the term 'Education of Learners from Disadvantaged Groups'. It states, "For achieving a cohesive society it could be essential to respond to specific educational needs of learners from different sections of the society with special emphasis on the Scheduled Castes, the Scheduled Tribes and other socially and economically disadvantaged groups."

## 34.2 CONSTITUTIONAL PROVISIONS REGARDING DEPRIVED SECTIONS

*Article 15.* It prohibits discrimination on grounds of religion, race, caste, sex or place of birth. Sub-section (4) of Article 15 states, "Nothing in this Article or in Clause (2) of Article 29 shall prevent the State from making any special provision for the development of any socially and educationally backward classes of citizens or for the Scheduled Castes and the Scheduled Tribes."

*Article 46.* It states, "The State shall promote with special care the educational and economic interests of the weaker sections of the people, and in particular, of the Scheduled and Castes and Scheduled Tribes and shall protect them from social injustice and all forms of exploitation."

*Article 338.* It makes provision for the appointment of a special officer for SCs and STs.

*Article 340.* It envisages the appointment of the commission to investigate the conditions of the backward classes.

## 34.3 EXPANSION OF EDUCATIONAL FACILITIES FOR SCHEDULED CASTES AND SCHEDULED TRIBES

There has been a great expansion of educational facilities for SCs and STs since independence. However it still lags behind general categories. It is hoped that with more incentives, there will be further improvement.

## 34.4 IMPORTANCE OF PROMOTION OF EDUCATION AMONG THE DEPRIVED SECTIONS

The Education Commission 1964-66 in chapter VI entitled 'Equalisation of Educational Opportunity and Social Change' very aptly observed, "One of the important social objectives of education is to equalise opportunity, enabling the backward or under-privileged classes and individuals to use education as a lever for the improvement of their conditions. Every society that values social justice and is anxious to improve the lot of the common man and cultivate all available talent must ensure progressive equality of opportunity to all sections of the population. This is the only guarantee for the building up of an egalitarian and humane society in which the exploitation of the weak is minimised". The Commission further stated, "The education of the backward classes in general and the tribal people in particular is a major programme of equalisation and of social and national integration. No expenditure is too great for this purpose." Alas! We have not paid heed to those words of wisdom. Non-implementation of this vital recommendation has led to disintegrative tendencies, hatred and strife.

The National Policy on Education, 1968, 1986 and modified Policy Formulation 1992 – all stress upon speedy action for the promotion of education of the deprived sections.

*Article 38(1)*. The State shall strive to promote the welfare of the people by securing and protecting as effectively as it may a social order in which justice, social, economic and political shall inform all the institutions of national life.

*Article 38(2).* The State shall, in particular, strive to minimize the inequalities in income and endeavour to elimates inequalities in status, facilities and opportunities, not only amongst individuals but also amongst group of people residing in different areas or engaged in different vocations.

*Article 45*. This relates to the provision of free and compulsory education for all children until they complete the age of 14 years.

## 34.5 MEASURES FOR THE PROMOTION OF EDUCATION OF THE DEPRIVED SECTIONS

*Preparatory Classes and Compensatory Instruction* – Many children belonging to the Scheduled Castes, Scheduled Tribes and economically weaker sections come from a comparatively poor environment. They may not be neat or smart. Their usage of standard language may be poor. Their vocabulary is under-developed as compared to their peers. They may not have formed the initial mathematical concepts. On the other hand they may be more enthusiastic to act. Because of the lack of congenial home environment, these children may not be in a position to complete their home assignments. Their parents are usually employed as landless labour or in other manual or agrarian activities. Therefore, such children are not able to conceptualise their future as educated persons.

There is the need to conduct some preparatory classes for children coming from the Scheduled Castes and Scheduled Tribes. The primary objective of conducting such classes is to raise the school entry ability level of such children. This is also helpful in having a somewhat homogeneous group in the class. The classes may be conducted two to three weeks in advance of the general admissions. Classes may be conducted on healthy habits, personal and environmental cleanliness, eating habits, etc. The children may also be helped in improving the pronunciation of the words and picking up standard language. For this, they may be motivated to participate in discussions, recitation and story-telling etc. Initial concepts of mathematics may also be introduced.

*Remedial Instruction* – Students coming from Scheduled Castes and Scheduled Tribes are also likely to be deficient in the scholastic areas. The school may provide some remedial education programmes. Adoption of instructional strategies, such as peer group learning, monitorial assistance, diagnostic testing and tutoring would help to improve the educational levels of these learners.

Provision of outdoor games and activities, co-curricular and work experience activities will also help in the retention of such children in the schools and create an interest in them for continued schooling.

*Role of the Teachers* – The teachers can play an important role in developing a favourable school climate conducive to the educational progress of Scheduled Castes and Scheduled Tribes. Some suggestions in this regard are given here.

1. The teacher's own example in his behaviour towards students belonging to these castes is the most effective and powerful way to build up a congenial climate.
2. The school staff should ensure non-discrimination between the children of Scheduled Castes, Scheduled Tribes and other communities.
3. The school staff should avoid the use of the caste names or derogatory words while calling roll calls or naming children.
4. Teachers should provide equal opportunities to all the children to participate in the curricular and co-curricular activities of the school, including games.
5. Frequent meetings between the staff, school teachers and parents of Scheduled Castes and Scheduled Tribes children should be arranged. The details of the schemes for promoting education amongst Scheduled Castes and Scheduled Tribes should be explained to the parents at these meetings. It should be impressed upon them that they must continue the education of their children.
6. Special attention should be paid to motivating parents to educate girls.
7. Teachers should suggest to illiterate parents the advantages gained by attending functional literacy classes in the centre.

**Other Measures**

These include :

1. A standing Committee of the Central Advisory Board of Education (CABE) under the Chairmanship of Minister of Human Resource Development may be constituted to monitor and review implementation of all educational programmes for the deprived sections.
2. Incentive schemes in operation for the promotion of the education of

the deprived sections may be evaluated and appropriate strategies evolved in the light of such studies.

3. For the curriculum, suitable changes should be made which reflect the contribution of the deprived sections in the national development. The curriculum should include the salient features of the culture of these groups.
4. Recruitment of teachers to the prescribed percentage should be ensured.

# 35

# Practical Work: Diverse Issues

## 35.1 POLICY RECOMMENDATIONS ON GIRLS' EDUCATION SINCE INDEPENDENCE: COMMITTEES, COMMISSIONS AND NATIONAL POLICIES ON EDUCATION

(*For importance, need, etc. of girls' education see Chapter 31*)

Police recommendations of the following are included here:

1. The University Education Commission (1948-49)
2. Constitutional Provisions (1949-50)
3. Secondary Education Commission (1952-53)
4. Smt. Durgabai Deshmukh Committee (1959)
5. Smt. Hansa Mehta Committee (1961)
6. M. Bhaktavatsalam Committee (1963)
7. Education Commission (1964-66)
8. Resolution on the National Policy on Education (1968)
9. Committee on the Status of Women (1974)
10. National Policy on Education (1986)
11. Ramamurti Report (1990)
12. Modified National Policy on Education (1992)
13. National Curriculum Frame work for School Education (2000)

### 1. University Education Commission (1948-49)

The University Education Commission was appointed to suggest reforms on University Education. Dr. S. Radhakrishnan who later on became the second President of India, was its chairman. It made the following observations as far as girls' education is concerned at the school stage.

There seem to be a definite prepondenrance of opinion that from the thirteenth or fourteenth year of age until about the eighteenth, separate schools for boys and girls are desirable.

### 2. Constitutional Basis and Policy Recommendations on Girls' Education (1949-50)

*Right to Equality : Article 15. Prohibition of discrimination on grounds of religion, race, caste, sex or place of birth.* (1) The State shall not discriminate against any citizen on grounds only of religion, race, caste, sex, place of birth or any of them.

Nothing in this article shall prevent the State from making any special provision for women and children.

### 3. Secondary Education Commission (1952-53) on Policy Recommendation on Girls Education

The Secondary Education Commission examined all aspects of secondary education in India and made recommendations accordingly. Here we quote extracts from the report relating to education of girls.

There was general agreement, however, that for girls—as well as for boys—education needs to be more closely connected with the home and the community. It should be less bookish in the narrow sense of the word and more practical and should explore the possibility of training the mind through the hands. It should do much more to prepare them for the part they will have to play later as parents and as citizens, i.e., the claims of family life should be considered as important as those of public life. For this reason, it was urged that the teaching of Home Science in Girl's School, (and wherever possible, for girls attending boy's schools) should be radically improved not necessarily with the idea that women's place is restricted to the home, but because it is essential that she should be educated to fulfil her two-fold duly to family and society. If greater attention is given to Home Science, with special emphasis on practical work of every day needs and problems, it will help to bridge the gulf between the school and the life of the home and the community, and be a better preparation for a girl's life after school, in which home making will necessarily play an important part. An educated girl who cannot run her home smoothly and efficiently, within her resources can make no worthwhile contribution to the happiness and the well-being of her family or to raising the social standards in her country.

In co-educational as well as mixed schools there should be provision for special co-curricular activities suited to girls, in addition to those activities in which they participate side by side with the boys – e.g. Girl Guiding, Home Nursing, Needle Work, etc.

It is also desirable that on the management of such schools there should be women representatives who will be able to see that the necessary facilities for girls are actually provided by the management.

*Summary of Recommendations*

1. While no distinction need be made between education imparted to boys and girls, special facilities for the study of Home Science should be made available in all girls' schools or in co-educational and mixed schools.
2. Efforts should be made by the State Governments to open separate schools for girls where there is demand for them.
3. Definite conditions should be laid down in regard to co-educational

or mixed sch/ols to satisfy the special needs of girl students and women members of the teaching staff.

**4 National Committee on Women's Education (1958-59) and Policy Recommendations in Girls Education**

The National Committee on Women's Education was appointed by the Government of India, Ministry of Education. Smt. Durgabai, Chairperson, Central Board of Social Welfare was the Chairperson of the Committee.

*Special recommendation needing top priority.* Steps should be taken to constitute as early as possible a National Council of Girls and Women Education.

*Primary Education (Age group 6 – 11)*

1. Concessions in kind (not in cash) should be given to all girls whether from rural or urban areas, of parents below a certain income level.
2. The Government should formulate a scheme for awarding prizes to the village which shows the largest proportional enrolment and average attendance of girls.

*Middle and Secondary Education (Age group 11 to 17)*

1. At the middle school stage, more and more co-educational institutions should be started.
2. But for the secondary stage, separate schools for girls should be established specially in rural areas, at the same time giving parents full freedom to admit their girls to boy's schools if they so desire.
3. All girls (and all boys also) of parents below a prescribed income level should be given free education upto the middle stage.
4. As far as possible, free or subsidised transport should be made available to girls in order to bring middle and secondary schools, within easy reach.

*Curriculum and Syllabi*

1. There should be identical curriculum for boys and girls at the primary stage with the proviso that, even at this stage, subjects like music, painting, sewing, needle work, simple hand-work and cooking should be introduced to make the courses more suitable for girls.
2. At the middle school stage, and more especially at the secondary stage, there is need for differentiation of curricula for boys and girls.

*Training and Employment*

1. Immediately steps should be taken to set up additional training institutions for women teachers in all such areas of the country where a shortage exists at present.

2. With a view to inducing women from urban areas to accept posts of teachers in rural schools, women teachers serving in rural areas may be provided with quarters. The public in general and the teachers in particular will have to be made to realise that it is unscientific to divide tasks and subjects on the basis of sex and to regard some of them as 'masculine' and others as 'feminine'. Similarly, the fact that the so-called psychological differences between the two sexes arise, not out of sex but out of social conditions will have to be widely publicised and people will have to be made to realise that stereo-types 'masculine' and 'feminine' personalities do more harm than good.

*Co-education*

1. Co-education should be adopted as the general pattern at the elementary stage.
2. At the secondary and collegiate stages, there should be full freedom to the managements and parents either to start common institutions or to establish separate ones for girls.
3. Steps should be taken to appoint women teachers in all educational institutions at the secondary and university stages, which are ordinarily meant for boys. Similarly, some men teachers should also be appointed in separate secondary schools and colleges for girls.

**5. Committee on Differentiation of Curricula for Boys and Girls (1961) or Hansa Mehta Committee**

Smt. Hasna Mehta was the chairperson of the Committee. Important observations and recommendations are :

1. There is no justification for the popularly held view that certain subjects are 'masculine' and others 'feminine'.
2. The existing gap between the education of boys and girls should be rapidly bridged
3. Co-education should be adopted as the general pattern at the elementary stage.
4. At the secondary and college stage there should be full freedom to the managements and parents either to start common institutions or separate ones for girls.
5. No differentiation should be made in the curricular for boys and girls at the primary and middle stage.
6. In all middle schools it is desirable to have mixed staff, but where girls do attend a middle school ordinary meant for boys, appointment of women teachers on staff should be obligatory.
7. Steps should be taken to expand the provision of facilities for middle school education for girls as far as possible.

**6. Committee to Look into the Causes for Lack of Public Support Particularly in Rural Areas for Girls' Education and to Enlist Co-operation (1963)**

M. Bhaktavatsalam, Chief Minister of Madras was the Chairman of the Committee. Major recommendations on girls' education are:

1. Enrolment drives for girls' education should be made.
2. Assistance to voluntary organisations engaged in the field of education of girls and women should be provided.
3. Women teachers should be appointed in large numbers in mixed schools.
4. Education should be made free for girls' education at the school stage.
5. While the curriculum can be the same for both boys and girls at primary and middle stages, provision should be made for offering of elective subjects which would be of special interest to girls.

**7. Education Commission 1964-66**

This was the first Education Commission that went into all aspects of education at all levels. Its recommendations became the bases of educational reforms in the country for a long time. The Commission is also known Kothari Commission after the name of its Chairman D.S. Kothari.

The Commission made the following recommendations on girls' education.

The education of girls at the primary stage requires special attention in fulfilling the constitutional directions and should be accelerated on the lines of the National Committee on Women's Education. (Hansa Mehta Committee 1961—See 35.5)

**8. Resolution on the National Policy on Education (1968)**

The education of girls should receive emphasis, not only on grounds of social justice but also because it accelerates social transformation.

**9. Committee on the Status of Women (1971-73)**

The Committee was appointed by the Ministry of Education and Social Welfare. Smt. P. Guha was the Chairperson of the Committee. The Committee made the following recommendations:

1. Co-education should be adopted as the general policy at the primary stage.
2. At the middle and secondary stages, separate schools may be provided in areas where there is a great demand for them.
3. There should be common course of general education for both sexes till the end of class X.
4. At the primary stage, simple needle craft, music and dancing should be taught to both the sexes.

5. From the middle stage differences may be permitted under work experience.
6. In classes XI-XII, girls should have full opportunity to choose vocational and technical courses for all students.
7. Sex education should be introduced from the middle stage.
8. Secondary education should be made free.
9. In all mixed schools, mixed staff should be appointed.
10. Adequate provision for separate common rooms and toilet facilities for girls should be made.

### 10. National Policy on Education (1986)

The new education policy will lay special emphasis on the removal of disparities and to equalise educational opportunity by attending to the specific needs of those who have been denied equality so far.

*Education for Women's Equality*

Education will be used as an agent of basic change in the status of woman. It order to neutralise the accumulated distortions of the past, there will be a well conceived edge in favour of women. The National Education System will play a positive, interventionist role in the empowerment of women. It will foster the development of new values through redesigned, curricula, textbooks, the training and orientation of teachers, decision-makers and administrators, and the active involvement of educational institutions. This will be an act of faith and social engineering. Women's studies will be promoted as a part of various courses and educational institutions encouraged to take up active programmes to further women's development.

The removal of women's illiteracy and obstacles inhibiting their access to, and retention in, elementary education will receive overriding priority, through provision of special support services, setting of time targets, and effective monitoring. Major emphasis will be laid on women's participation in vocational, technical and professional education at different levels. The policy of non-discrimination will be pursued vigorously to eliminate sex stereo-typing in vocational and professional courses and to promote women's participation in non-traditional occupations, as well as in existing and emergent technologies.

### 11. Ramamurti Committee (1990)

The Committee for Review of the NPE or the Ramamurti Committee entitled its report '*Towards an Enlightened and Humane Society*'. It included the following recommendations on girls' education.

*Removal of Regional Disparities in Girls Education*

(i) The issue of regional disparities needs to be incorporated into the operational design for universalising girls' access to elementary education.

(ii) Any effective strategy for raising the educational status of women in India would have to give priority to the educationally backward districts.

*Girls' Curriculum*

The curriculum in schools should include:

— Increase in the visibility of women and projection of a positive image of the role of women in history, their contribution to society in general and the Indian context in particular. For instance, history should project the contribution that women have made in the national movement.
— Special efforts should be made to strengthen mathematics and science education among girls.
— Undifferentiated curriculum for boys and girls.
— Elimination of negative stereotypes and biological and social concepts which have a sexist bias.
— Outmoded traditions and myths that hinder positive development of women and their role in national life should be objectively discussed in the classroom in a gender perspective.
— Basic legal information including protective laws regarding women and children and extracts from the Constitution to make the children aware of the fundamental rights and other basic concepts therein.
— Specific measures to improve the participation of girls in physical training and sports should be undertaken.

**12. NPE (1992 – Modified NPE 1986)**

No change in NPE – (1986)

**13. National Curriculum Framework for School Education (2000)**

Equality among sexes is a fundamental right under the Constitution of India. Emphasis in education has moved from 'Equality of Educational Opportunity' (NPE 1968) to 'Education for Women's Equality and Empowerment (1986). Besides, making education accessible to more and more girls, especially rural girls' removing all gender discrimination and gender bias in school curriculum, textbooks and the process of transaction is absolutely necessary.

## 35.2 POLICY RECOMMENDATIONS ON SPECIAL EDUCATION SINCE INDEPENDENCE

Important documents are as under :

1. Constitutional Provisions
2. Secondary Education Commission (1952-53)
3. Education Commission (1964-66)
4. National Policy on Education (1968)

5. National Policy on Education (1986)
6. Ramamurti Committee Report (1990)
7. National Curriculum Framework for School Education

**1. Constitutional Provisions**

*Direct Principles of State Policy*. Under these principles we may include the following articles which are applicable to all including those needing special education :

a) Article 38(1) requires the State to secure a social order for the promotion of welfare of the people.
b) Article 41 relates to the right to work, to education and to public assistance in some cases.
c) Article 45 is regarding provision for free and compulsory education for all children until they complete the age of fourteen years.

**2. Secondary Education Commission (1952-53)**

(*Extracts from the Report*)

The need for special types of schools for pupils who are handicapped in various ways has been recognised in all countries. In some of the advanced countries, a regular system of special schools has been established for mentally and physically handicapped children. There should be few schools in each state for such children where methods specially suited to their needs may be adopted. This is also necessary in the interest of the smooth progress of normal children.

These schools (schools for the blind, the deaf and dumb etc.) must necessarily be residential where the pupils can be kept for a number of years till they are fit to take up some useful occupation.

**3. Education Commission (1964-66)**

The Education Commission has equated the term special education with the education of the handicapped children. Under this category, it has included the following categories of children :

1. The blind
2. The deaf
3. The orthopaedically handicapped.

The recommendation of the Commission on the education of the handicapped children are given below:

1. The progress in providing educational facilities to handicapped children will be limited by two main considerations: lack of teachers and financial resources.
2. A reasonable target will, however be to provide, by 1986, education for about 15 percent of the blind, deaf and orthopaedically handicapped children and to about 5 percent of the mentally retarded ones.

3. As a part of the programme, it should be possible to have at least one good institution for the education of the handicapped children in each district.
4. Experimentation with integrated programmes is urgently required in our country and that every attempt should be made to bring in as many children into the integrated programme as possible.
5. It will be desirable to develop services on a pilot basis for other categories of children who have peculiar educational needs, viz., the partially sighted, the speech handicapped, the brain-injured and the mentally disturbed.
6. To develop the above programmes for the education of the handicapped children on proper lines, it will be necessary to emphasise the training of teachers, the co-ordination of the officers of the different agencies working in the field and to promote adequate research into the problem.

**4. National Policy on Education (1968)**

Educational for the physically and mentally handicapped children should be expanded and attempts should be made to develop integrated programmes enabling the handicapped to study in regular schools.

**5. National Policy on Education (1986)**

The policy includes the following directions on the handicapped children:
The objective should be to integrate the physically and mentally handicapped with the general community as equal partners, to prepare them for normal growth and to enable them to face life with courage and confidence. The following measures will be taken in this regard :

(i) Wherever it is feasible, the education of children with major handicaps and other mild handicaps will be common with that of others;
(ii) Special schools with hostels will be provided, as far as possible at district headquarters, for the severely handicapped children;
(iii) Adequate arrangements will be made to give vocational training to the disabled;
(iv) Teacher's training programmes will be reoriented, in particular for teachers of primary classes, to deal with the special difficulties of the handicapped children; and
(v) Voluntary effort for the education of the disabled, will be encouraged in every possible manner.

**6. Ramamurti Report or the Report to Review the NPE 1986 (1990)**

(i) People should be made aware of the problems of the handicapped, in terms of the magnitude and types of handicaps. The media should be effectively used for this purpose.

(ii) Every family with a handicapped child should be provided support through incentives, dialogue and periodic training and evaluation. Perents' groups and community education groups should be formed.

(iii) The educational system for the handicapped should be flexible. It should offer a range of education provisions—special schools for those who cannot be educated in general schools, special classes in general schools, and integrated education for the disabled of the types already in existence. Education should be through different options—formal, non-formal, open schools, home day schools, vocational centres etc.

(iv) Educational packages should be offered for hearing impaired children in a differentiated way.

(v) For making the boys and girls of impaired hearing economically independent, vocational training has to be specially organised.

(vi) For the moderately mentally retarded, special curricula should be developed and standardised not merely for the purpose of basic education in 3 R's but for training in self-care skills.

(vii) Vocational schools for the mentally retarded adults are not too many. For their benefits jobs in sheltered workshops, farms and industries should be provided as they are not capable of receiving open employment.

(viii) In pre-service teacher training programme, education of the handicapped, should be made part and parcel of the pedagogy and methodology.

(ix) A programme of sensitization should be implemented for in-service teachers as well.

(x) At least one resource faculty should be provided in each DIET to provide teacher training inputs in the context of education for the handicapped.

(xi) The role of the special schools should be clearly redefined.

(xii) Measures for dissemination of information regarding the technologies and techno-aids available for meeting the special needs of the handicapped should be taken.

(xiii) Sustained research should be undertaken to determine the needs of the physically handicapped and to produce technological aids.

**7. National Curriculum Framework for School Education (2000)**

The curriculum prepared by the NCERT. It includes the following policy perspectives :

1. The importance of individualising instruction for all learners with special needs requires unit concepts to integrate educational experiences.
2. Curriculum planning must interrelate the many facets of classroom

services, special support services and personnel and co-curricular activities in creating a new and vital programme which will facilitate curricular integration in its most specific situations.

3. Learners under this category have varied needs to be addressed.
4. Teachers must make sincere efforts to develop a relationship and an atmosphere that would generate self-motivated, self-actualising and self-monitoring learning.
5. Instructional materials need to be produced.
6. The system must ensure the empowerment of the learners with special needs and their parents by building partnership with them.
7. Compensatory and remedial measures in education to suit their needs assume special importance.

## 35.3 POLICY RECOMMENDATIONS ON EDUCATION OF THE DISADVANTAGED SECTIONS

1. *Constitutional Provisions on Disadvantaged Sections* (*See Chapter 34*).
2. *Education Commission on Disadvantaged Sections* (*See Chapter 3*).
3. *National Policy on Education (1986 and as amended in 1992).*

The NPE has dealt with this subject in Part IV under 'Education for Equality'. Writing on 'disparities', the policy states, "The New Education Policy will lay special emphasis on the removal of disparities and to equalise educational opportunity by attending to the specific needs of those who have been denied equality so far".

*Recommendations on the Education of Scheduled Castes*

**4.4** The central focus in the SCs' educational development is their equalisation with the non-SC population at all stages and levels of education, in all areas and in all the four dimensions – rural male, rural female, urban male and urban female.

**4.5** The measures contemplated for this purpose include:

(i) Incentives to indigent families to send their children to school regularly till they reach the age of 14;

(ii) Pre-metric Scholarship Scheme for children of families engaged in occupations such as scavenging, etc. to be made applicable from Class I onwards. All children of such families, regardless of incomes, will be covered by this scheme and time-bound programmes targeted on them will be undertaken;

(iii) Constant micro-planning and verification to ensure that the enrolment, retention and successful completion of courses by SC students do not fall at any stage, and provision of remedial courses to improve their prospects for further education and in employment;

(iv) The recruitment of teachers from Scheduled Castes;

(v) Provision of facilities for SC students in hostels at district headquarters, according to a phased programme;

(vi) Location of school buildings, balwadis and Adult Education Centres in such a way as to facilitate full participation of the Scheduled Castes;

**4.5** ***Revised Para (vii)*** *The utilisation of Jawahar Rozgar Yojna resources so as to make substantial educational facilities available to the Scheduled Castes; and*

**4.5 NPE 1986 Para (vii)** The utilisation of N.R.E.P. and R.L.E.G.P. resources so as to make substantial educational facilities available to the Scheduled Castes;

(viii) Constant innovation in finding new methods to increase the participation of the Scheduled Castes in the educational process.

### The Education of Scheduled Tribes

**4.6** The following measures will be taken urgently to bring the Scheduled Tribes on par with others :

**4.6** ***[Revised Para (i)]*** *Priority will be accorded to opening primary schools in tribal areas. The construction of school buildings will be undertaken in these areas on a priority basis under the normal funds for education, as well as under the Jawahar Rozgar Yojna, Tribal Welfare schemes, etc.*

4.6 **[NPE 1986 Para (i)]** Priority will be accorded to opening primary schools in tribal areas. The construction of school buildings will be undertaken in these areas on a priority basis under the normal funds for education, as well as under the N.R.E.P., R.L.E.G.P., Tribal Welfare schemes, etc.

(ii) The socio-cultural milieu of the ST has its distinctive characteristics including, in many cases, their own spoken languages. This underlines the need to develop the curricula and devise institutional materials in tribal languages at the initial stages, with arrangements for switching over to the regional languages.

(iii) Educated and promising Scheduled Tribe youths will be encouraged and trained to take up teaching in tribal aeas.

(iv) Residential schools, including Ashram Schools, will be established on a large scale.

(v) Incentive schemes will be formulated for the Scheduled Tribes, keeping in view their special needs and life styles. Scholarships for higher education will emphasise technical professional and para-professional courses. Special remedial courses and other programmes to remove psycho-social impediments will be provided to improve their performance in various courses.

(vi) Anganwadis, non-formal and Adult Education Centres will be opened on a priority basis in areas predominantly inhabited by the Scheduled Tribes.

(vii) The curriculum at all stages of education will be designed to create an awareness of the rich cultural identity of the tribal people as also of their enormous creative talent.

**Other Educationally Backward Sections and Areas**

**4.7** Suitable incentives will be provided to all educationally backward sections of society, particularly in the rural areas. Hill and desert districts, remote and inaccessible areas and islands will be provided adequate institutional infrastructure.

**Minorities**

**4.8** Some minority groups are educationally deprived or backward. Greater attention will be paid to the education of these groups in the interests of equality and social justice. This will naturally include the Constitutional guarantees given to them to establish and administer their own educational institutions, and protection to their languages and culture. Simultaneously objectivity will be reflected in the preparation of textbooks, and in all school activities, and all possible measures will be taken to promote an integration based on appreciation of common national goals and ideals, in conformity with the core curriculum.

(*See also Chapter 34*).

## 35.4 PREPARATION OF PROFILE FOR SCHOOL: GUIDELINES/HINTS

I. *Identification Data*

1. Name of the school
2. Complete address of the school
3. Name of the village/town/city
4. Rural or Urban
5. CD Block/Tehsil/Taluk
6. Name of the district
7. Name of the State/Union Territory
8. Date of establishment of the school

II. *Management*

(i) Government/Local Body/Private aided/Private unaided

(ii) Name of the Trust, if any.

III. *Stage/Type of School*

(i) Boys/Girls/Co-educational

(ii) Level – Primary/Upper Primary/Secondary/Higher Secondary

VI. *Area*

(i) Total area of the school campus

(ii) Total covered area of the school building

V. *Type of Building*

(i) Pucca/Partly pucca/Kachaha/Thatched huts/Tents/Partly tents/ Open space

- (ii) Major portion of the building is owned/rented/rent free
- (iii) Total number of rooms in the school
- (iv) Number of rooms used for instructional purposes
- (v) No. of laboratories with sizes indicating the subjects for which laboratories are available.
- (vi) Particulars of the workshops
- (vii) Number of books in the library
- (viii) Number of encyclopaedia, if any
- (ix) A reading room – yea/no, if yes, number of newspapers and magazines
- (x) Particulars of subject rooms
- (xi) Size of Principal's room
- (xii) Size of class rooms
- (xiii) Size of other rooms

VI. *Furniture*

- (i) Number of desks Single as well as double desks

VII. *Play ground facilities in the school*

- (i) Does the school have playground facility?
- (ii) Is the playground facility within the school premises or outside?
- (iii) Games played in the school
- (iv) Distinctions won by the school (Details)

VIII. *Water and Sanitary Arrangement*

- (i) Condition of lavatories
- (ii) Condition of urinals

IX. *Medical Check-up*

- (i) First Aid
- (ii) School Doctor
- (iii) Dispensary

X. *Incentive Schemes*

- (i) Mid-day meals
- (ii) Free Uniforms
- (iii) Bookbanks etc.

XI. *Staff Statement:* Teaching, non-teaching with qualifications etc.

XII. *Students strength*: Classwise and streamwise if it is Higher Secondary.

XIII. *Teaching-Leaning Material*

- (i) Syllabus
- (ii) Textbooks for teachers
- (iii) Maps
- (iv) Electronic media etc.
- (v) Games equipment. Home science equipment etc.

XIV. *School Time-Table*

- (i) Teachers
- (ii) Class

(iii) Vacant period

(iv) Games etc.

XV. *Vocational Courses:* Names and students in each course. Guidance facilities

XVI. Co-curricular Activities: Mention names

XVII. *School Results* Board's examination during the past five years. Internal result of one year only

XVIII. *School Inspection.* Main observations.

XIX. *School Environment.* Cooperation etc.

XX. *School Management.* Particulars of members

XXI. *School Funds.* Recurring and non-recurring

XXII. *School Community Relationships.* PTA, etc.

(*Note : List is not exhaustive*)

## 35.5 PREPARATION OF REPORTS FOR FIELD TRIPS: GUIDELINES FOR PREPARING THE REPORT

The report should include the following items :

1. Obtaining informal permission of the head for organising the trip.
2. Involvement of the students regarding the choice of place to be visited.
3. Formal approval of the Head.
4. Sending individual letters to parents through their wards seeking their permission—giving details of the place/places to be visited, clothes and other materials required by the students, approximate expenses.
5. Contacting the tourist office/offices through letters/personal visits according to convenience for collecting necessary information about the places-points of interest.
6. Contacting the transport authorities for hiring buses or using other modes of transport.
7. Contacting appropriate authorities for accommodation etc.
8. Dividing students into suitable groups and nominating group leaders.
9. Accompanying first-aid box, cameras, etc.
10. As far as possible, student singers, tit-bit tellers and photographers etc. also to find a place so that learning and entertainment may go together.
11. Observance or reasonable discipline. Freedom within limits to be given.
12. Asking students to keep brief notes of the interesting elements/places visited.
13. Keeping complete accounts of the income and expenditure on the tour.
14. Submitting a report to the Head.
15. Display of photographs and other details of the trip on the school Bulletin Board.

(*Note : This is just a suggestive list*).

